EPHESIANS

AN
EXPOSITIONAL
COMMENTARY

Books by Dr. Boice . . .

Witness and Revelation in the Gospel of John
Philippians: An Expositional Commentary
The Sermon on the Mount
How to Live the Christian Life (originally, *How to Really Live It Up*)
Ordinary Men Called by God (originally, *How God Can Use Nobodies*)
The Last and Future World
The Gospel of John: An Expositional Commentary (5 volumes in one)
"Galatians" in the *Expositor's Bible Commentary*
Can You Run Away from God?
Our Sovereign God, editor
Our Savior God: Studies on Man, Christ and the Atonement, editor
Foundations of the Christian Faith (4 volumes in one)
The Foundations of Biblical Authority, editor
The Epistles of John
Does Inerrancy Matter?
Making God's Word Plain, editor
Genesis: An Expositional Commentary (3 volumes)
The Parables of Jesus
The Christ of Christmas
The Christ of the Open Tomb
Standing on the Rock
The Minor Prophets: An Expositional Commentary (2 volumes)
Christ's Call to Discipleship
Daniel: An Expositional Commentary
Ephesians: An Expositional Commentary

EPHESIANS

AN
EXPOSITIONAL
COMMENTARY
JAMES
MONTGOMERY
BOICE

Ministry Resources Library

Zondervan Publishing House • Grand Rapids, MI

EPHESIANS: AN EXPOSITIONAL COMMENTARY
Copyright © 1988 by James Montgomery Boice

MINISTRY RESOURCES LIBRARY is an imprint of Zondervan Publishing House,
1415 Lake Drive, S.E., Grand Rapids, Michigan 49506.

Library of Congress Cataloging in Publication Data

Boice, James Montgomery, 1938–
    Ephesians : an expositional commentary / James Montgomery Boice.
      p.   cm.
    Includes bibliographical references and index.
    ISBN 0-310-21651-6
    1. Bible. N.T. Ephesians—Commentaries. I. Title.
BS2695.3.B65   1988   88-28169
227'.5077—dc19   CIP

Quotations from John R. W. Stott, *God's New Society: The Message of Ephesians*, copyright © 1979 by John R. W. Stott, are used by permission of InterVarsity Press, P.O. Box 1400, Downers Grove, IL 60515.

Quotations from D. Martyn Lloyd-Jones, *God's Ultimate Purpose: An Exposition of Ephesians 1:1 to 23* (Grand Rapids: Baker, 1979) and *God's Way of Reconciliation: Studies in Ephesians, Chapter 2* (Grand Rapids: Baker, 1972), are used by permission of Mrs. Bethan Lloyd-Jones, London, England.

All Scripture quotations, unless otherwise noted, are taken from the HOLY BIBLE: NEW INTERNATIONAL VERSION (North American Edition). Copyright © 1973, 1978, 1984, by the International Bible Society. Used by permission of Zondervan Bible Publishers.

Edited by Joseph Comanda
Designed by Louise Bauer

Printed in the United States of America

88 89 90 91 92 93 / CH / 10 9 8 7 6 5 4 3 2 1

*To him
who is able to do immeasurably more
than all we ask or imagine,
according to his power
that is at work within us*

Contents

Preface

"A mini-course in theology, centered on the church." That is what Paul's great letter to the Ephesians, written from Rome shortly after the midpoint of the first Christian century, is about.

But what a course! What theology!

Like Romans, Ephesians deals with the most fundamental Christian doctrines. But even more than that other great doctrinal book, it stresses the sovereignty of God in salvation and the eternal sweep of God's great plan, by which believers are lifted from the depth of sin's depravity and curse to the heights of eternal joy and communion with God. Like 1 and 2 Corinthians and the pastoral letters, Ephesians deals with the church. But even more than these very practical letters, Ephesians highlights the church's true spiritual dynamics and gives guidelines for the new relationships in which the reality of the new humanity can be seen. Like 1 Peter and James, Ephesians speaks of the Christian's spiritual warfare. But only in Ephesians is that warfare presented in such vivid imagery and unforgettable terms.

John Mackay called Ephesians "the greatest . . . maturest . . . [and] for our time the most relevant" of Paul's letters. Armitage Robinson called it "the crown of Saint Paul's writings."

I have never felt free to give quite such glowing accolades to this book, thinking always of Paul's other great writings. But there is no denying that Ephesians is deeply appealing, perhaps precisely because, as I have suggested in the introductory chapter, it presents the basic doctrines of Christianity comprehensively, clearly, practically, and winsomely. But this is something the reader can decide for himself. Study Ephesians! I recommend a careful reading of Paul's letter first, perhaps more than once, and then a quicker reading of this commentary. And I recommend prayer while doing both. I am sure you will find great blessing from Ephesians and, I trust, helpful insight too from what I have written.

These studies were first presented at the morning worship services of Tenth Presbyterian Church in Philadelphia, the congregation I have served as pastor since 1968. Because Ephesians is so much about the church and because I was preaching to my own church, I found it natural to illustrate some of the principles the book develops by lessons I have learned in Philadelphia. I hope this will not be distracting to the general reader and that, instead, it will prove useful.

I should say a word of special appreciation for the Tenth congregation. Over the last twenty years Tenth has grown into a large multifaceted congregation with many outreach and service ministries. As it has, I have found it impossible to keep up with everything that is happening in the church, and there are some who have been unhappy about this. Nevertheless, the great majority of the people have been supportive of my work, precisely in the sense Paul intended when he spoke of the pastor's task being "to prepare God's people for works of service, so that the body of Christ may be built up until we all reach unity in the faith and in the knowledge of the Son of God and become mature, attaining to the whole measure of the fullness of Christ" (Eph. 4:12–13).

Tenth Church has not attained to "the whole measure of the fullness of

Christ" yet, and I am sure that it never will in this life. But it has been built up, and this is the direction in which it is headed. The key factor in this forward motion is the desire and prayer of the congregation that I (and the other pastors) be free to "prepare God's people" through the weekly preaching and teaching.

I also want to thank Miss Caecilie M. Foelster, my secretary, who has typed the manuscript and assisted in the laborious task of proofreading and preparing the indexes.

"To him who is able to do immeasurably more than all we ask or imagine, according to his power that is at work within us, to him be glory in the church and in Christ Jesus throughout all generations, for ever and ever! Amen" (Eph. 3:20–21).

James Montgomery Boice

1

Introduction to Ephesians

(Ephesians 1:1–2)

Paul, an apostle of Christ Jesus by the will of God,
To the saints in Ephesus, the faithful in Christ Jesus:
Grace and peace to you from God our Father and the Lord Jesus Christ.

As I study books of the Bible I find that those who write commentaries invariably extol their particular book as deepest, most important, or most relevant. Writers on Ephesians are no exception. William Barclay calls Ephesians "the queen of the epistles." The English poet Samuel Taylor Coleridge termed this book "the divinest composition of man" because, as he believed, "it embraces, first, those doctrines peculiar to Christianity, and, then, those precepts common with it in natural religion." John Mackay, a former president of Princeton Theological Seminary who was converted at the age of fourteen through reading Ephesians, called it the "greatest . . . maturest . . . [and] for our time the most relevant" of all Paul's writings. "This letter is pure music," he said. Ruth Paxson called Ephesians "the Grand Canyon of Scripture," meaning that it is breathtakingly beautiful and apparently inexhaustible to the one who wants to take it in.[1]

All superlatives aside, I want to begin by emphasizing the simple clarity of this letter. If Ephesians *is* profound, it is so not for the mysterious nature of its unfathomable deep secrets, but for the clear way it presents the most basic Christian truths. There is nothing in Ephesians that is not taught elsewhere. In his unfinished but valuable exposition of this letter, B. F. Westcott included an appendix in which he discussed the letter's distinct doctrines. He found twenty-seven of them, running from God the Father, Christ, the Holy Spirit, and the Trinity through the will of God, the world and creation, the unseen world, angels, evil powers, and the devil to the church, the communion of saints, the sacraments, and the Christian ministry.[2] Not one of these doctrines is unique to Ephesians. They are just *basic Christianity*.

What is the appeal of this book? In my judgment it is just this: it presents the basic doctrines of Christianity comprehensively, clearly, practically, and winsomely.

I can put it another way. The focus for all the other doctrines in Ephesians

[1] William Barclay, *The Letters to the Galatians and Ephesians*, The Daily Study Bible (Edinburgh: St. Andrews, 1954), 71, 83; John R. W. Stott, *God's New Society: The Message of Ephesians* (Downers Grove, Ill.: InterVarsity, 1979), 15–16; John A. Mackay, *God's Order: The Ephesian Letter and This Present Time* (New York: Nisbet and Macmillan, 1953), 9–10, 33; Ruth Paxson, *The Wealth, Walk and Warfare of the Christian* (New York: Revell, 1939), 11–12.

[2] B. F. Westcott, *Saint Paul's Epistle to the Ephesians* (Grand Rapids: Eerdmans, n.d.), 126–50.

11

is the church as God's new society, so in a sense the book links these truths of Christianity to us God's people. In other words, it is practical. We are told who we are, how we came to be as we are, what we shall be, and what we must do now in light of that destiny. John R. W. Stott writes, "The whole letter is thus a magnificent combination of Christian doctrine and Christian duty, Christian faith and Christian life, what God has done through Christ and what we must be and do in consequence."[3]

THE CHURCH AT EPHESUS

The letter is addressed to the Ephesians, but there is some question about its destination in scholarly circles. The words "in Ephesus" are absent from three of the oldest Greek manuscripts: the Vatican and Sinaitic uncials and the Chester Beatty Papyrus, which predates them. Nor is it just a question of two missing words. We know from the account of Paul's travels in Acts that the apostle spent two years at Ephesus on his third missionary journey (Acts 19:10). Ephesians was written from prison (Eph. 3:1), presumably from Rome, which means that it was composed subsequent to this extended mission in the city. Since that is the case, it is surprising that the letter is without any of the personal greetings found in such letters as Romans, 1 and 2 Corinthians, Galatians, Philippians, and Colossians. To complicate matters further, in the second century the heretic Marcion referred to Ephesians as the letter of Paul to the Laodiceans, thereby suggesting that his copy contained the word "Laodicea" for "Ephesus" in verse 1.

There are two main theories to explain this situation. The first is based on the fact that the letter to the Colossians and the letter to the Ephesians are closely related (thirty-five verses in the two letters are substantially the same) and that in Colossians 4:16 Paul writes, "After this letter has been read to you, see that it is also read in the church of the Laodiceans and that you in turn read the letter from Laodicea." It is argued that Ephesians was actually this Laodicean letter and that the two churches were to exchange them.

That seems plausible, but unfortunately it does not explain how our letter came to be identified as our letter to the Ephesians or why there are no extant manuscripts that say "Laodicea."

The second explanation, probably the best, is that Ephesians was originally composed as a circular letter intended for all the seven churches of Asia— those established by Paul or his followers during the time of his ministry in Ephesus—and that the name Ephesus became identified with the epistle because it was the chief city. Whatever the explanation for the missing words in some manuscripts and the lack of personal greetings in all, there is no doubt that the letter was identified as a letter from Paul to the Ephesian Christians from the earliest centuries. In the commentary referred to earlier, Westcott cites references to Ephesians from Irenaeus, Tertullian, Origin, and Clement of Alexandria, as well as others.[4]

What was Ephesus like? Ephesus was the capital of proconsular Asia and as such was the political and commercial center of a large and prosperous region. That is why Paul spent so much time there. Ephesus was on the Cayster River, not far from the Aegean coast. Its port was large and so became the chief communication and commercial link between Rome and the East. Merchants flocked to it. It became a melting pot of nations and ethnic groups. Greek and

---

[3] Stott, *God's New Society*, 25.
[4] Westcott, xxiii–xxxii.

Roman, Jew and Gentile mingled freely in its streets. In Paul's day Ephesus played a role not unlike that of Venice in the Middle Ages or Constantinople today.

Ephesus boasted the largest of all Greek open-air theaters; it held 25 thousand spectators. There was a stadium for chariot races and fights with animals. Chiefly, however, Ephesus boasted of its great temple to Diana or Artemis. It was considered one of the seven wonders of the ancient world. It measured 425 by 220 by 60 feet (about four times the size of the Parthenon) and housed the statue of Diana, believed to have come down from heaven. This temple was a depository for huge amounts of treasure and was, in effect, the bank of Asia. It was served by hundreds of the priestesses of Diana, who were temple prostitutes.

To this city the apostle Paul came to preach—briefly on his second missionary journey and extensively on his third. In this city God was pleased to establish a faithful church. To the Christians of this city, attempting to live for God in the midst of utter paganism, the apostle directs this letter.

The Writer to His Readers

If Paul was writing this letter during his imprisonment in Rome, as we believe, he had already achieved a great deal in Christ's service. He could have begun his letter with a rehearsal of his many accomplishments or even a reminder of what he had personally endured to bring the gospel of Christ to Asia. Paul does not do this. Instead, he introduces himself (as he does in many of his other letters) as "an apostle of Christ Jesus by the will of God."

An apostle was one appointed by the Lord to be a recipient and authenticator of the New Testament revelation. As Paul said in writing to the Corinthians, he was one who spoke "not in words taught . . . by human wisdom but in words taught by the Spirit" (1 Cor. 2:13). This is important because it means that the book Paul wrote is not to be regarded as other books written by mere men or women but as God's own revelation. It is from God. Therefore it is all true; it speaks with authority.

However, in view of the emphasis upon God's sovereign, electing grace which follows in verses 3–23, I am inclined to think that in this letter Paul's emphasis does not lie so much on the fact that he *was* an apostle, as wonderful as that was, but on *how* he became one. It was not by his own will but "by the will of God." Indeed, if it had not been for God's sovereign and efficacious will, Paul would not only not have been an apostle, he would not even have been a Christian. Left to himself apart from the grace of God, he fought against God and attempted to destroy his church.

This is true of all of us. The gospel is a wonderful thing. It is the word of life in Christ. But however wonderful the gospel may be, we would never have responded to it or have become a part of that marvelous new creation the church, about which Paul is soon to speak, if God had not first called us from sin to Christ, as in the days of his flesh Jesus called the decaying Lazarus from the tomb. If we are going to talk about the basics of the gospel, as Ephesians does, we must start at this point and from the very beginning of our exposition be sure that we relate everything to God. God called Paul. God called the Christians at Ephesus. God calls us, if we are truly Christians.

D. Martyn Lloyd-Jones says, "Much of the trouble in the church today is due to the fact that we are so subjective, so interested in ourselves, so egocentric. . . . Having forgotten God, and having become so interested in ourselves, we become miserable and wretched, and spend our time in 'shallows and in miseries.' The message of the Bible from beginning to end is designed to bring us back to God, to humble us before God, and to enable us to see our true relationship to him." He adds, "And that is the great theme of this epistle."[5]

THE SAINTS AT EPHESUS

It is also the theme of the second part of verse 1 in which Paul turns from himself to his readers, identifying them as "the saints in Ephesus, the faithful in Christ Jesus." This phrase contains three definitions of believers, or what D. Martyn Lloyd-Jones calls "the irreducible minimum of what constitutes a Christian."[6]

1. *Christians are saints.* The biblical meaning of this word is different from what the church or even general secular society has made it. In the Roman Catholic Church a saint is a particularly holy person who is exalted to be a saint by ecclesiastical procedure. The person is nominated for the position. Then a trial is held in which one advocate pleads the virtues of the nominee (showing among other things that he or she was responsible for at least one miracle) and another advocate, called "the Devil's Advocate," tries to tear the person down. When the person's worthiness is properly established he or she is officially declared a saint. Similarly, the world looks upon a saint (if it sees one) as a particularly good person.

This is far from the biblical idea, as I have indicated. In the Bible to be a saint means to be set apart. It is something God does quite apart from human merit. We see this meaning of the word in Exodus where Moses was instructed to sanctify the laver and the altar of the Jewish tabernacle. He was to make saints of them. This does not mean that in some miraculous way Moses

changed the nature of the material that made up the laver or the stones that made up the altar. They did not become holier. It only means that he set them apart to a special, sacred use in the temple service. In the same way, when Jesus prayed in John 17, "For them I sanctify myself, that they too may be truly sanctified," he did not mean that he wished to become holier. He already was perfectly holy. He meant rather than he was dedicating himself (setting himself apart) to the task of making atonement for our sins on the cross so we could become set apart for God. A Christian is set apart when God reaches down through the person and power of the Holy Spirit, regenerates him, and thus draws him into the company of God's church.

Every Christian is a saint, and every saint is a Christian. Moreover, every true Christian is in some sense separated from the world. It does not mean that we are taken out of the world. That is not the way God operates. But it does mean that we are removed from it in the sense of not really belonging to the world any longer. If we are truly Christ's, we have a new nature, a new set of loyalties, and a new agenda. We belong to a different kingdom.

This also means, to carry it a step farther, that although being a saint does not primarily refer to being a good person, all saints will nevertheless be better than they would otherwise have been and will in increasing measures develop and show forth the character of Christ. In the second chapter of this letter we are going to see that the Christian has been saved by grace through faith alone—not by works (vv. 8–9). But we will also see that the one who has been saved is predestined "to do good works" through God's working within him (v. 10). Theologians

[5] D. M. Lloyd-Jones, *God's Ultimate Purpose: An Exposition of Ephesians 1:1 to 23* (Grand Rapids: Baker, 1979), 13.
[6] Ibid., 24.

state this by saying that no one is justified who is not also regenerated. That is, we are saved by faith alone, but we are not saved by faith which is alone. All Christians are saints, and all saints must increasingly be saintly.

2. *Christians are faithful.* When Paul calls the believers at Ephesus "faithful in Christ Jesus," he has two ideas in mind. The first and primary meaning of the word "faithful" is "exercising faith." That is, a Christian is one who has heard the gospel of God's grace in Jesus Christ and who has then exercised faith in that gospel or believed it.

This faith has three elements. First, there is an intellectual element. Faith involves content. For faith to exist, that content must be proclaimed and understood. Second, there is an emotional element. The content that is understood, if it is understood rightly, is not something that can simply be passed off as interesting but of little real importance. It involves the death of the very Son of God for me, a sinner. Faith at this level warms the heart and draws forth a loving response to God, who has revealed himself in Christ. Third, there is a volitional element. Having perceived and understood the gospel and having been affected by it, the true Christian now makes a personal commitment to Christ who died for him.

There is a beautiful example of this third element in the conversion of Thomas as recorded in John 20. At first Thomas had refused to believe, but then Jesus appeared to him. Jesus did more than convince Thomas intellectually of the truths of the atonement and resurrection—he also touched his heart—and Thomas immediately made a commitment, declaring, "*My* Lord and *my* God" (v. 28). All Christians are faithful in that sense, and all who are thus faithful are Christians.

The second meaning of the word "faithful" is "to continue in faith" or, as we might say, "to keep the faith." It involves the idea of perseverance in the Christian life, enduring to the end. Jesus said, "He who stands firm to the end will be saved" (Matt. 10:22). Usually, when Reformed Christians talk about the perseverance of the saints, they mean the perseverance of God with his saints. They wish to say that the only reason why any of us are ever able to stand firm to the end is that God is faithful to us. Well and good! But it is also true that precisely because God perseveres with us, we also must persevere. We must be faithful. It is therefore also proper to say that a Christian is one who is characterized by a full faith to the very end of life.

3. *Christians are in Christ.* This is an idea to be dealt with at greater length later, for it is characteristic of this book and indeed of Paul's writings generally. The phrases "in Christ," "in him," or the equivalent occur nine times just in Ephesians 1:3–23. They occur 164 times in all Paul's writings. The phrases mean more than just believing on Christ or being saved by his atonement. They mean being joined to Christ in one spiritual body so that what is true of him is also true for us. On this basis Paul goes so far as to say that "God raised us up with Christ and seated us with him *in the heavenly realms* in Christ Jesus" (Eph. 2:6). Harry Ironside considered this last idea so important that he used it as a title of his published expository addresses on Ephesians.[7]

This is a difficult concept, and the Bible uses numerous images to teach it to us: the union of a man and woman in marriage (Eph. 5:22–33), the union of the vine and the branches (John 15:1–17), the wholeness of a spiritual temple in which Christ is the foundation and

---

[7] H. A. Ironside, *In the Heavenlies: Practical Expository Addresses on the Epistle to the Ephesians* (Neptune, N.J.: Loizeaux Brothers, 1937).

we the individual stones (Eph. 2:20–22), the union of the head and other members of the body in one organism (1 Cor. 12:12–27).

But whether we understand it or not, union with Christ is in one sense the very essence of salvation. John Murray, an able expositor of this theme, wrote, "Union with Christ has its source in the election of God the Father before the foundation of the world and it has its fruition in the glorification of the sons of God. The perspective of God's people is not narrow; it has the expanse of eternity. Its orbit has two foci, one the electing love of God the Father in the counsels of eternity, the other glorification with Christ in the manifestation of his glory. The former has no beginning, the latter has no end."[8]

Apart from Christ our condition is absolutely hopeless. In him our condition is glorious to the extreme.

GRACE ABOUNDING

The last words of Paul's introduction are: "Grace and peace to you from God our Father and the Lord Jesus Christ" (v. 2). They may be applied to what we have said in this fashion.

When I was discussing the setting for this epistle I pointed out that in the three oldest manuscripts the words "in Ephesus" do not occur. That may indicate that in its original form the letter was an encyclical designed for several churches. But whether that is true or not, one copy of the letter was certainly directed to the Christians at Ephesus, and this means these faithful saints, who were "in Christ," were nevertheless also in the world—in Ephesus—and were obliged to live for Christ there. In the same way we must live for Christ in Philadelphia, in London, in New York, in Singapore, or wherever God has placed us. And our world is like Ephesus! Was Ephesus crassly commercial and materialistic? So are our cities. Was it pagan, preoccupied with sex, superstitious? So are we. What can keep Christian people faithful to God in such environments? What can enable them to be saintly continually?

There is only one answer. It is what Paul speaks of in his greeting: "grace and peace," and particularly grace, from God the Father. As the book goes on we are going to learn *what* we should be in this world. But from the very beginning there is no mystery about *how* we are to be it—by the will and strength of God, who alone can help us. We have no other strength, but by his grace we can triumph.

---

[8]John Murray, *Redemption Accomplished and Applied* (Grand Rapids: Eerdmans, 1955), 164.

2

All Good in Christ

(Ephesians 1:3)

Praise be to the God and Father of our Lord Jesus Christ, who has blessed us in the heavenly realms with every spiritual blessing in Christ.

I have been a pastor in one place or another for more than two decades, and during that time I have probably put together between 1,300 and 1,400 worship services. These services have had various elements, all important: the sermon, Scripture readings, hymns, prayers, congregational responses, and other items. I value each of these. But as I have reflected on the worship of Christian people over this long period, I have come to believe that one of the most important aspects of all the various parts of worship is hymn singing. Why? Because it is in hymn singing that the congregation itself actively voices praise to God.

The sermon is important. We learn from the sermon. But doctrine, if it is rightly understood, leads to doxology. If we discover who God is and what he has done for us, we will praise him.

PRAISE TO THE FATHER

Paul must have understood this well, for most of his letters begin early on with a hymn of praise (and prayer) to God. We all know that Paul's letters tend to divide into two sections: teaching and application or, as we could also say, faith and life. Doctrine is followed by duty. But usually, long before he

gets to the duty section, Paul revels in what God has done for us by praising him. Romans reviews basic doctrine and praises God for it. Second Corinthians is another example. The same thing occurs in Galatians (briefly), Philippians, Colossians, and other letters. Of all these letters, none is so overflowing with this initial praise to God for his great blessings as Ephesians.

This is a remarkable section of Paul's letter. To begin with, it is all one sentence—from verse 3 to verse 14. English translations generally break the words up for ease of reading, but in the Greek Paul simply begins with a note of praise to God for "every spiritual blessing" and then keeps going, adding phrase upon phrase and doctrine upon doctrine, as he lists these benefits. One commentators calls this "a magnificent gateway" to the epistle. Another calls it "a golden chain of many links." A third calls it "a kaleidoscope of dazzling lights and shifting colors."

John R. W. Stott, who lists these and other descriptions of Paul's great paragraph of praise, summarizes: "A gateway, a golden chain, a kaleidoscope, a snowball, a racehorse, an operatic overture and the flight of an eagle: all these metaphors in their different ways describe the impression of color, movement and grandeur which the sentence makes on the reader's mind."[1]

But it is not just a great panorama of color and movement that we are confronted with in these verses. We also meet with a vast display of doctrines. In fact, they are interconnected, which makes it hard to analyze the paragraph.

Some commentators have noticed that the work of God the Father is chiefly described in verses 3–6, the work of the Lord Jesus Christ in verses 7–10, and the work of the Holy Spirit in verses 11–14. They have divided the paragraph along Trinitarian lines. John Stott provides a temporal outline—the past blessing of election (vv. 4–6), the present blessing of adoption (vv. 5–8), and the future blessing of unification (vv. 9–10)—followed by a section on the "scope" of these blessings.[2] E. K. Simpson lists the blessings: election, adoption, redemption, forgiveness of sins, wisdom and understanding, the unification of things in Christ, and the seal of the Holy Spirit.[3] In his very extensive commentary, D. Martyn Lloyd-Jones abandons any attempt to provide a neat outline and simply goes through the section significant word or phrase by significant word or phrase.

Probably the Trinitarian framework is most helpful. Paul is saying that the blessings listed come from God the Father, become ours in Jesus Christ, and are applied by the Holy Spirit. We notice, for example, that God the Father is the subject of nearly every verb in the section, and that the phrase "in Christ" or "in him" occurs throughout.

ALL SPIRITUAL BLESSINGS

I have said that in Greek, Ephesians 1:3–14 is one sentence. But it is appropriate that the New International Version (and some others) make verse 3 a sentence to itself. It states a theme and highlights what is to come. The verse says God "has blessed us in the heavenly realms with every spiritual blessing in Christ" and praises him for it.

What are we to make of the word "spiritual" in this sentence? The word could mean either of two things. It could mean that the blessings come to us by means of the Holy Spirit. The last verses of this section (vv. 11–14) certainly teach that. Or it could mean that these are *spiritual* rather than *material* blessings. The phrase "in the heavenly realms" which also occurs in this sentence, suggests that Paul is probably thinking of "spiritual" in the second sense. That is, he is thinking of blessings related to heaven rather than earth and is declaring that these blessings are freely given to us.

It is not that God does not give material blessings as well. He does. Jesus promised that his disciples would be provided with all things needful (see Matt. 6:25–34). The apostle Paul said, "My God will meet all your needs according to his glorious riches in Christ Jesus" (Phil. 4:19). But these material provisions are relatively unimportant when measured against spiritual riches. Besides, although in this life we may have more or less material possessions, in spiritual terms we have not merely some but *all* blessings in Christ.

Ephesians 1:4–14 is a listing of these blessings. We will be looking at many of these in greater detail as our study unfolds, but it is worth looking ahead to the entire scope of them now.

1. *Election.* Paul says that "he [that is, God] chose us in him [that is, Christ]

---

[1] John R. W. Stott, *God's New Society: The Message of Ephesians* (Downers Grove, Ill.: InterVarsity, 1979), 32.

[2] Ibid., 36–50.

[3] E. K. Simpson, "Commentary on the Epistle to the Ephesians" in E. K. Simpson and F. F. Bruce, *Commentary on the Epistles to the Ephesians and the Colossians* (Grand Rapids: Eerdmans, 1957), 24–36.

before the creation of the world to be holy and blameless in his sight" (v. 4). This troubles some people, because they suppose that if God elects individuals to salvation, as this verse and others clearly declare he does, then the value of human choices is destroyed and the motivation for a holy life vanishes. This is not what happens. Instead of destroying the value of human choices, election gives us a capacity for choosing that we did not possess previously as unregenerate persons.

Before we were made alive in Christ we had a human will. But it was directed against God, not toward him. We could choose, but we always chose wrongly. When we were made alive in Christ we received a new nature, according to which God, who before was undesirable to us, now became desirable, and we willingly submitted ourselves to him. Again, so far as living a holy life is concerned, we are told in another text that God wills our holiness. So, far from being an excuse for unholiness, election actually guarantees the opposite. The only way we can know whether we are among the elect ultimately is whether we are living a holy life.

Election teaches that "salvation comes from the Lord" (Jonah 2:9). Indeed, Paul makes this very clear in this passage. He teaches that God "chose" (v. 4), "predestined" (v. 5), "gave" (v. 6), "forgave" (v. 7), "lavished grace" (vv. 7–8), "made known his will" (v. 9), "purposed" (v. 9), "included" (v. 13), and "marked" us with the seal of the Holy Spirit (v. 13). It is God's work from beginning to end.

2. *Adoption.* The second spiritual blessing in Christ is adoption, for "in love he predestined us to be adopted as his sons through Jesus Christ" (v. 5). Adoption means becoming God's sons and daughters with all the privileges implied. On this basis we are said to be "heirs of God and co-heirs with Christ"

(Rom. 8:17) and have the privilege of bringing all things to God in prayer and of being heard by him.

3. *Redemption.* Redemption means being delivered from the slavery of sin by the death of Christ, which Paul indicates by saying: "In him [that is, Christ] we have redemption through his blood" (v. 7). In antiquity a person could become a slave in one of three ways. He could be born a slave; children of slaves were automatically slaves too. He could become a slave by conquest; the citizens of a city or nation captured by another city or nation would be enslaved. He could become a slave through debt; a person who could not pay a debt could be enslaved as the last possible resource for payment.

Significantly, the Bible speaks of people being slaves of sin in each of these ways. We are born in sin, receiving a sinful nature from our parents ("Surely I was sinful at birth, sinful from the time my mother conceived me," Ps. 51:5). We are conquered by sin ("Keep your servant also from willful sins; may they not rule over me," Ps. 19:13). We are also slaves of sin through debt ("The wages of sin is death, but the gift of God is eternal life in Christ Jesus our Lord," Rom. 6:23).

Redemption means Jesus delivering us from this slavery to sin by his work on the cross. Before, we were held captive and could not break free to do God's bidding. We did not even want to. Now we are freed to serve God by Jesus' death. As Peter writes, "It was not with perishable things such as silver or gold that you were redeemed from the empty way of life handed down to you from your forefathers, but with the precious blood of Christ, a lamb without blemish or defect" (1 Peter 1:18–19).

4. *Forgiveness of sins.* Paul links forgiveness of sins to redemption, writing, "In him we have redemption through his blood, the forgiveness of sins" (v.

7). But although they are closely linked, forgiveness of sins is something different from redemption. Redemption means being freed from sin's power, so that it no longer rules over us. Forgiveness means having God wipe the slate clean. The Bible seems to go out of its way to magnify the wonder of this forgiveness. David wrote, God "forgives all my sins" (Ps. 103:3). Jeremiah quotes God as saying, "I will forgive their wickedness and will remember their sins no more" (Jer. 31:34). John declared, "If we confess our sins, he is faithful and just and will forgive us our sins and purify us from all unrighteousness" (1 John 1:9).

5. *The revelation of God's purpose in history.* Now Paul reaches the greatest heights of wonderment and rapture when he speaks of God's great purpose in history, namely, "to bring all things in heaven and on earth together under one head, even Christ" (vv. 9–10). Paul lived in a very broken world, as we do. He saw Greek pitted against Roman, Jew against Gentile, rich against poor, aristocrat against commoner. He saw people struggling for themselves and, above all, struggling against God. "Is this to go on forever?" he might have asked. Fortunately, Paul knew the answer to that question. The disharmony of the world is not to go on forever, for the same God who has predestined us to salvation in Jesus Christ has also predestined all things to be brought together in submission to him.

Paul wrote to the Philippians: "At the name of Jesus every knee [shall] bow, in heaven and on earth and under the earth, and every tongue [shall] confess that Jesus Christ is Lord, to the glory of God the Father" (Phil. 2:10–11).

6. *Sealing by the Holy Spirit.* Seals authenticate documents and declare that the promises contained in them are good. This is what the Holy Spirit does for Christians. So when Paul says, "Having believed, you were marked in him with a seal, the promised Holy Spirit" (v. 13), he is saying that God's gift of the Holy Spirit is an authentication that believers are truly God's and that none of the promises God has made to them will fail.

7. *An inheritance.* The Holy Spirit, though a seal on the document, so to speak, is actually more than certification of God's promises. He is himself a portion of our inheritance. Paul speaks of this when he terms the Holy Spirit "a deposit guaranteeing our inheritance until the redemption of those who are God's possession" (v. 14). This is a nice turn of phrase. According to this verse, Christians are God's inheritance. But the Holy Spirit, who is God, has been given to us as a down payment on the fullness of the inheritance which is already ours in Jesus Christ.

In Jesus Only

The last part of verse 3 tells us that the spiritual blessings given by God are "in Christ," which means, "in Jesus only." In the last chapter I alluded to the importance of the phrases "in Christ," "in him," or their equivalents, pointing out that they occur, in all, 164 times in Paul's writings. This is a difficult idea, but there is hardly a more important concept in the New Testament, since it is only by means of our union with Christ that any of these great spiritual blessings come to us. Even our election is in Christ, for God "chose us *in him* before the creation of the world" (v. 4).

We will be coming back to the phrase again and again as we work through this letter, and we will be looking at some of the more mystical aspects of the phrase then. Here it is more important to stress that these blessings can only be given to us through Jesus.

D. Martyn Lloyd-Jones puts it well: "If you leave out the 'in Christ,' you will never have any blessings at all. . . . Every blessing we enjoy as Christian people comes to us through the Lord Jesus Christ. God has blessings for all sorts and conditions of men. For instance, the Sermon on the Mount gives our Lord's teaching that God 'maketh his sun to rise on the evil and on the good' (Matt. 5:45). There are certain common general blessings which are enjoyed by the whole of humanity. There is what is called 'common grace,' but that is not what the apostle is dealing with here. Here he is dealing with particular grace, with special grace, the blessings that are enjoyed by Christian people only. The evil as well as the good, the unjust as well as the just, enjoy common blessings, but none but Christians enjoy these special blessings. People often stumble at this truth, but the distinction is drawn very clearly in the Scriptures. The ungodly may enjoy much good in this world, and their blessings come to them from God in a general way, but they know nothing of the blessings mentioned in this verse. Paul is writing here to Christian people, and his concern is that they should understand and grasp the special blessings and privileges possible to them as Christians; and so he emphasizes that all those blessings come in and through the Lord Jesus Christ, and in and through him alone. You cannot be a Christian without being 'in Christ.' Christ is the beginning as well as the end. He is Alpha as well as Omega.

There are no blessings for Christians apart from him."[4]

What does anyone have apart from Jesus Christ? Paul answers just a chapter further on in this letter: "Separate from Christ, [you are] excluded from citizenship in Israel and [are] foreigners to the covenants of the promise, without hope and without God in the world" (Eph. 2:12).

What is the situation when we are "in" him? We have "every spiritual blessing" and so praise God the Father, as Paul himself does, exuberantly. We will ask for our daily bread here, and other things besides. But if we suffer want here, in the final analysis it will be all right, because we still possess every spiritual blessing "in the heavenly realms." John Calvin summed it up wisely: "Whatever happens to us, let us always assure ourselves that we have good cause to praise our God, and that even if we are poor and miserable in this world, the happiness of heaven is enough to appease us, to sweeten all our afflictions and sorrows, and to give us such content that we may nevertheless have our mouths open to bless God for showing himself so kindhearted and liberal towards us as even to adopt us as his children, and to show us that the heritage which has been purchased for us by the blood of his only Son is ready for us, and that we cannot miss it, seeing that we go to it with true and invincible constancy of faith."[5]

---

[4]D. M. Lloyd-Jones, *God's Ultimate Purpose: An Exposition of Ephesians 1:1 to 23* (Grand Rapids: Baker, 1979), 58–59.

[5]John Calvin, *Sermons on the Epistle to the Ephesians* (1562; reprint, Carlisle, Pa.: Banner of Truth Trust, 1975), 21.

3

Election

(Ephesians 1:4–6)

For he chose us in him before the creation of the world to be holy and blameless in his sight. In love he predestined us to be adopted as his sons through Jesus Christ, in accordance with his pleasure and will—to the praise of his glorious grace, which he has freely given us in the One he loves.

It is wonderful to be told, as Paul does tell us in the third verse of Ephesians 1, that God "has blessed us . . . with every spiritual blessing in Christ." But as soon as that is said we immediately want to ask how such great blessing actually becomes ours. Paul describes it as "spiritual" blessing "in the heavenly realms." But we are not in heaven; we are on earth. How can we possess the blessings God has for us?

We can imagine a number of wrong ways. The blessings of heaven might be thought to be possessed by *force*, which is what Satan tried to do. He tried to conquer heaven; he was conquered instead. We might try to *earn* these great blessings. But with what would we earn them? Heaven's blessings must be bought by heaven's coin. We possess no spiritual currency. Perhaps we can *inherit* them when the owner dies. Alas, the owner is the eternal God, who does not die. Perhaps God is gracious and is only waiting for us to *ask* him for these blessings. Even this will not work. For according to Scripture, we are not the kind of persons who, unaided by God, will even ask him for blessings. On the contrary, we despise God's blessings. We want our will and

our way and left to ourselves, we would never ask God for anything.

Then how is it that some people receive these blessings, as Paul says they do? The answer is in verses 4–6. It is the result of God's own sovereign act, election. Paul says, "For [the Greek word is *kathōs*, meaning 'just as' or 'because'; it links verses 4 and 3, as an explanation] he chose us in him before the creation of the world to be holy and blameless in his sight. In love he predestined us to be adopted as his sons through Jesus Christ, in accordance with his pleasure and will—to the praise of his glorious grace, which he has freely given us in the One he loves."

This teaches that the blessings of salvation come to some people because God has determined from before the creation of the world to give them to them—and for that reason only.

ELECTION AND HUMAN DEPRAVITY

This doctrine is difficult for many persons, of course. But before we deal with their objections we would do well to consider the various views that people hold about election. There are three of them.

22

The first position is a *denial of election* outright. No one is saved because of some supreme hidden purpose of God, these objectors say. We can speak of grace, for God chose to reveal himself to fallen men and women and to provide a way of salvation through the death of his Son, the Lord Jesus Christ. That he did so proves him to be gracious. But having spoken of the grace of God in this sense, we must stop there and turn the entire situation over to human beings. God graciously offers salvation, but people must choose this salvation of their own free will. Election simply does not enter into it.

The strength of this view is that it conforms to what we all naturally like to think about our abilities. The difficulty is that, whether we like it or not, the Bible does teach this doctrine. John R. W. Stott calls election "a divine revelation, not a human speculation."[1] D. Martyn Lloyd-Jones refers to this teaching as "a statement, not an argument."[2] In his study of election J. C. Ryle begins by listing eleven texts (including Ephesians 1:4) that teach election in the simplest and most undeniable language and urges his readers to consider them well.[3]

It is hard to imagine anyone doing this and then continuing to deny that election is the Bible's teaching.

According to the second view, election is taught in Scripture but it is *election based on foreknowledge*. This is a mediating position, held by those who acknowledge that election is taught but who do not want to admit to a doctrine which they consider unjust and arbitrary. They would argue that God elects some to salvation and its blessings but that he does so on the basis of a choice, a response of faith, or some other good that he foresees in them.

This is patently impossible. One problem is that an election like that is not really election. In such a reconstruction God does not preordain an individual to anything; the individual actually ordains himself.

Another, greater problem is, if what the Bible tells us about the hopeless condition of man in sin is true, what good could God possibly see in anyone to cause him to elect that one to salvation? Goodness is from God. Faith is from God. If God is eliminated as a first cause of goodness or faith or a God-directed human choice (whatever it may be), how could there ever be any faith for God to foresee?

Calvin put it like this: "How should [God] foresee that which could not be? For we know that all Adam's offspring is corrupted and that we do not have the skill to think one good thought of doing well, and much less therefore are we able to commence to do good. Although God should wait a hundred thousand years for us, if we could remain so long in the world, yet it is certain that we should never come to him nor do anything else but increase the mischief continually to our own condemnation. In short, the longer men live in the world, the deeper they lunge themselves into their own damnation. And therefore God could not foresee what was not in us before he himself put it into us."[4]

When people have trouble with election—and many do—their real prob-

---

[1] John R. W. Stott, *God's New Society: The Message of Ephesians* (Downers Grove, Ill.: InterVarsity, 1979), 37.

[2] D. M. Lloyd-Jones, *God's Ultimate Purpose: An Exposition of Ephesians 1:1 to 23* (Grand Rapids: Baker, 1979), 86.

[3] John Charles Ryle, "Election," in *Old Paths: Being Plain Statements on Some of the Weightier Matters of Christianity* (Cambridge: James Clarke, 1977), 462–63.

[4] John Calvin, *Sermons on the Epistle to the Ephesians* (1562; reprint, Carlisle, Pa.: Banner of Truth Trust, 1975), 31–32.

lem is not with the doctrine of election, although they think it is, but with the doctrine of depravity that makes election necessary.

The question to settle is: how far did the human race fall when it fell? Did man fall upward? That is the view of secular evolutionists, that we are all getting better and better. Did man fall part way but not the whole way, so that he is damaged by sin but not ruined? That is the view of Pelagians or Arminians. It affirms that we are affected by sin but insists that we nevertheless possess the ability to turn from it and believe in Christ when the gospel is offered—by our own power. Or did man fall the whole way so that he is no longer capable of making even the smallest movement back toward God unless God first reaches down and performs the miracle of the new birth in him? That is the view of Scripture.

The Bible says that we are "dead in . . . transgressions and sins" (Eph. 2:1).

It says, "There is no one . . . who seeks God" (Rom. 3:11).

Jesus declared, "No one can come to me unless the Father who sent me draws him" (John 6:44).

It is written in Genesis: "The LORD saw how great man's wickedness on the earth had become, and that every inclination of the thoughts of his heart was only evil all the time" (Gen. 6:5).

What good could God possibly foresee in hearts that are dead in transgressions and sins and inclined only to evil all the time? What good could God anticipate in people who cannot come to him and do not even seek him unless he first draws them to himself? If that is the situation, as the Bible says it is, then the only way any man or woman can be saved is by the sovereign election of God by which he first chooses some for salvation and then leads them to faith.

The third position is *election pure and simple*. It teaches that we are too hopelessly lost in sin ever to partake of God's great spiritual blessings on our own. Instead, God in his mercy chose us and then made his choice effectual. First he made our salvation possible by sending the Lord Jesus Christ to die for our sin. Then he made us capable of responding to him by sending the Holy Spirit to open our eyes to the truth and glory of the gospel. Thus, all the blessings we enjoy must be traced back to this sovereign electing purpose of God toward us in Jesus Christ. And Paul does exactly that in these opening verses of Ephesians.

ARMINIAN OBJECTIONS

Objections to the Bible's teaching about election have been around for a long time, and there are many of them. Here I consider two: that election is arbitrary and that it is unjust.

When election is described as arbitrary we need to understand precisely what we are talking about. If we are basing the accusation on any supposed quality in man that is imagined to call forth election, then there is a sense in which election *is* arbitrary. From our perspective there is no reason why one individual rather than another should be elected. But generally that is not the way the change is made. Generally the objector means that election is arbitrary, not from our perspective, but from God's perspective. It amounts to saying that God has no reason for what he does. He is utterly arbitrary in picking one individual rather than another. It could as easily have been the other way around. Or God could have picked no one.

That last sentence indicates the way through this problem. For as soon as we think of the possibility of no one being saved we run against the very purpose Paul talks about in Ephesians 1:6, namely, that salvation is "to the praise of his [God's] glorious grace." That is, God purposed to glorify himself by saving some. Since that is so, election is not arbitrary. It has a purpose from God's point of view.

But why one person rather than another? Why more than one? Or why not everyone? These are good questions, but it does not take a great deal of understanding to recognize that they are of another order entirely. Once we admit that God has a purpose in election, it is evident that the purpose must extend to the details of God's choice. We do not know why he elects one rather than another, but that is quite a different thing from saying that he has no reasons. In fact, in so great an enterprise, an enterprise which forms the entire meaning of human history, it would be arrogant for us to suppose that we could ever understand the whole purpose. We can speculate. We can see portions of God's purpose in specific instances of election. But on the whole we will have to do as Paul does and confess that predestination is simply "in accordance with [God's] pleasure and will" (v. 5).

The second objection is that election is unjust. It is unjust for God to choose one rather than another, we are told. All must be given an equal chance. But is it possible that a person can still so misunderstand what is involved as to think in these categories? An equal chance! We have had a chance, but we have wasted it by rejecting the gospel. And it makes no difference how many "chances" are given, or to how many. Apart from God's sovereign work no one follows Jesus. So far as justice is concerned, what would justice decree for us, if justice (and nothing but justice) should be done? Justice would decree our damnation! Justice would sentence us to hell!

It is not justice we want from God; it is grace. And grace cannot be commanded. It must flow to us from God's sovereign purposes decreed before the

foundation of the world, or it must not come at all.

BLESSINGS OF ELECTION

Election is not the problem some have made it to be. In fact, it is actually a great blessing of the gospel. It is so in at least four areas.

1. *Election eliminates boasting.* Critics of election talk as if the opposite were true. They think it is the height of arrogance, something hardly to be tolerated, for a person to claim that he or she has been chosen to salvation. They suppose it is a claim to be worth more or to have done something better than other people. But, of course, election does not imply that at all. Election means that salvation is utterly of God. As Paul says, "*he* chose," "*he* predestined," "*he* has freely given," and this is "to the praise of *his* glorious grace" and not to our glory.

Only election eliminates all grounds for boasting. Suppose it were otherwise. Suppose that in the final analysis a person could get to heaven on the basis of something he or she had done. In that case, that individual could claim some part (small or large) of the glory. In fact, it would be the critical part, the part that distinguished him or her from those who were not saved. That is why salvation's blessings have to be ours by election alone.

2. *Election gives assurance of salvation.* Suppose it were otherwise. Suppose the ultimate grounds of salvation were in ourselves. In that case, salvation would be as unstable as we are. We might be saved one moment and lost the next. As Calvin says, "If . . . our faith were not grounded in God's eternal election, it is certain that Satan might pluck it from us every minute."[5]

Calvin found security of salvation in the "adoption," which verse 5 says God's election provides for us. Adop-

---

[5] Ibid., 29.

tion means that we are taken into God's family so that we become his children and he becomes our heavenly Father. Calvin points out that when we pray to God we must call him Father, for that is what Jesus taught us to do (see Matt. 6:9). But how can we do that, he asks, unless we are sure that he really is our Father? If not, then our prayers are mere hypocrisy and the first words we utter in them ("Our Father . . . ") are a lie. "We must be thoroughly resolved and persuaded in ourselves that God counts us as his children. And how may that be but by embracing his mercy through faith, as he offers it to us in his gospel, and by assuring ourselves also that we are grounded in his eternal election?"[6]

3. *Election leads to holiness*. A person might say, "Well, if I am elect, I suppose I'll be saved regardless of what I do; therefore, I'll enjoy myself and sin all I please." Those who say that either are not elect or else are elect but are not yet regenerate. Why? Because, as verse 3 says, election is to holiness. That is, election to salvation and election to holiness go together. They are never separated. So, as John Stott says, "Far from encouraging sin, the doctrine of election forbids it and lays upon us instead the necessity of holiness."[7] If we are not growing in holiness, we are not elect. We are still in our sins.

4. Finally, *election promotes evangelism*. Some think that election makes evangelism unnecessary. "For if God is going to save certain individuals any-way," the argument goes, "then he will save them, and there is no point in my having anything to do with it." It does not work that way. The fact that God elects to salvation does not eliminate the means by which he calls those elect persons to faith. One of those means is the proclamation of the gospel to sinners by those who already believe (1 Cor. 1:21). The very Paul who wrote this letter was the first great missionary.

Moreover, it is only as we recognize the importance of election that we gain hope in evangelism. Think about it. If the hearts of men and women are as opposed to God and his ways as the Bible says they are, and if God does not elect people and then call them effectively by means of the Holy Spirit so that they respond in saving faith, what hope could you or I possibly have of winning them? If God cannot call effectively, it is certain that you and I cannot. On the other hand, if God is doing this work on the basis of his prior election of some, then we can speak the word of truth boldly, knowing that all whom God has previously determined to come to faith will come to him.

We do not know who God's elect are. The only way we can find them out is by their response to the gospel and by their subsequent growth in holiness. Our task is to proclaim the Word boldly, knowing that all whom God has elected in Christ before the foundation of the world will surely come to Jesus.

---

[6] Ibid.
[7] Stott, *God's New Society*, 38.

4

Redemption

(Ephesians 1:7–10)

In him we have redemption through his blood, the forgiveness of sins, in accordance with the riches of God's grace that he lavished on us with all wisdom and understanding. And he made known to us the mystery of his will according to his good pleasure, which he purposed in Christ, to be put into effect when the times will have reached their fulfillment—to bring all things in heaven and on earth together under one head, even Christ.

Unitarians tell Christians that the word "Trinity" does not appear in the Bible. They are right. It does not. But although the *word* "Trinity" is not there, the *doctrine* of the Trinity certainly is. It is here prominently in the first chapter of Ephesians. I have already pointed out that in Greek, Ephesians 1:3–14 is one extended sentence and that it is difficult to outline it for that reason. Paul seems to pile one great truth upon another in his desire to express adequate praise to God for salvation. Still, there is obvious progression in these phrases, and the most obvious progression is in their orderly mention of God the Father, God the Son, and God the Holy Spirit. The work of the Father is principally stated in verses 3–6, the work of the Son in verses 7–10, and the work of the Spirit in verses 11–14.

Here we will focus on Christ's principal work which is redemption. All three persons of the Trinity are involved in this work, but Christ's role is central. The work of the Father was primarily in planning our salvation. The work of the Holy Spirit is in applying it to individuals. Jesus' principal work was to achieve salvation by his redemptive death for us on Calvary's cross.

BOUGHT WITH A PRICE

Redemption is central to Christianity. More than that, it is probably the single most beloved term in all the Christian's vocabulary. In the early part of this century B. B. Warfield, the distinguished professor of didactic and polemic theology at Princeton Theological Seminary, delivered an address to incoming students in which he argued that "there is no one of the titles of Christ which is more precious to Christian hearts than 'Redeemer.'" This is because, he said, Redeemer "is the name specifically of the Christ of the cross. Whenever we pronounce it, the cross is placarded before our eyes and our hearts are filled with loving remembrance not only that Christ has given us salvation, but that he paid a mighty price for it."[1]

In his address Warfield proved his thesis not, as we might suppose, by impressive theological arguments but

---

[1] B. B. Warfield, " 'Redeemer' and 'Redemption,' " in *The Person and Work of Christ* (Philadelphia: Presbyterian and Reformed Publishing, 1950), 325. The address was given on 17 September 1915.

by references to the church's hymns in which, he maintained, the true devotional heart of God's people is most evident. He cited such hymns as:

Let our whole soul an offering be
To our Redeemer's name.

While we pray for pardoning grace
Through the dear Redeemer's name.

Almighty Son, Incarnate Word,
Our Prophet, Priest, Redeemer,
Lord.

O for a thousand tongues to sing
My dear Redeemer's praise.

All glory, laud and honor
To thee, Redeemer, King.

The church our blest Redeemer
saved
With his own precious blood.

Warfield listed twenty-seven such selections—as well as lines by William Dunbar, William Shakespeare, Christina Rossetti, and Henry Vaughan. And then, lest we should miss the point, he did the same thing with hymns using the word "ransom," which, as he pointed out, is near in meaning to "redemption."

There are three words for "redemption" in the New Testament, two closely related to each other and the third quite different.

The first is *agorazō*. It comes from the noun for a Greek marketplace, an *agora*. It means "to buy" or "to buy in a marketplace." This word emphasizes the price Jesus paid for our salvation. However, as soon as we mention the word "price" many people object, arguing that any mention of a price in regard to salvation destroys grace. "Salvation is not sold," such persons argue. "Salvation is free. To think of God extracting a price for his forgiveness is to make God cheap, begrudging, and mercenary." Because of this reasoning some scholars have tried to change the idea of redemption from that of "buy-

ing" to mere "deliverance," that is, to "setting someone free" without the accompanying idea of a price or ransom. They point to Luke 24:21. There the Emmaus disciples speak of Jesus, saying, "We had hoped that he was the one who was going to redeem Israel." That refers to a political deliverance, not a commercial transaction. They could also point to Ephesians 1:13–14 in this paragraph, which says, "The promised Holy Spirit . . . is a deposit guaranteeing our inheritance until the redemption of those who are God's possession." Here redemption refers to deliverance from a life of sin and decay.

But that is not the whole story, of course. For one thing, the Emmaus disciples simply misunderstood what Jesus had come to do, just as those who speak of redemption as mere deliverance today also misunderstand it. We know this because later Jesus began to unfold for the disciples how it was necessary that he should "suffer and rise from the dead on the third day, and [that] repentance and forgiveness of sins . . . be preached in his name to all nations" (Luke 24:46–47). The price of redemption is Christ's death. That is what Christ himself is telling us in this passage.

Again, the idea of deliverance by payment of a price was common in the Old Testament period. The Jews spoke of *gaal* ("to redeem") and *goel* (usually translated "kinsman redeemer"). It was a principle of Jewish law that property should remain within a family whenever possible. So if a Jewish person lost his property through debt or some other means, there was a provision whereby he might receive it back again through the obligation placed upon a close relative. This relative, called the kinsman-redeemer, was to purchase the property and restore it to the family. Boaz did this for land that had belonged to the husband of Ruth.

A second Hebrew word is *kofer*,

which means "a ransom price." If a farm animal killed a person, the animal could be killed in payment for the life taken. Or if there was negligence, the owner of the animal could be compelled to forfeit his life. There would be no advantage to anyone in that, however. So there was an arrangement whereby if the man who owned the animal could settle on a price with the relatives of the person who had been killed, he could redeem either himself or the animal. This price of redemption was the *kofer*.

The point is that the idea of redemption by payment was firmly fixed in the Old Testament cultural world. It would therefore be natural that the New Testament writers, most of whom were Jews and all of whom were acquainted with that world, would use those concepts.

Again, it is not only in the Old Testament, Hebrew world that we find this idea. We find it in the New Testament, Greek world too. In Adolf Deismann's *Light from the Ancient East* and Leon Morris's *Apostolic Preaching of the Cross* there are examples of what was almost a standard formulation for the manumission of slaves in this period.[2] It might read:

> _____ pays to the Pithian Apollo the sum of _____ minae for the slave _____ on the condition that he (she) shall be set free.

This occurs so frequently that it is evident that the idea of delivering a person by the payment of a price was common in Greek culture.

However, the real reason why we must retain the idea of a price in discussing redemption is that the key New Testament texts all refer to it. There is Matthew 20:28, for example. Jesus says, "The Son of man did not come to be served, but to serve, and to give his life as a ransom for many."

What was Jesus talking about here? Obviously, he was saying that he was going to buy us out of slavery to sin at the cost of his life. Titus 2:14 is similar. It speaks of Jesus who "gave himself for us to redeem us from all wickedness and to purify for himself a people that are his very own, eager to do what is good." When this verse says that Jesus "gave himself for us" it means that he gave his life to redeem us. His life was the price. Finally, there is 1 Peter 1:18–19, perhaps the clearest text of all: "For you know that it was not with perishable things such as silver or gold that you were redeemed from the empty way of life handed down to you from your forefathers, but with the precious blood of Christ, a lamb without blemish or defect." In this verse the idea of Christ's life being the price of redemption is inescapable.

BOUGHT OUT AND FREED

The second New Testament word for "redemption," which helps to make the concept rich, is *exagorazō*. This is the same word as the one we have been studying but with the addition of the prefix *ex*, meaning "out of." *Exagorazō* means "to buy *out of* the marketplace," with the thought that one thus purchased might never return there again.

This is a particularly blessed thought for Christians because it has to do with the effective and permanent nature of redemption. When we are speaking in spiritual terms the redemption we have in mind is from sin, and the promise of this word is that we might never be sold under the power of sin again. In secular terms, we can imagine a case where a well-meaning, merciful person might purchase a slave to work in his or her household but then tire of the slave's performance or abilities and thus sell him again. In ancient times

---

[2] Adolf Deismann, *Light from the Ancient East: The New Testament Illustrated by Recently Discovered Texts of the Graeco-Roman World* (Grand Rapids: Baker, 1978), 327–30; Leon Morris, *The Apostolic Preaching of the Cross* (Grand Rapids: Eerdmans, 1956), 22–23.

that must have happened repeatedly, so that a slave's position was never really secure. Not so with Christ! Jesus purchased us so that we might be taken out of the marketplace and never have to return. "Once saved, always saved" is the way some put it. Having been purchased at the infinite cost of the blood of God's own Son, there is no one who can possibly top the price and thus purchase us away from him.

The third word for redemption in the New Testament is unrelated to the other two: *luō* (plus the derivatives *lutroō, lutron, lutrosis,* and *apolutrosis*). It means "to loose, set free or deliver"— by the payment of a price. Here too is a beautiful and encouraging thought for Christians. For it is not merely that we are bought out of the marketplace of sin, never to be returned there. A person could be bought on the slave block, never be sold on the block again but nevertheless continue for the remainder of his life as a slave. This is not what Jesus Christ does for us. He buys us from sin to set us free. This is what enabled Charles Wesley to write:

> Long my imprisoned spirit lay
> Fast bound in sin and nature's
>   night;
> Thine eye diffused a quick'ning ray,
> I woke, the dungeon flamed with
>   light;
> My chains fell off, my heart was
>   free,
> I rose, went forth and followed
>   thee.

So long as we know that the death of the Lord Jesus Christ has accomplished that for us, we will continue to love him and serve him as our "dear Redeemer."

Fellowship of the Redeemed

Ephesians 1:7–8 speaks of redemption "in accordance with the riches of God's grace that he lavished on us with all wisdom and understanding." As we have been studying the work of re-demption effected by Christ, we have begun to open up some of these riches. But there is more! The last verses of this section speak of the fellowship of the redeemed and of God's great purpose in redemption, saying, "And he made known to us the mystery of his will according to his good pleasure, which he purposed in Christ, to be put into effect when the times will have reached their fulfillment—to bring all things in heaven and on earth together under one head, even Christ" (vv. 9–10).

Paul's use of the word "mystery" here is ironic, for what he is saying is a mystery to many who read this text. It need not be. In Bible language a mystery is something that formerly was unknown but is now revealed. What Paul reveals in this verse is that God's ultimate purpose in redemption is "to bring all things in heaven and on earth together" again under Jesus Christ.

In the first volume of his multivolume study of Ephesians, D. Martyn Lloyd-Jones has an excellent study of these verses in which he points out rightly that the key to understanding them is a word which, strangely enough, most of the translations omit. It is the word "again," and it occurs in Greek in connection with the verb "bring together under one head." The verb is a strange one. The root of the verb is *kephalē*, which means "head." Variations of the word can mean the "headstone" or "cornerstone," the "main point" of an argument, a "summary," or even a "scroll" in which all things are summed up. The verb in Ephesians 1:10 is an expansion of this word (*anakephalaioō*), but, as I said, the word "again" (*ana*) is linked to it. The word really says that it is God's purpose "to bring together, unite, [or] sum up" all things "again" in Jesus Christ. In other words, everything was together in Jesus once, ceased to be united to him through the Fall, but is to be reunited in him *again* by redemption.

This is not a doctrine of universalism, the doctrine that all fallen creatures will be saved. That is repudiated in other places, including places that quote Jesus himself (see Matt. 25:41, 46; Mark 9:47–48; John 3:36; 5:28–29; 12:48). It is the teaching rather that all things will be subjected to Christ—some willingly as those who have been redeemed by Jesus joyfully exult in his rule, some unwillingly as evil is nevertheless restrained and all are forced to acknowledge Jesus as Lord of all.

Lloyd-Jones writes, "The perfect harmony that will be restored will be harmony in man and between men. Harmony on the earth and in the brute creation! Harmony in heaven, and all under this blessed Lord Jesus Christ who will be the head of all! Everything will again be united in him. And wonder of wonders, marvellous beyond compare, when all this happens it will never be undone again. All will be reunited in him to all eternity. That is the message; that is God's plan. That is the mystery which has been revealed unto us. . . . These things are so marvellous that you will never hear anything greater, either in this world or the world to come."[3]

KEEPING WORDS ALIVE

At the beginning of this study I referred to the address of B. B. Warfield in which he extolled redemption as being among the most blessed terms in the Christian's vocabulary. But to be faithful to his essay, I must acknowledge that toward the end of that message he bemoaned the fact that (even in his day) this was ceasing to be the case. On the one hand, the concepts had been under attack by liberal scholars who scorned the simple gospel of redemption and were trying to divest the great theological terms of Scripture of their meaning. On the other hand (although Warfield did not spell this out specifically), they were being neglected by Christian people. Maybe they were regarded as too theological, too abstract, or too impractical.

Warfield said, "It is a sad thing to see words like these die, . . . and I hope you will determine that, God helping you, you will not let them die thus, if any care on your part can preserve them in life and vigor. But the dying of the words is not the saddest thing which we see here. The saddest thing is the dying out of the hearts of men of the things for which the words stand. . . . The real thing for you to settle in your minds, therefore, is whether Christ is truly a Redeemer to you, and whether you find an actual Redemption in him. . . . Do you realize that Christ is your Ransomer and has actually shed his blood for you as your ransom? Do you realize that your salvation has been bought, bought at a tremendous price, at the price of nothing less precious than blood, and that the blood of Christ, the Holy One of God? Or, go a step further; do you realize that this Christ who has thus shed his blood for you is himself your God? So the Scriptures teach:

"The blood of God outpoured upon
  the tree!
So reads the Book. O mind,
  receive the thought,
Nor helpless murmur thou hast
  vainly sought
Thought-room within thee for such
  mystery. . . .

Draw near and listen to this
  sweetest sweet—
Thy God, O mindling, shed his
  blood for *thee!*[4]

---

[3] D. M. Lloyd-Jones, *God's Ultimate Purpose: An Exposition of Ephesians 1:1 to 23* (Grand Rapids: Baker, 1979), 206–7.

[4] Warfield, " 'Redeemer' and 'Redemption,' " 347–48.

5

Salvation's Seal

(Ephesians 1:11–14)

In him we were also chosen, having been predestined according to the plan of him who works out everything in conformity with the purpose of his will, in order that we, who were the first to hope in Christ, might be for the praise of his glory. And you also were included in Christ when you heard the word of truth, the gospel of your salvation. Having believed, you were marked in him with a seal, the promised Holy Spirit, who is a deposit guaranteeing our inheritance until the redemption of those who are God's possession—to the praise of his glory.

As I was preparing this study of Ephesians 1:11–14 late one year, the Philadelphia papers and the news broadcasts were filled with talk of the move of the city's professional football team, the Eagles, to Phoenix, Arizona. The story broke on a Tuesday, and for the rest of the week every minor development was reported exhaustively. On Friday night one television channel gave the first fifteen minutes of its thirty-minute news allotment to this story and even returned to it later in the program. This is the kind of thing that interests the people of this world.

In Ephesians 1 Paul presents the greatest news story there has ever been, as he traces the plan of salvation that began in the mind of God even before the beginning of this world and which will be continued throughout all eternity. As he tells it, it is bigger and wiser and grander than anything we can possibly imagine. This story has three movements, like a symphony. The first movement is the sovereign election of God according to which he has chosen to bless a special people with every possible spiritual blessing in his Son Jesus Christ. The second movement is the accomplishing of that purpose through the redeeming death of Jesus. It is through that death that these especially chosen people have forgiveness of sins and are brought under Christ's lordship.

The final movement—the one we are to study now—concerns the work of the Holy Spirit by which those who have been chosen by the Father and redeemed by the Lord Jesus Christ are actually "linked up" to salvation. The theological term for this is "application." The Holy Spirit is said to "apply" the benefits of Christ's work savingly.

THE EFFECTUAL CALL

We have already seen enough in our study of the opening paragraph of Ephesians to appreciate how comprehensive and profound this is. As I pointed out earlier, Ephesians 1:3–14 is actually a single sentence that embraces most of the essential doctrines of Christianity. It deals with the doctrines of God, the Trinity, election, the work of

Christ, forgiveness, the gospel, grace, creation, the consummation of world history when all things are brought together in subjection to Christ—and others besides. In this collection of doctrines Paul also talks about the Holy Spirit, and his elaboration of this subject is even more comprehensive than the ideas presented previously. What we have in verses 11–14 is a rich statement of the chief doctrines of the Holy Spirit and his work.

The first work of the Holy Spirit is what theologians term "the effectual call." It is what is referred to in verse 11: "In him *we were also chosen*, having been predestined according to the plan of him who works out everything in conformity with the purpose of his will." At first reading, this seems to be saying the same thing as verse 4, where Paul wrote that God "chose us in him before the creation of the world." That is, it seems to refer to the eternal election of believers to salvation. But that would be redundant. Actually, in this verse Paul is carrying the argument a bit further, showing how, having first "predestined" to salvation, God now chooses those who have been chosen, thereby working out his purposes in their particular lives. This is accomplished by the Holy Spirit, who opens our eyes to understand what Christ has done for us, grants faith to believe on him, and moves our wills to embrace him as our personal Savior.

This effectual call by the Holy Spirit is necessary because, apart from it, no one would turn from sin to Christ. Instead, all would turn from Christ, deeming his lordship something to be repudiated and the just demands of God something to be abhorred. Apart from the Holy Spirit the world crucifies Christ. That is why Jesus sent the Holy Spirit: to "convict the world of guilt in regard to sin and righteousness and judgment: in regard to sin, because men do not believe in me; in regard to

righteousness, because I am going to the Father, where you can see me no longer; and in regard to judgment, because the prince of this world now stands condemned" (John 16:8–11).

GLORIFICATION OF JESUS

The second function of the Spirit, according to these verses, is the glorification of Christ. In verse 12 Paul continues the thought of verse 11, saying that the Spirit calls God's elect "in order that we, who were the first to hope in Christ, might be *for the praise of his glory*." That sentence is written of Paul and his companions, but the same thing is said later of all Christians. All this is "to the praise of his glory" (v. 14).

In some ways the most important thing that can be said about the Holy Spirit is that it is the Holy Spirit's work to glorify Christ, as he himself said in John 15:26 ("When the Counselor comes, whom I will send to you from the Father, the Spirit of truth who goes out from the Father, he will testify about me") and John 16:13–14 ("He will not speak on his own; he will speak only what he hears. . . . He will bring glory to me by taking from what is mine and making it known to you").

Whenever the church has forgotten this it has tended to call attention to the Holy Spirit rather than Christ and has fallen into an unhealthy and often divisive subjectivism. When people ask, "Do you have the Holy Spirit?" "Have you had a second experience of the Holy Spirit?" "Have you received the gift of tongues [or whatever other evidence of the presence of the Spirit is being particularly stressed at that time]?"—then the church is divided! When the church has remembered that the role of the Spirit is to glorify Christ, then all the other activities of the Holy Spirit—sanctification, inspiration, the giving of gifts, even the work of creation and anything else that might be mentioned—are seen within that framework, and the church is drawn together around Jesus.

We can learn a practical lesson at this point. Since the work of the Holy Spirit is to glorify Christ, we may conclude that any emphasis upon the person and work of the Holy Spirit that detracts from the person and work of Christ is not of the Spirit. It is the work of another spirit, the spirit of antichrist (see 1 John 4:2–3). On the other hand, wherever Christ is exalted—in whatever way—there the third person of the Trinity is at work, and we may recognize that work and thank him for it.

We may notice one more thing, namely, that the work of the Holy Spirit in glorifying Christ is not apart from us since, as Paul says in verse 12, *"we . . . [are] for the praise of this glory."* Sometimes Christians fall into an overly subjective approach to Christianity, making their faith chiefly a succession of experiences. Sometimes they also commit the opposite error of making their faith abstract and viewing the work of God apart from their own involvement in it. They forget that God works through means. In conversion he works through the Bible and the Spirit who illumines its teachings to us. In glorifying Jesus he works through the Spirit *and ourselves*—by leading us to Christ and by increasingly producing the character of Jesus in our lives.

Are you glorifying Jesus in what you say and by the way you live? If not, you have no part in the Spirit, since that is what he is sent to do in Christians.

One New Man of Two

The third work of the Holy Spirit is the making of one new people, the church, out of those who were diverse peoples beforehand. This theme comes in for full and repeated treatment in

chapter 2. But even here it is so prominent that John R. W. Stott, for one, organizes the outline of Ephesians 1 around it. He speaks of "the future blessing of unification" in verses 9 and 10, and of "the scope of these blessings" in verses 11–14, showing that the blessings given by God through Christ belong equally to Jewish and gentile believers.[1] The parallelism is perfect. In verses 11 and 12 Paul speaks of himself and other Jewish believers, saying that such were "chosen . . . for the praise of his glory." In verses 13 and 14 he speaks of the gentile believers, to whom he is writing the letter, saying that they *"also were included . . . to the praise of his glory."*

This was an important thing in Paul's day because of the hostility that existed between Jews and Gentiles—between Greeks and Romans, rich and poor, slaves and free men, too, for that matter. In Paul's day (as in ours) the world was sharply divided along many scores of lines. People were divided by distrusts and hatreds. But into this divided world came a new breed of people, people whose lives were transformed by the Holy Spirit and who were united in Christ in spite of their differences. In chapter 2 Paul speaks of a "barrier," a "dividing wall of hostility." But that has been broken down by Jesus Christ. Now those who once were many rival peoples have become "one new man" and "one body" (Eph. 2:15–16).

What a great thing this is! And what a great way for the Holy Spirit to glorify Jesus Christ, in whose name this new society is founded!

I am sorry for churches made up of one class of people, as many American churches are, for they lack opportunity to show this new unification of people effectively. Church growth specialists

[1]John R. W. Stott, *God's New Society: The Message of Ephesians* (Downers Grove, Ill.: InterVarsity, 1979), 41, 45.

tell us that this is the best way for churches to grow, people being most attracted to those who are like themselves, and it may be so. Churches may grow fastest when everyone they are working with is alike. But at what cost is this growth purchased! I would rather have less growth and more glory given to Christ. I would rather have smaller totals but a larger body in the sense of a larger number of the types and conditions of people who are included in it.

WORD AND SPIRIT

The fourth aspect of the doctrine of the Holy Spirit in these verses is the connection between the Holy Spirit and the Word of God, the Bible, which Paul alludes to here in speaking of "the word of truth, the gospel" (v. 13). Just as the Holy Spirit glorifies Christ and may not be separated from him, so also does the Holy Spirit always speak through and with the Word of God, the Bible, and is not to be separated from it. The Holy Spirit never speaks or works apart from Scripture.

This was one great discovery of the Protestant Reformers. Luther, Calvin, and others had a strong belief in the work of the Holy Spirit in bringing men and women to faith and in leading and preserving them in that faith once they had believed. They believed in the Holy Spirit's work because the Bible taught it. They rejoiced in such verses as John 3:8 ("The wind blows wherever it pleases. You hear its sound, but you cannot tell where it comes from or where it is going. So it is with everyone born of the Spirit"), 1 John 5:6 ("The Spirit . . . testifies, because the Spirit is the truth") or 1 Corinthians 2:12–14 ("We have not received the spirit of the world but the Spirit who is from God, that we may understand what God has freely given us. This is what we speak, not in words taught us by human wisdom but in words taught by the

Spirit, expressing spiritual truths in spiritual words. The man without the Spirit does not accept the things that come from the Spirit of God, for they are foolishness to him, and he cannot understand them, because they are spiritually discerned").

But when they thought of these verses, with their strong emphasis on the work of the Holy Spirit, the Reformers also remembered many other verses that taught the importance of the Bible in knowing the mind of God, and they recognized that it is through the Bible, as the Holy Spirit illumines it to our minds, that God speaks.

Apart from a general revelation of God in nature (which by itself saves no one), we may say that God reveals himself in three ways: (1) there is a revelation of God in history, centered in the atoning work of Christ; (2) there is a revelation of God in writing, the Bible, which tells us of God's acts; and (3) there is a revelation of God to the mind and heart of the individual by the Holy Spirit, who interprets the written revelation to us and applies its blessings to our hearts. None of this happens apart from the Bible or the truth of the gospel, which it contains, which is what Paul says here. So we can never give too much attention to the Bible. The Bible is the means God uses to call and bless people, as the Holy Spirit, who is God, reveals the Lord Jesus Christ and his work through its pages.

MARKED WITH A SEAL

The final work of the Spirit mentioned here is his work of sealing God's people. The text says, "Having believed, *you were marked in him with a seal*, the promised Holy Spirit, who is a deposit guaranteeing our inheritance until the redemption of those who are God's possession" (vv. 13–14).

In his commentary Charles Hodge points out rightly that there are three purposes for which a seal is used and that each illustrates the Spirit's work: (1) a seal is used to confirm an object or document as being true or genuine, (2) a seal is used to mark a thing as one's property, and (3) a seal is used to make something fast or secure.[2] The first may be illustrated by the seal of the United States which appears on paper currency or by the seal affixed to a passport. The second is like a name plate on the flyleaf of a book. The third is illustrated by the seal of the Sanhedrin placed upon the tomb of Christ.

Each of these illustrates something important about the Spirit's work. The Holy Spirit verifies that the one receiving him really is God's child, as Paul says in Romans 8:16 ("The Spirit himself testifies with our spirit that we are God's children").

D. Martyn Lloyd-Jones thinks that this is the chief point of Paul's reference in Ephesians 1:14 and spends five chapters on it.[3] The Holy Spirit is also God's claim on us that we truly are his possession. The phrase "God's possession" is used explicitly in verse 14. Finally, the Holy Spirit makes the Christian secure in his new faith and relationship. This comes through in the idea of the Spirit's being "a deposit [or down payment] guaranteeing our inheritance" until our full redemption. Like a down payment on the purchase of a property, he is proof of God's good faith and an earnest of the full amount to come.

Sealing with the Holy Spirit answers to all our needs. It assures us of God's favor. It shows that we belong to him. It renders our salvation certain.

To God Be Glory

The last words of this great opening sentence of the apostle Paul are "to the praise of his glory." It is an appropriate end, just as it was an appropriate beginning. In verse 3 Paul began by exclaiming, "Praise be to the God and Father of our Lord Jesus Christ, who has blessed us in the heavenly realms with every spiritual blessing in Christ." Then, after he has enumerated those blessings, he returns to the place from which he set out, saying that this is "to the praise of his glory."

And there is this too. When Paul began to speak of God's blessings to us in salvation he went back before the creation of the world to God's eternal will, saying that salvation began when God chose us in Jesus Christ (v. 4). He then showed how that will of God unfolded itself in history, first in the work of the second person of the Godhead in providing redemption from sin, and then in the work of the third person of the Godhead in applying that work to the individual. At this point he introduces the idea of God's purpose, showing it to be that God himself might be glorified. In other words, everything we have in Christ comes from God and returns to God, beginning in his will and ending in his glory. It is God-centered from beginning to end.

---

[2]Charles Hodge, *A Commentary on the Epistle to the Ephesians* (1856; reprint, Grand Rapids: Baker, 1980), 63.

[3]D. M. Lloyd-Jones, *God's Ultimate Purpose: An Exposition of Ephesians 1:1 to 23* (Grand Rapids: Baker, 1979), 243–300.

6

Prayer for the Saints

(Ephesians 1:15–19)

For this reason, ever since I heard about your faith in the Lord Jesus and your love for all the saints, I have not stopped giving thanks for you, remembering you in my prayers. I keep asking that the God of our Lord Jesus Christ, the glorious Father, may give you the Spirit of wisdom and revelation, so that you may know him better. I pray also that the eyes of your heart may be enlightened in order that you may know the hope to which he has called you, the riches of his glorious inheritance in the saints, and his incomparably great power for us who believe.

If God is in charge of everything and has "foreordained whatsoever comes to pass"—in the words of the Westminster Shorter Catechism—what is the point of praying? In fact, what is the point of doing anything? Why witness? Why study the Bible? Why do good works? If what is going to happen is going to happen anyway, none of these things count. We might as well do as we please and let God do what he wants.

The reasonable answer to this objection is that although God does do as he pleases, he uses means like prayer, witnessing, Bible reading, and the doing of good works. So it is just as correct to say with James "You do not have, because you do not ask God" (James 4:2), as it is to say, "The will of God is done." If we do not pray, the good things for which we pray will not happen, since it is through prayer that God brings the blessing.

The first chapter of Ephesians teaches this lesson clearly. It would be hard to find a passage of Scripture that stresses the sovereignty of God in salvation more strongly (except perhaps Romans 8). Yet it also emphasizes the importance and urgency of prayer just as strongly. Indeed, those two themes give the chapter its shape.

In the first half of the chapter, in one long sentence running from verse 3 to verse 14, Paul praises God for the salvation of which he is both the author and accomplisher. God the Father chose; God the Son redeemed; God the Holy Spirit applied that salvation in a personal way. But then, in the second half of the chapter we have a prayer. The gist of this prayer is that God, who has planned and accomplished this salvation, might complete it as his people grow in knowledge of him.

For Paul, the knowledge that God was working was an inducement to prayer, not an excuse for neglecting it. It was because God *was* at work that he could pray with confidence.

To Know Him Better

Paul's statements of what he is praying for follow a typical Greek construction. In this construction he says what

37

he is praying about first. Then he uses a purpose clause to indicate why he is praying in this way. He does it twice in this passage. In verse 17 he says that he is praying that God might give the Ephesians "the Spirit of wisdom and revelation" *in order that* they "may know him better." Then in verses 18 and 19 he says that he is praying that "the eyes of [their hearts] may be enlightened" *in order that* they may know "the hope to which he has called [them], the riches of his glorious inheritance in the saints, and his incomparably great power for us who believe." Put together, it is really one great prayer for knowledge: knowledge of God and a fuller knowledge of the elements of salvation, consisting in our hope, our inheritance, and the power available to us through the Lord Jesus Christ.

The chief idea is that we might know God.

Some years ago I was in a question-and-answer session following a meeting of the post-college group at Tenth Presbyterian Church, and I was asked, "Dr. Boice, what do you think is the greatest lack among evangelical Christians in America today?" It was the first time I had been asked that question, but it was asked at a timely moment. I had been doing work on the attributes of God and had this in mind. So although at an earlier period in my ministry I might have said, "To be faithful to the teachings of Scripture, to show love for one another," or some such thing, in this case I replied, "I think that the greatest need of the evangelical church today is for professing Christians really to know God." My opinion has not changed in the years since. As I read a verse like Ephesians 1:17, I sense that from the beginning this has been the prayer of true pastors for God's people.

The reason this is so important is that we often settle for something quite less.

Some of us settle for very little knowledge. We take pride in singing, "I need no other argument, I need no other plea; I only know that Jesus died and that he died for me." We want to go to heaven ignorantly.

Some settle for mere knowledge of the Bible. This is good, of course, for the Bible is God's Word and there is no knowledge of God apart from it. Still, although we must know Scripture, this in itself is not the fullness of what God has for us.

Other Christians settle for knowledge about God. They are theologians of sorts. They can discuss God's attributes. But it is possible to know a great deal about God without knowing God. It is possible to know much theology and still not be a Christian. Jesus said, "This is eternal life: that they may know *you*, the only true God, and Jesus Christ, whom you have sent" (John 17:3).

It is interesting to find this prayer that the Ephesians might "know [God] better" on the lips of the apostle, for it was Paul who had taught the doctrine of God to the Ephesians. He had taught the truths we find in this letter, indeed, in this very chapter: that God is a Trinity (Father, Son, and Holy Spirit), that God created the world, that he elected a people to salvation even before creation, and that he worked in Jesus Christ to accomplish that salvation by the cross. Paul has spoken of predestination, redemption, adoption, sanctification, and glorification. He has reminded the Ephesians of the final subjection of all things to God through Jesus at the last day. This is a seminary course's worth of theology, and it has come from Paul.

We might very well ask, "What do you mean, Paul, when you pray that the Ephesians might come to know God better? You have taught them all these things already. Do you mean that they do not know them? Or that there is some hidden, esoteric information still to come?"

"No," Paul would answer. "You have misunderstood me. I am not praying that the Ephesians might come to know more *about* God, though they probably do have a great deal more to learn, but rather that they might know *him*. Knowing him and knowing about him are quite different."

What then does it mean to know God? This is not an easy question to answer, any more than it is easy to answer the same question about a person. Whole books have been written about it. In one of these books, *Knowing God,* British scholar J. I. Packer suggests the following three elements: "First, knowing God is a matter of *personal dealing*. . . . It is a matter of dealing with him as he opens up to you, and being dealt with by him as he takes knowledge of you. . . . Second, knowing God is a matter of *personal involvement,* in mind, will and feeling. . . . The believer rejoices when his God is honored and vindicated, and feels the acutest distress when he sees God flouted. . . .

"Equally, the Christian feels shame and grief when convicted of having failed his Lord. . . . Third, knowing God is a matter of *grace*. It is a relationship in which the initiative throughout is with God—as it must be, since God is so completely above us and we have so completely forfeited all claim on his favour by our sins."[1]

That being the case, Packer concludes, "What matters supremely . . . is not . . . the fact that I know God, but the larger fact which underlies it—the fact that *he knows me.*"[2] This, of course, is the perspective of Paul in this opening chapter of Ephesians. He prays that we might know God precisely because it is God who has first set his love upon us and elected to know us savingly.

THE SCOPE OF SALVATION

The second time Paul prays for knowledge for the Ephesians he shifts his focus slightly, turning from knowledge of God himself to knowledge of those elements of salvation he has achieved for us. He makes three requests: (1) that we might know "the hope to which he has called [us]," (2) that we might know "the riches of his glorious inheritance in the saints," and (3) that we might know "his incomparably great power for us who believe."

1. *The hope to which he has called us.* In this phrase Paul links the words "hope" and "call." This is significant. In Scripture the word "hope" usually looks toward the last things or to the completion of what has already been begun. By linking the idea of the "call" to "hope" Paul is saying that the calling of God, which he has been talking about extensively in the opening half of this chapter, is not without a context (as if God was merely calling to us in a fog). God has called us to something and for something. Earlier he said that God chose us "to be holy and blameless in his sight" (v. 4), "to be adopted as his sons through Jesus Christ" (v. 5), and to be "for the praise of his glory" (v. 12). That calling is part of our hope along with our hope of being taken into heaven, seeing God, and being made like the Lord Jesus Christ.

What a great knowledge this is! Once we really understand it, it will inevitably transform how we look at this world with its sin and suffering and how we look at others who by the grace of God also share this destiny.

D. Martyn Lloyd-Jones tells the story of Philip Henry, the father of Matthew Henry the commentator. He and a

[1]J. I. Packer, *Knowing God* (Downers Grove, Ill.: InterVarsity, 1973), 34–36.
[2]Ibid., 37.

We can know God because He knows us.

young lady had fallen in love with each other. She belonged to a "higher" level of society than he did, and although she had become a Christian and therefore regarded such things differently, her parents saw the disparity in social status as an obstacle to the marriage. "This man Philip Henry," they said, "where has he come from?"

To this question the future Mrs. Henry gave the immortal reply, "I do not know where he has come from, but I know where he is going."[3]

In Christian circles the worth of a person is determined not by his or her background (we are all only sinners saved by grace) but by where we are going. We are going to Zion. We are going to be like the Lord Jesus Christ in every way.

Knowing this gives Christians confidence. It gives us the assurance that we really are God's children and that his hand is on us, leading us to a certain and blessed destiny. In common speech we generally "hope" for uncertain things. In the Bible the word is used of that which is certain because it is grounded on what God has done for us in the work of Christ. That is why the Bible speaks of "a living hope" (1 Peter 1:3), a "blessed hope" (Titus 2:13), and a hope which is "sure" (Heb. 6:11).

My hope is built on nothing less
Than Jesus' blood and righteousness;
I dare not trust the sweetest frame,
But wholly lean on Jesus' name.

On Christ, the solid Rock, I stand;
All other ground is sinking sand.

2. *The riches of his glorious inheritance in the saints.* The Greek behind this phrase allows two interpretations. It can refer either to God's inheritance of us—we are his possession—or to our inheritance of what he has given to us in salvation. The second interpretation is

more likely, because of the context (Paul is praying that we might know our call and destiny) and because of a parallel text in Colossians 1:12, in which Paul prays that we might "share in the inheritance of the saints in the kingdom of light."

If the riches of our inheritance involve the future realization of what we already have in part, what is the difference between this petition and the first petition in which Paul asks that we might know the hope to which we have been called? The answer is in the difference between the words "hope" and "riches." In the first case, the emphasis is upon hope, which is a certain thing. The issue is assurance. In the second case, the emphasis is upon riches. Here the issue is the scope of the blessings God has for us.

How little we know of those blessings! We know little enough of the blessings God has for us here, blessings like prayer, Bible study, the joys of Christian fellowship, meaningful work, the sacraments. But if that is true of earthly things, how much truer is it of heavenly things! What do we know of heavenly joys? the new Jerusalem? the beatific vision? Indeed, even Paul wrote, "Now we see but a poor reflection . . . then we shall see face to face. Now I know in part; then I shall know fully, even as I am fully known" (1 Cor. 13:12). We know little; and we know imperfectly. But we should know more—and will, as we pray for one another and progress in grace.

Some critics charge that a concern for what is to come makes Christians of little earthly use. The opposite is the case. We know what we are to become and therefore we live differently here. It is the citizens of heaven who make the greatest differences on earth.

3. *His incomparably great power for us*

---

[3] D. M. Lloyd-Jones, *God's Ultimate Purpose: An Exposition of Ephesians 1:1 to 23* (Grand Rapids: Baker, 1979), 324.

who believe. In his commentary on Ephesians John R. W. Stott points out that in the framework of these verses the Christian is living somewhere between the call of God, which is past, and the riches of our inheritance, which (in their fullness) are still future. We live in the here and now, and the question for the present is how we are to live as God's children. How can we live as citizens of heaven in a world whose citizens do not acknowledge God's sovereignty?

Paul's answer is to know God's power by experience. This is so important to him that he picks up on this idea and completes the chapter with it. It is, he says, "that power . . . which he exerted in Christ when he raised him from the dead and seated him at his right hand in the heavenly realms, far above all rule and authority, power and dominion, and every title that can be given, not only in the present age but also in the one to come (vv. 19–21).

The important idea here is that this is to be experiential knowledge, just as in Paul's opening petition the knowledge of God is to be experiential. Paul was not going to be any more satisfied with an intellectual knowledge of God's power on the part of the Ephesians than he was going to be satisfied with a mere intellectual knowledge of God. It is important to know both these things intellectually; indeed, that is the starting point. But beyond this, he wanted them to know God and the power of Christ's resurrection in their lives.

TIME WITH GOD

How are you and I to experience that power? If we are to live in the power of Christ's resurrection, we must come to know God. That is what Paul prays for first. And if we are to know God, we must spend time with him in Bible study, prayer, and meditation. You cannot get to know a person without spending time with him or her. No more can you get to know God without spending time with him.

Harry Ironside tells of meeting a very godly man early in his ministry. The man was dying of tuberculosis, and Ironside had gone to visit him. His name was Andrew Fraser. He could barely speak above a whisper. His lungs were almost gone. Yet he said, "Young man, you are trying to preach Christ, are you not?"

"Yes, I am," replied Ironside.

"Well," he said, "sit down a little, and let us talk together about the Word of God." He opened his Bible, and until his strength was gone he opened up one passage after another, teaching truths that Ironside at that time had never seen or appreciated. Before long tears were running down Ironside's cheeks, and he asked, "Where did you get these things? Can you tell me where I can find a book that will open them up to me? Did you get them in a seminary or college?"

Fraser replied, "My dear young man, I learned these things on my knees on the mud floor of a little sod cottage in the north of Ireland. There with my open Bible before me, I used to kneel for hours at a time and ask the Spirit of God to reveal Christ to my soul and to open the Word to my heart, and he taught me more on my knees on that mud floor than I ever could have learned in all the seminaries or colleges in the world."[4]

That is the secret. It is not intelligence, outstanding instruction, or academic degrees. It is time spent with God. It is to people who sit at Jesus' feet that God opens his heart.

---

[4]H. A. Ironside, *In the Heavenlies: Practical Expository Addresses on the Epistle to the Ephesians* (Neptune, N.J.: Loizeaux Brothers, 1937), 86–87.

7

Jesus Over All

(Ephesians 1:19–23)

That power is like the working of his mighty strength, which he exerted in Christ when he raised him from the dead and seated him at his right hand in the heavenly realms, far above all rule and authority, power and dominion, and every title that can be given, not only in the present age but also in the one to come. And God placed all things under his feet and appointed him to be head over everything for the church, which is his body, the fullness of him who fills everything in every way.

A person does not need to read very much of the New Testament to realize that large portions are future-oriented. We are told of Christ's past work, providing salvation for his people, but we are also told that he will return in power to subdue his enemies and subject all things to God. One of the earliest Christian prayers, reflected in 1 Corinthians 16:22 and Revelation 22:20, is, "Come, Lord Jesus." The church looks forward to that future day and longs for Christ's victory.

Unfortunately, a concern for future things has often obscured for some Christ's present exalted position in the universe. It is true, as the author of Hebrews writes, that "at present we do not see everything subject to him" (Heb. 2:8). But, as he also writes, "We see Jesus . . . crowned with glory and honor" (v. 9). Paul was thinking along these lines at the end of the first chapter of Ephesians. He had been speaking of the greatness of our salvation— grounded in the electing purpose of God from eternity, accomplished in history by the atoning death of Jesus Christ, and applied to individuals per-

sonally by the Holy Spirit. He prayed for the Ephesians, asking that they might be more fully grounded in God's truth. He said that he wanted them to know the power of Christ. But when he got to the thought of God's power Paul's mind expanded to marvel at the greatness of that power, and his thoughts turned to the present exalted status of Christ in whom that power has already been displayed.

In speaking of Jesus' present exaltation he referred: (1) to his resurrection from the dead, (2) to his ascension and enthronement over evil, and (3) to his headship over the church his body.

GOD'S MIGHTY STRENGTH

In studying the first part of this prayer (vv. 15–23) I pointed out the importance of knowledge for sound faith. Paul makes his concern for sound knowledge plain. He prayed that the Christians at Ephesus might know God better (v. 17) and that they might know the hope to which he had called them, the riches of his glorious inheritance in the saints, and the incomparable greatness of his power to all who believe (vv. 18–19). It is impossible to look at those verses without realizing that Christianity is a religion of knowledge. It is for the head as well as for the heart.

But having said this, we must also stress that Christianity is not just "head" knowledge. It is not a religion of ideas only. It is not merely a philosophy. Some Christians treat the faith as if it were, taking care to master Bible doctrines, thinking that when they have done this they have done all that needs to be done. They believe that in knowing the truth they have it all. This did not satisfy the apostle, and it should not satisfy us either. For important as sound theological and doctrinal knowledge is, it is given that we might know God better and thus live in his power and be victorious over sin in this life. Christianity is knowledge, yes. But it is also power, power from beginning to end. Without the power of God not one individual would ever become a Christian. The salvation of the soul is a resurrection, the recovery of a person from the dead. Without God's power not one individual would ever triumph over sin, live a godly life, or come at last to the reward God has for all his own in heaven.

So we begin to see why this is so important and why Paul develops and emphasizes it as he does. It is by the power of God displayed in Jesus Christ that we are to live Christianity.

RESURRECTION POWER

When Paul thinks of the greatness of the display of God's mighty power in Christ, he looks first at the resurrection. Jesus had predicted that God would raise him from the dead after the leaders of the people had arrested, abused, and crucified him. He said, "The Son of Man will be betrayed to the chief priests and teachers of the law. They will condemn him to death and will hand him over to the Gentiles, who

will mock him and spit on him, flog him and kill him. Three days later he will rise" (Mark 10:33–34). It seemed impossible. For centuries people had lived and died. So far as anyone could see, death was the end of them. Yet Jesus said that after he died (indeed, after three days in the tomb) he would return to life triumphantly.

What power on earth could possibly accomplish this miracle? Obviously, no power on earth could. Only a heavenly power could—and did! On the third day God raised Jesus Christ from the dead, as he said he would. God thus vindicated Jesus' claims, declared that Christ's atonement for sin was accepted, and revealed that all who are united to Christ by faith can live triumphantly through that power.

We sometimes speak of Christ's resurrection as the forerunner of our own resurrection—and the proof of it. Because he lives, we shall live also. That is true enough. It is a glorious certainty. But it is not only at the end of things, that is, at our own resurrection, that the power of God displayed in Christ is to be seen in us. It is to be seen in our present victories over sin in this life. In his study of this passage D. Martyn Lloyd-Jones speaks of victory over worldliness, the flesh and the devil— our three great adversaries. The world constantly bombards us with its values. We get them from television, newspapers, films, the competitive world in which we earn our livings and from casual conversations. How are we to be victorious over this great enemy? It is by the power of God displayed in the resurrection of Jesus Christ from the dead. This power is able to transform us "by the renewing of our mind[s]" (Rom. 12:2). It is what makes us "new creation[s]" (2 Cor. 5:17).

Our second great adversary is the flesh, which in biblical language means the nature of sinful man untouched by the Holy Spirit. The flesh is a formidable enemy. It draws us to inactivity when we should be reading the Bible, praying, or performing good works. It locks us into sinful patterns of behavior when we should be living a Christlike life. How can we triumph over these strong forces? It is only by the power of God displayed in the resurrection of Jesus from the dead.

Third, there is the devil. What a foe he is! Many people, even Christians, regard the devil almost as an invention or at least as one at whom we may laugh. But when Satan met our first parents in Eden it was no laughing matter. They had been created perfect with not even a disposition to evil. Yet when Satan appeared, so great were his power, wiles, and subtlety that it was only a short time before he had brought about the fall of both Eve and Adam. Thus did sin (and death, the consequence of sin) pass upon the race. No wonder Peter writes, "Your enemy the devil prowls around like a roaring lion looking for someone to devour" (1 Peter 5:8). No wonder Paul told the Ephesians, "Put on the full armor of God so that you can take your stand against the devil's schemes" (Eph. 6:11). Lloyd-Jones says, "Because of these things we need to be enlightened with respect to the power of God working in us. Nothing else can enable us to stand against the wiles of the devil."[1]

ALL THINGS UNDER JESUS

With all these spiritual enemies, is Christ's power adequate to overcome them? We might doubt that it can—were it not for this next step in Christ's exaltation. God's mighty strength was not exhausted in the resurrection of Jesus from the dead but also worked to seat him "at his right hand in the heavenly realms, far above all rule and authority, power and dominion, and every title that can be given, not only in the present age but also in the one to come" (vv. 20–21).

Christ's exaltation over "all rule and authority" involves all earthly powers and angels. But in the context of the Christian's struggle to live a godly life (and in the context of this book as a whole) the emphasis is certainly upon the hostile spiritual powers of the corrupt world system. The Bible teaches that demonic powers stand behind evil rulers so that, as Paul says later in this book, we struggle not merely "against flesh and blood, but against the rulers, against the authorities, against the powers of this dark world and against the spiritual forces of evil in the heavenly realms" (Eph. 6:12). These spiritual forces have been made subject to Christ. So when we are told that Jesus has been exalted over them we do not need to fear attacks from these forces any more than from our flesh or the surrounding world system.

How are we to be victorious over Satan? James tells us: "Submit yourselves, then, to God. Resist the devil, and he will flee from you" (James 4:7). We cannot resist Satan in our own strength. But if we first submit ourselves to God so that the power of God demonstrated in the exaltation of Christ above all rule and authority flows through us, the devil will flee from us as he fled from Christ at the conclusion of his temptation in the wilderness.

THE CHURCH, HIS BODY

The third step in Christ's exaltation through God's power is in verses 22–23: "And God placed all things under his feet and appointed him to be head over everything for the church, which is his body, the fullness of him who fills everything in every way." These verses

---

[1] D. M. Lloyd-Jones, *God's Ultimate Purpose: An Exposition of Ephesians 1:1 to 23* (Grand Rapids: Baker, 1979), 420.

continue the thought of Jesus being exalted above all rule and authority since "*all* things" have been placed under his feet. But they carry the thought further by reference to "the church" for whose benefit this subjugation has been made. Jesus has been exalted over the spiritual forces of evil as a conqueror. He is exalted over the church as its proper and greatly honored head.

This is the first time in Ephesians that the word "church" has occurred, but from the beginning Paul has had the church in mind. Ray C. Stedman outlines Ephesians around this theme: (1) the origin of the church, (2) the nature of the church, (3) the function of the church, and (4) the church's essential relationship to its Lord.[2] Since the letter is chiefly about the church, it is worth looking at this first reference to the church carefully.

Unfortunately, there is difficulty in knowing how to translate verse 23, which deals with it. The difficulty stems from the fact that the words translated "the fullness of him who fills everything in every way" can have three meanings.

1. The first interpretation takes the phrase to be *a description of Christ* so that we should read: ". . . the church, which is the body of him (that is, Christ) who is the fullness of him (that is, God) who fills all in all." John Stott, who discusses each of these three options carefully, notes that "at first sight this is an attractive interpretation."[3] Certainly the idea of God filling all things is biblical (Jer. 23:24), and the fullness of the Godhead *is* said to dwell in Jesus Christ (Col. 1:19; 2:9). To translate the verse this way would be to end the chapter with a grand wrap-up of all things in Christ, who is the fullness of God, and God, who is the fullness of all things. The difficulty with this view is that although the Godhead is said to dwell fully in Christ, in the sense that he is fully God, Scripture never elsewhere says that Christ is God's fullness. That would be to say that the Father is subsumed in the Son, which is not accurate.

2. The second interpretation (like the third, which follows) takes "fullness" as *referring to the church*. What makes it distinct from the third view is that here the meaning is supposed to be active, that is, the church is that *which fills or completes Christ*, while in the last possibility the meaning is supposed to be passive, that is, the church is that which Christ fills.

If the church fills or completes Christ, the verse is teaching the startling truth that without the church Christ is in some sense incomplete. That cannot be meant ontologically, of course; if Christ is God (as he is), there can be no real incompleteness or imperfection about him. But that is not what proponents of this view mean. They only wish to carry out the images of the church as the body or bride of Christ, which this letter develops. A head without the body is incomplete. A husband without his wife is incomplete, just as a wife without her husband is also incomplete. John Calvin held to this interpretation. He wrote, "By this word 'fullness' he means that our Lord Jesus Christ, and even God his Father, account themselves imperfect unless we are joined to him. . . . It is his will to have us joined to him, yes, even on the condition that he should be perfected in us by our being united in that manner. As if a father should say, My house seems empty to me when I do not see my child in it. A husband will say, I

---

[2] Ray C. Stedman, *Body Life* (Glendale, Calif.: Regal, 1972), 7.
[3] John R. W. Stott, *God's New Society: The Message of Ephesians* (Downers Grove, Ill.: InterVarsity, 1979), 61–62. Stott discusses these views on pp. 61–66.

seem to be only half a man when my wife is not with me."[4]

D. Martyn Lloyd-Jones also endorses this view in guarded fashion: "There is a sense in which we as the church are his fullness. . . . A head alone is not complete. A head needs a body, and you can not think of a head without a body. So the body and the head are one in this mystical sense. As such we Christian people are part of 'the fullness' of the Lord Jesus Christ."[5]

3. The final interpretation of this phrase takes it in the passive sense of being *that which Christ fills.* John Stott holds to this view. I think he does so rightly, although, as I say, each of the views is possible. Stott holds to this view chiefly because of the analogy of Scripture, which nowhere else says that the church completes Christ but which often says that he fills it. It also fits the flow of this chapter, which climaxes with Christ in his glory, just as it began with him. In view of the teaching about Christ's exaltation in these last verses, it is more natural to say that Jesus fills the church as he also fills the universe than to say (unnaturally) that the church somehow completes him. Since Paul is talking about God's power displayed in Christ, it is natural for him to portray Christ as filling and thus empowering the church, which is his body.

BANNER OF THE CROSS

The church is to be a transforming power—indeed, through the presence of the risen Christ within, the greatest of all powers in this world. Those who belong to the church are changed; apart from the power of Christ in their lives they do not even belong to it. Then,

having been changed and having become members of the church, they are to work through the power of Christ in the church to transform the world powerfully. The victory is not achieved by arms. It is not achieved by marches or by the force of power politics. It is the victory of transformed lives as, through the church which Christ fills, the rule of Christ is extended forcefully throughout the world.

Edward Gibbon, the author of the classic study *The Decline and Fall of the Roman Empire*, saw this in the early church and wrote about it movingly: "While that great body [the Roman Empire] was invaded by open violence, or undermined by slow decay, a pure and humble religion gently insinuated itself into the minds of men, grew up in silence and obscurity, derived new vigour from opposition, and finally erected the triumphant banner of the Cross on the ruins of the Capitol. Nor was the influence of Christianity confined to the period or to the limits of the Roman empire. After a revolution of thirteen or fourteen centuries, that religion is still professed by the nations of Europe, the most distinguished portions of human kind in arts and learning as well as in arms. By the industry and zeal of the Europeans it has been widely diffused to the most distant shores of Asia and Africa; and by the means of their colonies has been firmly established from Canada to Chile, in a world unknown to the ancients."[6]

That is the way Christ's banner is erected: by pure and humble means, *but powerfully*, as the strength of Christ appears in those who are his followers.

---

[4]John Calvin, *Sermons on the Epistle to the Ephesians* (1562; reprint, Carlisle, Pa.: Banner of Truth Trust, 1975), 122–23.

[5]Lloyd-Jones, *God's Ultimate Purpose*, 430–31.

[6]Edward Gibbon, *The Decline and Fall of the Roman Empire* (New York: Harcourt, Brace, 1960), 143.

8

The Way We Were

(Ephesians 2:1–3)

As for you, you were dead in your transgressions and sins, in which you used to live when you followed the ways of this world and of the ruler of the kingdom of the air, the spirit who is now at work in those who are disobedient. All of us also lived among them at one time, gratifying the cravings of our sinful nature and following its desires and thoughts. Like the rest, we were by nature objects of wrath.

Several years after I came to Philadelphia as pastor of Tenth Presbyterian Church, a committee met to develop our own Sunday school literature. We were unhappy with the existing materials. Either they were strong pedagogically but weak theologically, or they were strong in doctrine and Bible content but weak in teaching. Chiefly we were disappointed by their failure to teach the great doctrines of the Bible.

Eventually we produced our own curriculum, which followed a three-year cycle. The first year covered basic doctrines: sin, salvation, Bible study, prayer, the Christian life. The second year covered the same areas but from the perspective of the church and in terms of personal relationships. Here we talked about the church and how one becomes a member of it. We taught about Christian behavior and about Jesus as the Christian's example. The third year focused on God's plan in history and the place of today's believers in that plan.

There is a sense in which Paul did the same thing as he moved from the first to the second chapter of Ephesians— and later from the third to the remain-ing chapters. In chapter 1 Paul looked at salvation from God's point of view, showing how he has blessed us with all blessings in Christ and how one day all things shall be subjected to Christ. In chapter 2 he talks about salvation from the perspective of the individual Christian. He shows what we were before God's work in calling us to Christ, what God did for us in Christ, and what we are now to become and do as the result of that working.

Chapter 1 gives us the past, present, and future of God's great plan of salvation. Chapter 2 gives us the past, present, and future of the persons Christ saves.

WELL, SICK, OR DEAD?

Some years ago a movie circulated in American theaters entitled *The Way We Were*. It was a nostalgic look at the past, which is the way most people want to remember earlier years. In the first verses of this chapter Paul, too, looks at the past. Only his view is not nostalgic. On the contrary, it is filled with the utmost realism. This caused Paul to paint one of the most pessimistic pictures of human nature found any-

47

where. John R. W. Stott says, "Paul first plumbs the depths of pessimism about man." However, after he has done this he also "rises to the heights of optimism about God" and of how his grace saves sinners.[1]

How are we to assess human nature? In the whole history of the human race there have only been three basic answers to that question.

The first view is that people basically are okay. In medical terms we would say that they are well or healthy, as opposed to being sick or dead. Many would admit that human nature is not as healthy as it may perhaps one day be. We live in an evolving world, so they believe. Past centuries have witnessed wars, starvation, disease, economic hardships. But people have survived, and both they and their world are getting better. At the worst, people are not quite perfect.

If man's nature is only as lightly flawed as this outlook supposes, then surely it should have been perfected by now. Little flaws should have been eliminated. That they have not been eliminated—that we still have wars, starvation, disease, and economic turmoil—suggests that the matter is more serious than the "healthy" view allows.

The second view is that man is not well; he is sick, even mortally sick, as some would say. That is, there is indeed something wrong with human beings. But the situation is not hopeless. People are at least alive, and as long as they are alive . . . well, where there is life, there is hope. There is no need to call the mortician yet.

The third view, the biblical view (which Paul articulates in classic language in this passage), agrees that man is not well. In fact it makes a more serious diagnosis: man is dead—dead so far as his relationship to God is concerned. He is "dead in . . . transgressions and sins" (v. 1), as God warned he would be in Eden before Adam's fall. Like a spiritual corpse, a sinner is unable to make a single move toward God, think a single thought about God, or even correctly respond to God—unless God is first present to bring the spiritually dead person to life, which is what Paul says he does do.

In Christian doctrine the crux of this matter is in how we regard the human will. Is it free to choose God, even in its fallen state? Some Christians believe this. Or is it unable to choose God, being bound by sin, as others say? This matter has been debated at length in the long history of the Christian church, and the church has always come out on the side of what Martin Luther called the will's "bondage." There have been different ways of expressing this. Luther expressed it in different terms from Augustine, Calvin in different terms from Luther. Jonathan Edwards had his own original contribution. But all were united in saying that apart from the utterly unexpected grace of God in quickening the human mind and soul, no one ever willingly turns to God or embraces the offer of salvation. Sin enslaves us. Instead of turning to God, we run from him. No other view does justice to what the Bible teaches concerning the radical nature of sin and the totality of grace in salvation.

Jonathan Edwards probably saw the matter most clearly. He said that the problem is not with the will itself, since the will is simply the mind choosing what the mind deems best. The problem is with man's moral nature, which is opposed to God, and with the sinful "motives" that flow from that corrupt nature. Edwards declared that the will is always free; we always choose what

---

[1]John R. W. Stott, *God's New Society: The Message of Ephesians* (Downers Grove, Ill.: InterVarsity, 1979), 69.

we judge best in a given situation. But as sinners we always judge *wrongly*. We think God undesirable. Hence, we always resist him and reject the gospel.

WALKING CORPSES

Jonathan Edwards lived many centuries after the apostle Paul, but when I read the second chapter of Ephesians, I sense that Paul would have liked Edwards' analysis. I say this because the kind of death Paul talks about in Ephesians 2:1–3 is a strange one—one in which, although dead, the sinner nevertheless walks about quite actively in sin. He is dead toward God. But he is alive to all wickedness. Paul uses strong, active words here. Although spiritually dead, the sinner *follows* the ways of the world and of the devil and spends his time *gratifying* the cravings of his sinful nature.

Some years ago I heard John H. Gerstner compare this to what horror stories call a zombie. For the benefit of those who do not read such literature, a zombie is a person who has died but who is nevertheless up walking around. To make matters even more gruesome, the body is not only dead, but decaying, putrifying. It is the most disgusting thing many people can imagine. But that is what Paul says the human condition is before God. In their opposition to God, men and women are walking corpses. They are the living dead.

Gerstner said, "They are an offense to God's nostrils. These decaying spiritual corpses stink."

Moreover, sinners are trapped by the very things that are destroying them. In church liturgy it is customary to speak of temptations coming to us from "the world, the flesh, and the devil." These are the categories of sinful activity Paul speaks of. Only it is not mere tempta-

tion that the apostle has in mind, but actual captivity by these forces so that the person involved constantly moves and operates only within their influence. I spoke of the world, the flesh, and the devil in the last chapter, showing the resurrection power of God over each of them. But here Paul speaks of these things, not to show our victory over them or liberation from them through the power of God in Christ, but rather our enslavement to them apart from that power.

We are enslaved to the world, because apart from the "renewing of our minds" (Rom. 12:2) we are unable to perform in any other way. The world mocks Christians at this point, saying, "See how narrow these people are! They are locked up to their Bibles. What slavery!" But actually, it is the world that is enslaved. Such persons are entirely controlled by the world's thought-system. As D. Martyn Lloyd-Jones writes, "They think as the world thinks. They take their opinions ready-made from their favourite newspaper. Their very appearance is controlled by the world and its changing fashions. They all conform; it must be done; they dare not disobey; they are afraid of the consequences."[2]

Paul says that in our transgressions, sins, and disobedience we all "followed the ways of this world" (v. 2).

We are enslaved by the devil too, because, as that verse also says, we "followed . . . the ruler of the kingdom of the air, the spirit now at work in those who are disobedient." In this verse the word "spirit" is not a synonym for "devil," as if it meant "the evil spirit." Spirit is in the genitive case, while "ruler" is in the accusative, which means that the phrase should be translated: "the ruler of the kingdom of the air, [who is also the ruler of] the

[2]D. Martyn Lloyd-Jones, *God's Way of Reconciliation: Studies in Ephesians, Chapter 2* (Grand Rapids: Baker, 1972), 21–22.

spirit who is now at work in those who are disobedient." This tells how the devil enslaves men and women. It is not that he is personally present. He is only one creature and can only be present in one place at one time. It is rather through the evil spirit or outlook present in the world that he rules us.

The third area of human slavery is to the flesh, whose sinful cravings we are always at work to gratify (v. 3). Flesh refers, not to our skin, but to our fallen sinful nature, embracing both our fleshly desires and our wicked thoughts. We have fleshly sins of the more obvious sort: gluttony, laziness, lust, greed. But we also have inner, intellectual sins: pride, sinful ambition, hostility to the revealed truth of God, malice, and envy. Sadly we are trapped by these things. In our fallen state, we cannot turn from sin and seek after God; we cannot even stop sinning. We are on a path of self-destruction. Like lemmings, we seem oblivious to our danger as we rush pell-mell toward the sea.

OBJECTS OF WRATH

After the description of these verses we find ourselves wondering if anything worse could possibly be said about fallen men and women. It seems as if nothing more could be added. Yet Paul does add something, something so horrible, so overwhelming that the other descriptions actually fade into the background when placed next to it. He says that in our sin we are "by nature objects of [God's] wrath" (v. 3).

I hear someone saying, "Wrath? Did you say, wrath? If that is what you say, I can hardly believe you are serious. How can anyone possibly talk about the wrath of God today? I know the idea is in the Bible, in obscure places, but surely it is something Christians today should be embarrassed about and try as hard as possible to repudiate. Speak of God's love. Speak of mercy, even justice. But not wrath, at least not if you

want to be taken seriously by people living in our century." I hear the objection, but it is an example of the very bondage about which Paul has been writing. The worldly mind does not take God's wrath seriously because it does not take sin seriously. Yet if sin is as bad as the Bible declares it to be, nothing is more just or reasonable than that the wrath of a holy God should rise against it.

In the Old Testament there are more than twenty words used to express God's wrath. More than six hundred important passages deal with it. In the New Testament the chief terms are *thumos* (from a root which means "to rush along fiercely" or "be in a heat of violence") and *orgē*, the term used in Ephesians 2:3. *Orgē* comes from a root meaning "to grow ripe for something" and indicates God's gradually building and intensifying opposition to sin. *Orgē* is the word most often used for "wrath" in the New Testament.

Taken together these passages indicate that God's wrath is consistent, controlled, and judicial. That is what makes it so frightening. The doctrine of wrath does not mean that God merely gets angry from time to time, lashes out in anger, and then forgets about it. It is rather that his wrath is an inevitable and growing opposition to all that is opposed to his righteousness.

There is a present dimension to God's wrath. In Romans 1 Paul shows that whenever the truth about God is rejected, it leads to a darkening of the understanding (v. 21); a debasement of one's religious awareness and a corresponding debasement of one's person (v. 23); sexual perversions, lies, envies, hatred, murder, strife, deceit, disobedience to parents, and other consequences (vv. 24–32). We can express it by saying that the holiness of God never allows any sin to thrive.

There is also a future dimension to God's wrath, as the author of Hebrews indicates: "Anyone who rejected the law of Moses died without mercy on the testimony of two or three witnesses. How much more severely do you think a man deserves to be punished who has trampled the Son of God under foot, who has treated as an unholy thing the blood of the covenant that sanctified him, and who has insulted the Spirit of grace? For we know him who said, 'It is mine to avenge; I will repay,' and again, 'The Lord will judge his people.' It is a dreadful thing to fall into the hands of the living God" (Heb. 10:28–31).

How horrible a state! What is to be done for those who are enmeshed in sin and, unable to escape from it, are being carried along to the inevitable outpouring of the just wrath of the avenging God?

A RADICAL REMEDY

Humanly speaking nothing can be done. The sinner cannot save himself. Even a redeemed person, who has seen the truth of salvation in the gospel, cannot save another sinner. The state of the unsaved man or woman is humanly hopeless. But what is impossible for men is possible for God. A radical problem requires a radical remedy, and God supplies it.

This is where the next verses of the letter come in. For no sooner has the apostle spoken of the way we were then he joyfully breaks in, "But because of his great love for us, God, who is rich in mercy, made us alive with Christ even when we were dead in transgressions—it is by grace you have been saved" (vv. 4–5). Dead in transgressions? Dead in sins? Indeed we were! But God performs resurrections. He reaches down to where ruined, miserable, trapped sinners are living, and he brings them to spiritual life again. He calls them; and his voice, which quickens the dead, brings them running to that which beforehand they both shunned and feared.

George Whitefield, the great Calvinistic evangelist, compared this to Christ's raising of Lazarus: "Come, ye dead, Christless, unconverted sinners, come and see the place where they laid the body of the deceased Lazarus; behold him laid out, bound hand and foot with grave-clothes, locked up and stinking in a dark cave, with a great stone placed on the top of it. View him again and again; go nearer to him; be not afraid; smell him. Ah! how he stinketh. . . . Was he bound hand and foot with grave-clothes? So art thou bound hand and foot with thy corruptions: and as a stone was laid on the sepulchre, so is there a stone of unbelief upon thy stupid heart. Perhaps thou hast lain in this state, not only four days, but many years, stinking in God's nostrils. And, what is still more effecting, thou art as unable to raise thyself out of this loathsome, dead state, to a life of righteousness and true holiness, as ever Lazarus was to raise himself from the cave in which he lay so long. Thou mayest try the power of thy own boasted free-will, and the force and energy of moral persuasion and rational arguments (which, without all doubt, have their proper place in religion); but all thy efforts, exerted with never so much vigor, will prove fruitless and abortive, till that same Jesus, who said, 'Take away the stone,' and cried 'Lazarus, come forth,' also quicken you."[3]

Apart from that quickening voice of God there would be no hope for anyone. But because of it even the worst and most determined rebel may be saved.

---

[3] Cited by John H. Gerstner, *A Predestination Primer* (Grand Rapids: Baker, 1960), 19–20.

9

But God

(Ephesians 2:4–5)

But because of his great love for us, God, who is rich in mercy, made us alive with Christ even when we were dead in transgressions—it is by grace you have been saved.

It is customary in preparing English translations of the New Testament to rearrange the Greek phrases. This is appropriate, because English syntax is different from Greek syntax and the rearrangements present better for the English mind what the Greek is saying. Still, I wish the translators of the New International Version had not rearranged the phrases of Ephesians 2:4. For in the Greek text this classical statement of the gospel begins with the two words "but God," and that dramatic beginning is weakened when the words "because of his great love for us" are interposed.

D. Martyn Lloyd-Jones rightly says in his commentary, "These two words, in and of themselves, in a sense contain the whole of the gospel."[1] They tell what God has done, how God has intervened in what otherwise was an utterly hopeless situation. Before God's intervention we were as Ephesians 2:1–3 describes us: "As for you, you were dead in your transgressions and sins, in which you used to live when you followed the ways of this world and of the ruler of the kingdom of the air, the spirit who is now at work in those who are disobedient. All of us also lived

among them at one time, gratifying the cravings of our sinful nature and following its desires and thoughts. Like the rest, we were by nature objects of wrath."

This is a deplorable, desperate, heinous condition. *"But God!"* The intervention of those words and what they represent make all the difference.

I want to ask four questions as I seek to expound these words: (1) Who is this God? (2) What has he done? (3) Why has he done it? And (4) What must I then do?

WHO IS THIS GOD?

It is important that we begin by discussing the nature of the God about whom Paul writes, for there are different ideas of God and not all ideas of who he is fill the bill. Many people think of God as a benevolent but nevertheless basically weak being. He would like to help us (and does somewhat), but he cannot do much. He is limited by evil and controlled by circumstances. Others think of God as powerful, but as distant and austere. He could help, but he does not care. People have thousands of conflicting and inadequate ideas about God. But the

[1]D. Martyn Lloyd-Jones, *God's Way of Reconciliation: Studies in Ephesians, Chapter 2* (Grand Rapids: Baker, 1972), 59.

God about whom Paul is writing is not the God of this type of human imagining. He is the God of the Bible, the God of the Lord Jesus Christ. He is the God Paul has already presented gloriously in the first chapter.

What do we know about this God? We know a number of things.

1. *God is sovereign.* The most important thing that can be said about the God of the Bible is that God is sovereign. In fact if God is not sovereign, God is not God. Sovereignty means rule, so to say that God is sovereign is to say that God rules his creation. He made it, and he is in control of it. Nothing occurs without his permission. Nothing ever rises up to surprise him. What God has ordained from the beginning comes to pass. Because he knows this, Paul can speak as he does in the first chapter. For here he is not merely talking about what God has done in the past. That might be established merely by observation. He is also talking about the future, showing that God is at work to exalt Jesus as head of all things and subject everything to him. Paul speaks positively and certainly about the future because God is in control of it just as he has controlled the past. The future is certain because the all-powerful, sovereign God determines it.

2. *God is holy.* Nothing is more apparent in Paul's opening description of God's great plan of salvation, unfolding over the ages, than that God is a moral God. He is not indifferent to issues of right and wrong, justice and injustice, righteousness and sin. On the contrary, it is because of his opposition to everything sinful that his great plan of salvation was devised and is being executed. Sin will be punished; righteousness will be exalted in his universe.

3. *God is full of wrath against sin.* This point flows from God's holiness. It is the outworking of his holiness against all that is opposed to it. This is why our condition is so frightful. Paul describes us as being "dead in [our] transgressions and sins" (Eph. 2:1). That is bad, of course. But it would not be frightful apart from God's wrath against those transgressions. Apart from wrath we might simply conclude that this is just the way things are. God is God; we are people. He is holy; we are not holy. Let God go his way, and we will go ours. Ah, but it does not work like that. God does not simply take his own path. This is his universe. He is the holy God, and our sin has introduced a foul blemish into it. He is opposed to sin and is determined to stamp it out.

This is the God of the Bible and of the Lord Jesus Christ, the God about whom Paul is writing. This God is what we need, though we do not know it in our sinful state. Instead of coming to him to find new life and righteousness, we run from him to wickedness and spiritual death.

What Has God Done?

But God! It is wonderful to discover that although we run from God, preferring wickedness and death to righteousness and life, God has not run from us. Instead, he has come to us, and has done for us precisely what needed to be done. In a word, he has saved us. He has rescued us from the desperate, deplorable condition described at the beginning of the chapter.

When we were discussing the state of men and women before God intervenes to save them, I pointed out that our position as sinners (apart from God) is hopeless for three reasons. First, we are *"dead* in [our] transgressions and sins." This means that we are no more able to help ourselves spiritually than a corpse is able to improve its condition. Even when the gospel is preached we are no more able to respond to it than a corpse can respond to a command to get up— unless God speaks the command. Dead means hopeless. When a person dies, the struggle is over. Second, we are *enslaved* by sin. This spiritual death is a strange thing. Although we are dead in sin so far as our ability to respond to God is concerned, we are nevertheless alive enough to be quite active in the practice of wickedness. In fact, we are enslaved to wicked practices. We are enslaved to sin. Third, we are under God's just sentence for our transgressions so that, as Paul says, we are "by nature objects of wrath" (v. 3).

But God! Here is where the beauty and wonder of the Christian gospel comes in. We were hopelessly lost in wickedness. But God has intervened to save us, and he has saved us by intervening sovereignly and righteously in each of these areas.

Notice how this works out. We were dead in sins, but God "made us alive with Christ even when we were dead in transgressions" (v. 5). As I suggested at the close of the last chapter, our experience as Christians is like that of Jesus' friend Lazarus. We were dead to any godly influence. But God can awaken the dead, and that is what he has done for us. Like Lazarus, we have heard the Lord calling us to "come out" (John 11:43); his voice brought forth life in us, and we have responded, emerging wonderfully from our spiritual tomb. Now life is no longer as it was. Life is itself new, and in addition we have a new Master and a new standard of righteous living to pursue.

Again, not only were we dead in our sins, we were also enslaved by them. Even though we might have desired to do better, we could not. Instead our struggles to escape only drew us down, plunging us deeper and deeper into sin's quicksand. But God! God has not only called us back to life; he has also, Paul writes, "raised us up with Christ and seated us with him in the heavenly realms in Christ Jesus" (v. 6). There are no slaves in heaven. So if we have been raised up with Christ and been made to sit in the heavenly realms in him, it is as free men and women. Sin's shackles have been broken, and we are freed to act righteously and serve God effectively in this world.

Third, God has dealt with the wrath question. In our sins we are indeed "objects of wrath" (v. 3). But since Jesus has suffered in our place for our sin and we have been delivered from it, we are no longer under wrath. Instead we are objects of "the incomparable riches of [God's] grace, expressed in his kindness to us in Christ Jesus" (v. 7).

John R. W. Stott puts it like this: "These two monosyllables ['but God'] set against the desperate condition of fallen mankind the gracious initiative and sovereign action of God. We were the objects of his wrath, *but God out of the great love with which he loved us* had mercy upon us. We were dead, and dead men do not rise, *but God* made us alive with Christ. We were slaves, in a situation of dishonour and powerlessness, *but God* has raised us with Christ and set us at his own right hand, in a position of honour and power. Thus God has taken action to reverse our condition in sin."[2]

The words "but God" show what God has done. Besides, they draw our thoughts to God and encourage us to trust him in all things.

Am I ignorant of God? Indeed, I am. " 'No eye has seen, no ear has heard, no mind has conceived what God has prepared for those who love him'—*but God* has revealed it to us by his Spirit" (1 Cor. 2:9–10).

Am I tempted to sin? Indeed, I am. "Temptation . . . is common to man: *but God* is faithful, who will not suffer you to be tempted above that ye are able; but will with the temptation also

---

[2]John R. W. Stott, *God's New Society: The Message of Ephesians* (Downers Grove, Ill.: InterVarsity, 1979), 79–80.

make a way to escape, that ye may be able to bear it" (1 Cor. 10:13, KJV).

Am I foolish, weak, ignoble? Yes, that too. *"But God* chose the foolish things of the world to shame the wise; God chose the weak things of the world to shame the strong. He chose the lowly things of this world and the despised things—and the things that are not—to nullify the things that are, so that no one may boast before him" (1 Cor. 1:27–29).

Have I been the victim of other people's sin and ill will? Probably, or at least I will be sooner or later. Still I will be able to say, "You intended to harm me, *but God* intended it for good to accomplish what is now being done" (Gen. 50:20).

May I put it quite simply? If you understand those two words—"but God"—they will save your soul. If you recall them daily and live by them, they will transform your life completely.

Why Did God Do It?

The third question I want to ask is: Why? Why did God do all that Paul and these other passages tell us he has done? There is only one answer: grace. He has done this because it has pleased him to do it. I say "one answer." Yet, strictly speaking, Paul expresses the thought not with one but with four words.

1. *Love* (v. 4). God has done this, Paul says, "because of his great love for us." C. S. Lewis described this love by saying, "God, who needs nothing, loves into existence wholly superfluous creations in order that he may love and perfect them. He creates the universe, already foreseeing—or should we say 'seeing'? there are no tenses in God— the buzzing cloud of flies about the cross, the flayed back pressed against the uneven stake, the nails driven through the mesial nerves, the repeated

torture of back and arms as it is time after time, for breath's sake, hitched up. . . . Herein is love. This is the diagram of Love Himself, the inventor of all loves."[3]

2. *Mercy* (v. 4). Mercy is related to love; it flows from it. But mercy has the sense of favor being shown to those who deserve the precise opposite. If nothing but a proper code of rewards and retribution were followed, sinners would receive God's wrath. That they do not is because God is merciful. Instead of condemning them, as he had every right to do, he reached out and saved them through the death of Jesus Christ.

3. *Grace* (v. 5). This is the word that seems chiefly to have been on Paul's mind, for he repeats it in an almost identical sentence in the latter half of this same paragraph. Verse 5 says, "It is by grace you have been saved." Verses 8 and 9 say similarly, "For it is by grace you have been saved, through faith—and this not from yourselves, it is the gift of God—not by works, so that no one can boast." Grace means that there is no cause in us why God should have acted as he did. We think the opposite. We think God owes us something. Even after we become Christians we often find ourselves thinking in these terms. "Certainly God owes everyone at least a chance," we say. Or when God fails to do something we think he should do, we say, "It just isn't fair." So long as we think that way we do not understand grace. Grace is God's favor to the utterly undeserving.

4. *Kindness* (v. 7). Compared to the others this word seems a bit weak, but it is not. It flows from the character of God, who is not weak. Kindness means much in our daily living as believers. In the course of our lives we often sin grievously and foolishly. But God does not strike us down when we do. He

---

[3]C. S. Lewis, *The Four Loves* (New York: Harcourt, Brace & World, 1960), 176.

does not turn on us. Instead he is astonishingly kind. He protects us from the worst of sin's consequences, and he speaks softly to draw us back onto the path of obedience and virtue.

Why has God acted thus? Paul's answer is that God *is* love, mercy, grace, and kindness. God acts this way because that is what he is like. We can only marvel that he is love, mercy, grace, and kindness in addition to being sovereign, holy, and full of wrath against sin. We praise him for it.

What Must I Do?

We are saved by God's grace alone, but once we are saved, we inevitably want to serve the one who has been so loving to us. Are you still unsaved? If so, let this utterly unmerited love of God in Jesus Christ move and woo you. In Romans we read, "But God demonstrates his own love for us in this: While we were still sinners, Christ died for us" (Rom. 5:8). Are you already a believer? If so, let this great love of God move you to the heights of consecration and activity. The hymn writer said,

Love so amazing, so divine,
Demands my soul, my life, my all.

This is what John Calvin had in mind as he drew to the close of his exposition of these verses. He summarized wisely, "Now let us cast ourselves down before the majesty of our good God with acknowledgment of our faults, praying him to make us so to feel them that it makes us not only confess three or four of them, but also go back even to our birth and acknowledge that there is nothing but sin in us, and that there is no way for us to be reconciled to our God, but by the blood, death and passion of our Lord Jesus Christ.

"And therefore as often as we feel any regrets to turn aside from the grace of God, and to cite us before his judgment seat, let us have no other refuge than the sacrifice by which our Lord Jesus Christ has made atonement between God and us. And whenever we are weak, let us desire him to remedy it by his Holy Spirit, which is the means that he has ordained to make us partakers of all his gracious gifts. And let us so continue in the same that we may be an example to others and labour to draw them with us to the faith and unity of the doctrine, and by our life and good conversation show that we have not in vain gone to so good a school as that of the Son of God."[4]

---

[4]John Calvin, *Sermons on the Epistle to the Ephesians* (1562; reprint, Carlisle, Pa.: Banner of Truth Trust, 1975), 154.

10

Risen With Christ

(Ephesians 2:4–7)

But because of his great love for us, God, who is rich in mercy, made us alive with Christ even when we were dead in transgressions—it is by grace you have been saved. And God raised us up with Christ and seated us with him in the heavenly realms in Christ Jesus, in order that in the coming ages he might show the incomparable riches of his grace, expressed in his kindness to us in Christ Jesus.

Have you ever coined a word because you wanted to describe something for which no existing English word seemed adequate? Some people have done this. Nearly two hundred and forty years ago, in 1754 to be exact, Horace Walpole coined the word "serendipity," which he defined as "the faculty of making happy and unexpected discoveries by accident." I find that word in my twelve-volume *Oxford English Dictionary*, but even today it is not in the smaller Webster's *Collegiate Dictionary*.

Another coined word is C. Northcote Parkinson's "injelititis." It means "induced inferiority," the "disease seen in those who intentionally attempt little and achieve nothing."

The apostle Paul also coined words from time to time. In Ephesians 2:5–6 there are three of them. Paul had been discussing the radical change in our situation brought about by the unmerited kindness of God. Before our conversion we were "dead in . . . transgressions and sins," but now we have been "made . . . alive with Christ." Before, we were dead; now we are alive. Before, we were enslaved by our sins and carnal nature; now we are emancipated. Before, we were objects of wrath; now we experience God's love. What words can adequately describe this great change? What terms can express it? Since nothing like this had been known in the history of the world before Christ, it is not surprising that in Paul's day adequate words did not yet exist to describe what happened.

So Paul invented some. He took the Greek prefix *syn*, meaning "together with," and combined it with three words used elsewhere to describe what God did with Jesus after his crucifixion: (1) "make alive," (2) "raise up," and (3) "sit down" by him in heaven. The results were this:

1. *Syzōpoieō*, which means "to make together with";
2. *Synegeirō*, which means "to raise up together with";
3. *Synkathizō*, which means "to sit down together with."

Taken together, these words make one of the most significant statements in the Bible of what has happened to Christians as a result of their union

57

with Jesus Christ in God's great work of salvation.

A Difficult Doctrine

As with most New Testament teachings, the seeds of the doctrine of the union of believers with Christ are in the recorded words of Jesus—often as metaphors. On one occasion Jesus compared our union with him to the union of branches and a vine: "Remain in me, and I will remain in you. No branch can bear fruit by itself; it must remain in the vine. Neither can you bear fruit unless you remain in me. I am the vine; you are the branches. If a man remains in me and I in him, he will bear much fruit; apart from me you can do nothing" (John 15:4–5). Other metaphors refer to eating Christ, as one would eat bread (John 6:35; Matt. 26:26–28), or drinking him, as one would drink water or wine (John 4:1–14; Matt. 26:26–28).

How Christ's followers will be received or rejected by the world also suggests this union, for it is said to be a reception or rejection of Christ himself: "He who listens to you listens to me; he who rejects you rejects me" (Luke 10:16).

In the great prayer Jesus uttered for his followers just before his arrest and crucifixion, the Lord referred to this mystical union explicitly: "I have given them the glory that you gave me, that they may be one as we are one: I in them and you in me" (John 17:22–23).

The doctrine received its greatest development and emphasis in the writings of Paul. At times, as in Ephesians 2, Paul seems to have coined words to express it. At other times he speaks merely of being "in him," "in Christ" or "in Christ Jesus," phrases which occur 164 times in his writings. By his use of these phrases, Paul teaches that we were *chosen* "in him before the creation of the world" (Eph. 1:4), *redeemed* "in him" (Eph. 1:7), *justified* "in [him]" (Gal. 2:17), *sanctified* "in [him]" (1 Cor. 1:2) and *enriched* "in every way" (1 Cor. 1:5)—all by virtue of that mystical union.

This doctrine is so important that one commentator rightly called it "the heart of Paul's religion."[1] John Murray wrote, "Union with Christ is the central truth of the whole doctrine of salvation."[2] Arthur W. Pink is even more emphatic: "The subject of spiritual union is the most important, the most profound, and yet the most blessed of any that is set forth in sacred Scripture." But he also rightly notes that "sad to say, there is hardly any which is now more generally neglected. The very expression 'spiritual union' is unknown in most professing Christian circles, and even where it is employed it is given such a protracted meaning as to take in only a fragment of this precious truth."[3]

The mere fact that this teaching is prominent throughout the New Testament does not mean that we understand it. Many cannot escape feeling that when Paul speaks of our being "made . . . alive with Christ" or "raised up with Christ" or "seated . . . in the heavenly realms in Christ" somehow this is all just word games. They ask, "What does it mean to say that we are made alive in Christ? In what sense have I actually been raised with him or seated with him in heaven?"

Two Types of Union

One way to understand it is to see our union with Christ as a *federal* or *covenantal* union. This refers to what we might call our technical position before God as a result of Christ's work for us.

---

[1] James S. Stewart, *A Man in Christ: The Vital Elements of St. Paul's Religion* (New York: Harper and Brothers, n.d.), 147.

[2] John Murray, *Redemption Accomplished and Applied* (Grand Rapids: Eerdmans, 1955), 170.

[3] Arthur W. Pink, *Spiritual Union and Communion* (Grand Rapids: Baker, 1971), 7.

It is described in detail in Romans 5:12–21, in which we are said to have been in Adam before our salvation but to be in Christ afterward. Adam had been established by God as a representative or federal head of the human race. He was to stand for us so that, if he continued in righteousness, we would also be considered as having continued in righteousness in him. But if he fell by transgressing God's command, we would be considered as having sinned in him—and his judgment, death, would pass to us. Adam did sin, and that is what happened. Death passed upon the race. It is proof that God considered us to have been in Adam and to have fallen by his transgression.

By contrast, Jesus stood firm, not merely demonstrating a practical and perfect righteousness in his own life but also dying for those who would be united to him by faith. Thus, those judged sinners because of Adam's sin are now judged righteous because of Christ's righteousness. Because he is justified, we are justified. Because he is raised, we are raised. Because he is exalted to heaven, we too are exalted to heaven. As Jesus is seated at the right hand of the Father in glory, so also are we seated.

This doctrine is called "federalism," because it is analogous to the way a citizen is involved in the actions of his country or federal government. As citizens of a country, we suffer the liabilities and enjoy the benefits of actions taken by earlier generations of citizens.

But that is only one way of explaining what the Bible means by our mystical union with Christ, and it is not always necessarily the most useful way of thinking of it—certainly not in studying Ephesians 2:4–7. A second way to describe our union with Christ is as a *vital* or *experiential* union. This refers to the actual effects in us of this relationship. The chief New Testament teaching in this respect is Christ's illustration of the vine and branches, referred to earlier. When Jesus compared himself to a vine and us to branches, he was not thinking of a mere technical position attained as a result of his work. He was thinking of an actual difference in our lives. As a result of our union with him we are enabled to pray to God and receive the things we pray for (John 15:7) and to bear spiritual fruit to God's glory (v. 8).

ALL THINGS NEW

This is the sense in which Paul's coined words in Ephesians 2:4–7 must be taken and in which they yield their richest treasures.

1. *Made alive together with Christ.* Of the three words, this term most clearly requires an experiential rather than a federal interpretation. The point is that we were once dead and that we now live, as a result of our union with Christ. A dead person is unconscious of what is around him, inactive, and in a process of bodily decay. This was true of us spiritually. We were unconscious of God, inactive in God's service, and decaying morally. Now we are alive to God, working for God, and growing in practical righteousness. This is the most profound transformation imaginable, and it is true of all Christians. If this change has not taken place, the person involved is not a real Christian.

D. Martyn Lloyd-Jones describes this change as God's giving us a new disposition, not new faculties: "The difference between the sinner and the Christian, the unbeliever and the believer, is not that the believer, the Christian, has certain faculties which the other man lacks. No, what happens is that this new disposition given to the Christian directs his faculties in an entirely different way. He is not given a new brain; he is not given a new intelligence, or anything else. He has always had these; they are his servants, his instruments, his 'members,' as Paul calls them in the sixth chapter of Romans; what is new is a new bent, a new disposition. He has turned in a different direction; there is a new power working in him and guiding his faculties. This is the thing that makes a man a Christian."[4]

We cannot explain this other than to say that it happens by our union with Christ. Jesus told Nicodemus, "The wind blows wherever it pleases. You hear its sound, but you cannot tell where it comes from or where it is going. So it is with everyone born of the Spirit" (John 3:8).

2. *Raised up together with Christ*. The words "raised up" are sometimes used of the resurrection, and quite properly. But here the words apply, not to the resurrection but to what we more normally call the ascension. Having been raised from the dead, Jesus was taken up into heaven, and we are said to have been raised up to heavenly places in him.

How so? This concept is a bit more difficult to grasp, but we can explain it this way. Our being raised from the dead with Christ means that we have been given new life or, as Martyn Lloyd-Jones wrote, a "new disposition." Our being taken up into heaven with Christ, our ascension, means that we have been given a new environment. We are no longer creatures only of this world, bound by what we can see and touch and smell and hear and taste. We are now creatures of the greater, heavenly realm who now, because of our union with Christ, think and work and speak in spiritual categories. Martyn Lloyd-Jones says that the Christian "is lifted up into an entirely new 'thought realm.' And he judges everything now in the light of it. He has a new standard of values; he assesses

things in an entirely different way. What he wants to know about anything now is, not what sort of a 'kick' he will get out of it, not what sort of pleasure will it bring him; but rather, what is its value to his soul?"[5]

More than that, the Christian recognizes that he belongs more to heaven than he does to earth. Charles Hodge derives this from the key phrase "in the heavenly realms," which he rightly says relates to "the kingdom of heaven" as opposed to "the kingdoms of this world" or "the kingdom of Satan.' "We are within the pale of God's kingdom; we are under its law; we have in Christ a title to its privileges and blessings and possess—alas! in what humble measure—its spirit." He says, somewhat whimsically, that "though we occupy the lowest place of this kingdom, the mere suburbs of the heavenly city, still we are in it."[6]

Again, this is by union with Christ. Apart from that union we would not even be aware of God's kingdom, let alone be a part of it. We would adjust our thoughts of heaven (such as they might be) to our worldly orientation, rather than the other way around.

3. *Seated with God in the heavenly realms in Christ Jesus*. The last of these three coined words carries the thought of what it means to be united with Christ to the highest peak, showing that we are not only raised in him but that we have also been seated with him in heaven next to God the Father. The verb is in an aorist or past tense. It means that we have already been made to sit with God in Christ. That is our position now. That is where we have arrived, and we are to live accordingly.

There are many aspects of this. The seat next to God in which we have been

---

[4]D. Martyn Lloyd-Jones, *God's Way of Reconciliation: Studies in Ephesians, Chapter 2* (Grand Rapids: Baker, 1972), 79.

[5]Ibid., 91.

[6]Charles Hodge, *A Commentary on the Epistle to the Ephesians* (1856; reprint, Grand Rapids: Baker, 1980), 115.

seated with Christ is a throne, which means that we reign with him. We are extensions of Christ's presence and authority in the world. This is the seat described in Psalm 110:1, "The LORD says to my Lord: 'Sit at my right hand until I make your enemies a footstool for your feet'" (cf. Matt. 22:44; Acts 2:34–35; Heb. 1:13; 10:13). This seat speaks of victory. It involves security, privilege, rejoicing, accomplishment.

Still, I do not think this is what Paul chiefly had in mind. Let me explain what I think he meant. Do you remember that beautiful account of the Last Supper included by the apostle John in his Gospel? Do you remember how he describes himself as reclining next to Jesus? As John describes it, Jesus had announced that one of the Twelve would betray him, and Peter, disturbed at this revelation, motioned to John to ask Jesus which of the disciples he was speaking about. John then wrote of himself, "Leaning back against Jesus, he asked him, 'Lord, who is it?'" (John 13:25). Jesus answered, "It is the one to whom I will give this piece of bread when I have dipped it in the dish" (v. 26). He then dipped the bread and gave it to Judas Iscariot. John was seated by Jesus and was therefore the one who received the revelation.

Now read Ephesians. "God raised us up with Christ and *seated us with him* in the heavenly realms in Christ Jesus, *in order that* in the coming ages *he might show the incomparable riches of his grace,* expressed in his kindness to us in Christ Jesus" (vv. 6–7). That place, in Christ at the right hand of God the Father, is the place of intimacy and revelation. It is where God opens up his heart. And notice: It is where we are now. We are seated with God in Christ in the heavenly realms now. Now God is speaking to us intimately.

This is the great privilege Paul had chiefly in mind as he composed this portion of Ephesians.

ARE YOU IN CHRIST?

I close with these questions. First, have you been made alive with Christ? Has God put his new principle of life within you? Do you sense a new spiritual disposition in what you do? Are you born again? If you cannot answer these questions affirmatively, by all means seek after God until you can. For that is Christianity. Christianity is not mere doctrine or a sense of having been forgiven or even believing that God will forgive you. Christianity is Christ— Christ alive in his people, Christ in us. No one who has been made alive with Christ can ever be the same afterward. No one who has been united to Christ can ever again die to God or take up with old sins as before.

Second, have you been raised with Christ so that your orientation is now heavenly, rather than being only earthbound? If you are a Christian, you must think of things in relationship to God. You must know yourself to be a member of his kingdom and responsible to his laws. You must live for him and represent him wherever he sends you.

Finally, have you been seated with God in Christ in the heavenly realms? That is, have you made your true, blessed, and intimate home with God? Do you talk to him there? Does he talk to you? That is a far more intimate place than "the garden" described in C. Austin Miles's hymn, though the sentiments are the same:

> He walks with me, and he talks
> with me,
> And he tells me I am his own;
> And the joys we share as we tarry
> there,
> None other has ever known.

If you have enjoyed that intimacy, you will no longer set your affections on things on this earth but on God's glory.

11

Saved by Grace Alone

(Ephesians 2:8–9)

For it is by grace you have been saved, through faith—and this not from yourselves, it is the gift of God—not by works, so that no one can boast.

Our text is one of the best known passages in the Bible—and rightly so, for it contains the greatest message that any person can hear. It is probably one of the most widely memorized texts, along with John 3:16 and the Twenty-third Psalm. John 3:16 says, "For God so loved the world that he gave his one and only Son, that whoever believes in him shall not perish but have eternal life." Ephesians 2:8–9 says the same thing theologically: "For it is by grace you have been saved, through faith— and this not from yourselves, it is the gift of God—not by works, so that no one can boast."

The text has three parts. The first part tells how it is that God saves us: "It is by grace." The second part speaks of the channel through which this grace of God comes to us: It is "through faith." The last part, which is a contrast, tells how God does *not* save us, and it explains why: It is "not by works, so that no one can boast."

ALL OF GRACE

A number of years ago one of my predecessors at Tenth Presbyterian Church, Donald Grey Barnhouse, published a small booklet on these verses in which he illustrated this teaching. He began by commenting on the difficulty of forming adequate definitions even of common things, like a chair, let alone theological concepts. Therefore, rather than give a theological definition of grace such as "God's unmerited favor" or "the kindness and love of God toward sinful men and women," he told this story.

During the last century, in the worse slum district of London, there was a social worker whose name was Henry Moorehouse. One evening as he was walking along the street he saw a little girl come out of a basement store carrying a pitcher of milk. She was taking it home. But when she was a few yards from Moorehouse she suddenly slipped and fell. Her hands relaxed their grip on the pitcher and it fell on the sidewalk and broke. The milk ran into the gutter, and the little girl began to cry as if her little heart would break. Moorehouse quickly stepped up to see if she was hurt. He helped her to her feet, saying, "Don't cry, little girl." But there was no stopping her tears.

She kept repeating, "My mommy'll whip me; my mommy'll whip me."

Moorehouse said, "No, little girl, your mother won't whip you. I'll see to that. Look, the pitcher isn't broken in many pieces." As he stooped down beside her, picked up the pieces, and began to work as if he were putting the pitcher back together, the little girl stopped crying. She had hope. She came from a family in which pitchers had been mended before often. Maybe this stranger could repair the damage. She watched as Moorehouse fitted several of the pieces together until, working too roughly, he knocked it apart again. Once more she began to cry, and Moorehouse had to repeat, "Don't cry, little girl. I promise you that your mother won't whip you."

Once more they began the task of restoration, this time getting it all together except for the handle. Moorehouse gave it to the little girl, and she tried to attach it. But, naturally, all she did was knock it down again. This time there was no stopping her tears. She would not even look at the broken pieces lying on the sidewalk.

Finally Moorehouse picked the little girl up in his arms, carried her down the street to a shop that sold crockery, and bought her a new pitcher. Then, still carrying her, he went back to where the girl had bought the milk and had the new pitcher filled. He asked her where she lived. When he was told, he carried her to the house, set her down on the step, and placed the full pitcher of milk in her hands. Then he opened the door for her. As she stepped in, he asked one more question, "Now, do you think your mother will whip you?"

He was rewarded for his trouble by a bright smile as she said to him, "Oh, no, sir, because it's a lot better pitcher than we had before."[1]

Here is an illustration of the grace of God in salvation. The Bible teaches that men and women were created in the image of God. But when our first parents, Adam and Eve, sinned by disobeying God's righteous law, that image was broken beyond repair. This does not mean that there is no value at all to human nature. Even a broken pitcher is not without value. Archaeologists use pieces of broken pottery to date civilizations uncovered by their digs. I have seen bits of pottery used as ashtrays or even some on which pictures have been printed. Broken pottery is not worthless. But it is worthless so far as carrying milk is concerned. In the same way, human nature in its broken state is useless for pleasing God or earning heaven. The Bible says, "There is no one righteous, not even one; there is no one who understands, no one who seeks God. All have turned away, they have together become worthless; there is no one who does good, not even one" (Rom. 3:10–12).

Yet men keep trying to please God by their character. Like Moorehouse in his first attempts to help the little girl, they keep trying to put the pieces of their broken righteousness back together. They cannot achieve God's perfect standards of righteousness, but they see parts of their character that are good from their perspective, and they try to work with those. The result is a patchwork of shards, which God condemns.

But here is where the grace of almighty God comes in. The Lord Jesus Christ came to this world, which was weeping in its failure and sin, and he became the means by which an utterly hopeless situation was transformed. There is nothing in the Bible to indicate that Jesus ever attempted to patch up fallen human nature. He did not come to assist us or reform us. He came to re-create us. He said, "You must be born again" (John 3:7). Instead of trying to piece together the broken pieces of our fallen nature, Jesus gives us a new nature: "If anyone is in Christ, he is a new creation" (2 Cor. 5:17). And to paraphrase the words of the little girl, "It's a lot better nature than we had

[1]Donald Grey Barnhouse, *How God Saves Men* (Philadelphia: The Bible Study Hour, 1955), 7–9.

before." It is nothing less than the nature of the holy and eternal God within his people.

And it is all of grace. In Barnhouse's story the little girl did not do anything to deserve Moorehouse's favor. She did not pay for her new pitcher and milk. She did not hire Moorehouse's services; she had nothing to hire him with. She did not even prevail upon his sympathies because she was pretty or miserable or homely or pathetic. Moorehouse did as he did solely because it pleased him to do it. He did not even expect a reward from the girl's parents. Thus did Jesus come not "to call the righteous, but sinners" to repentance (Matt. 9:13). He died for us and saved us solely because of his good pleasure.

The great nineteenth-century Baptist preacher Charles Haddon Spurgeon wrote, "Because God is gracious, therefore sinful men are forgiven, converted, purified and saved. It is not because of anything in them, or that ever can be in them, that they are saved; but because of the boundless love, goodness, pity, compassion, mercy and grace of God."[2]

What Is Faith?

"But just a minute!" someone says. "You have been speaking of the grace of God in salvation, and that is all very wonderful. I admit that I cannot put the pieces of my life back together. I cannot meet God's standards of perfection. If I am to be saved, salvation must come graciously from God in Jesus Christ. But that is still remote, abstract. How does a salvation as great and free as that become mine personally?"

The answer of Ephesians 2:8–9 is that it becomes ours "through faith."

Here, of course, we must dispense with the world's common misunderstandings of faith.

The most common misunderstanding is to think of faith as *subjective feelings.*

Some years ago in a rather extended discussion about religion a young man told me that he was a Christian. As we talked, I discovered that he did not believe that Jesus Christ was fully divine. He said he was God's Son, but only in the sense that we are all God's sons. He did not believe in the resurrection. He did not believe that Jesus died for our sin or that the New Testament contains an accurate record of his life and ministry. He did not acknowledge Christ as Lord of his life. When I pointed out that these beliefs are involved in any true definition of a Christian, he answered that nevertheless he believed deep in his heart that he was a Christian. The thing he called faith was only a deeply held gut feeling.

Another substitute for faith is *credulity.* Credulity is the attitude of a person who will accept something as true apart from evidence, simply because he or she earnestly wishes it to be true. Rumors of miraculous cures for some incurable disease sometimes encourage this attitude in many unfortunate people. This is faith of a sort, but it is not what the Bible means by faith.

A third substitute is *optimism.* In this view faith is a positive mental attitude as a result of which the thing believed in is supposed to happen. An example would be a salesman who so intensely believes in his ability to sell that he actually becomes successful at it, or the congressman who believes that he can become President of the United States and does so by faith in himself (and hard work). Of course, there is some value in a positive mental attitude. A positive attitude to one's work really will help one to do better at it. Faith in oneself really is self-fulfilling to a degree. Yet this is not faith in the biblical sense of the term.

Norman Vincent Peale has made much of this outlook. He popularized it

---

[2] Charles Haddon Spurgeon, *All of Grace* (Chicago: Moody, n.d.), 41.

originally in a best-selling book called *The Power of Positive Thinking*. He taught that the Bible contained a technique for "spiritual power" that could make us successful. For him, the heart of the gospel was to be found in a few strong statements about faith in the New Testament, verses like "Everything is possible for him who believes" (Mark 9:23) and "If you have faith as small as a mustard seed, you can say to this mountain, 'Move from here to there' and it will move. Nothing will be impossible for you" (Matt. 17:20–21). All we had to do, he said, was memorize these verses and allow them to sink down into our subconscious minds and transform us, and we would become believers in God and in ourselves. Then we would be able to do what we previously thought impossible. Peale concluded, "According to your faith in yourself, according to your faith in your job, according to your faith in your God, this far you will get and no further."[3]

But here is the difficulty. Apparently, in Peale's mind faith in oneself, faith in one's job, and faith in God are essentially the same thing, and this really means that the object of faith is irrelevant. John R. W. Stott, who analyzes Peale's outlook, says, "To Dr. Peale faith is really another word for self-confidence."[4]

Against these distortions we must reply that real faith is not based upon a person's individual attitudes and feelings. In the context of these human definitions, faith is unstable. In the context of biblical teaching, faith is reliable; for it is faith in the trustworthy God, who reveals himself reliably.

Faith in the biblical sense actually has three elements, which I call: knowl-edge, heart response, and commitment. In Spurgeon's work on grace, which I referred to earlier, the great Baptist preacher speaks of knowledge, belief, and trust, but the elements he is thinking of are essentially the same.

1. *Knowledge.* This must be first because it is impossible to believe in a thing unless we know what it is we are believing. In the biblical sense this knowledge is of the gospel. It is knowledge of the very things Paul has been writing about in Ephesians 2: that in our natural state we are all dead in transgressions and sins, that we are objects of God's just wrath, but that God nevertheless has reached out to save us through the work of Jesus Christ—and that this is of grace. The work of Christ consists in his dying for sin in our place. Calvin wrote, "We shall possess a right definition of faith if we call it a firm and certain knowledge of God's benevolence toward us, founded upon the truth of the freely given promise in Christ, both revealed to our minds and sealed upon our hearts through the Holy Spirit."[5]

2. *Heart response.* But faith is not mere intellectual assent to certain truths. It is also a response to such knowledge. Therefore, Calvin also says, "It now remains to pour into the heart what the mind has absorbed. For the Word of God is not received by faith if it flits about in the top of the brain, but when it takes root in the depth of the heart that it may be an invincible defense to withstand and drive off all the stratagems of temptation."[6]

3. *Commitment.* The final element is commitment or, as Spurgeon says, trust. It means casting yourself upon Christ, resting on his promises and accepting his finished work on your

[3]Norman Vincent Peale, *The Power of Positive Thinking* (New York: Prentice-Hall, 1952), 99.
[4]John R. W. Stott, *Your Mind Matters* (Downers Grove, Ill.: InterVarsity, 1972), 35–36.
[5]John Calvin, *Institutes of the Christian Religion,* ed. John T. McNeill, trans. Ford Lewis Battles (Philadelphia: Westminster Press, 1960), 1:551.
[6]Ibid., 583.

behalf. It is saying, as Thomas did, "My Lord and *my* God!" (John 20:28).

Marriage provides an illustration. A good marriage is the culmination of an extended process of learning about someone, responding to him or her, and then making a commitment. Courtship may be compared to faith's first element: knowledge. It is a time for getting to know each other, for seeing whether the other person possesses those characteristics that will be good in the marriage. It is a very important step. If the other person is not of good character or cannot be trusted, there will be trouble later on. The second stage is comparable to the second element in faith: the movement of the heart. This corresponds to falling in love, which is quite obviously an important step beyond mere knowledge. Finally, there is the point of verbalized commitment contained in the marriage ceremony. At this point the couple promise to live together and love each other regardless of what their future circumstances might be. So also do we commit ourselves to Christ for this life and for eternity.

How God Does *Not* Save Us

There is one last idea in Ephesians 2:8–9. It tells how God does not save sinners: "not by works, so that no one can boast." This makes "faith" something other than a work; for although faith is a channel by which the grace of God comes to us, it is not a deserving action or attitude on our part. In speaking on this text I have sometimes referred to the previous phrase in verse 8 ("and this not from yourselves, it is the gift of God") as referring to faith,

teaching that even faith is God's gift. This is probably not what Paul had in mind, because "faith" (*pistis*) is feminine, and "this" (*touto*) is neuter. The statements in verse 8 probably refer to the whole of the previous sentence, teaching that the salvation which is ours through faith is not of ourselves but rather is God's gift.

Still, although Paul is writing that "faith" is not from ourselves, the point is nevertheless valid in that we do not contribute to our salvation even in so vital a matter as the faith by which Christ's work is received. If faith were a virtue, then we would be able to boast in heaven. We would be there because of the grace of God *plus faith*, and another would not be there because in his case faith was lacking.

No, not even faith is a work. Nothing that you or I can do, however great or small, can get us into salvation. If we think there is, we are still trusting ourselves and our own ability rather than Christ, and we cannot be saved. Salvation is by grace alone. All we can do (but also *must* do) is take the pitcher God puts in our hand—and thank him because it is a lot better than anything we ever had before. Will you not do that? It is the way a person becomes a Christian and thus passes out of death into life. Say, as we do in the hymn,

Nothing in my hands I bring,
Simply to thy cross I cling;
Naked, come to thee for dress,
Helpless, look to thee for grace;
Foul, I to the Fountain fly;
Wash me, Savior, or I die.

Rock of Ages, cleft for me,
Let me hide myself in thee.

12

God's Workmanship

(Ephesians 2:10)

For we are God's workmanship, created in Christ Jesus to do good works, which God prepared in advance for us to do.

Since the Protestant Reformation in the sixteenth century those who follow in the steps of Martin Luther have been strong to assert that justification is by grace through faith and not by human works. But does this mean that works no longer have any place in Christianity? Does this doctrine of justification by grace—Luther's doctrine—actually lead to bad conduct?

Here is the place where sound Protestant and Roman Catholic theology part company. Many Roman Catholics insist that justification is by the grace of God through faith. (Ephesians 2:8 says so.) But they answer questions about the relationship between faith and works differently than Protestants do. Catholic theology says that works enter into justification in the sense that God justifies us in part by producing good works in us, so that we are justified by faith plus those works. Sound Protestant theology also insists on works, but it says that works follow justification as a consequence and evidence of it.

Catholic theology says: "Faith plus works equal justification."

Protestants reply: "Faith equals justification plus works."

Of course, there is an *unsound* Protestant theology that eliminates the necessity of works altogether, maintaining that a person can be saved and show no evidence of his spiritual regeneration. But this must be rejected.

GOOD WORKS

This subject comes before us in the last sentence of the first great paragraph of Ephesians 2, which we have been studying: "For we are God's workmanship, created in Christ Jesus to do good works, which God prepared in advance for us to do" (v. 10).

More than one commentator has pointed out that there is a striking repetition of the word "works" in verses 9 and 10. The first mention of works is negative. It tells us in no uncertain terms that we are not saved "by works," by anything we did or can do. It was all God's work of grace in us, so we have no reason to boast, no grounds for feeling a sense of accomplishment. This verse utterly repudiates the idea that works contribute in any measure to our justification. Grace and works are mutually exclusive possibilities. Either we are saved by God's grace alone or we are trying unsuccessfully to save ourselves by our own works. There are no other possibilities. However, no sooner has Paul rejected the role of works in justification than he immediately brings it in again, saying that God has created us precisely "to do good works." This is stated in such strong language—"works, which God prepared in advance for us to do"—that we are correct in saying that if there are no works, the person involved is not justified.

FAILURE OF GOOD WORKS

Before we talk about the necessity of works that flow out of a believer through Christ and because of the believer's spiritual union with him, it is necessary to look at the works human beings are capable of apart from Christ and see that there is no hope in them. This is because God's standard can be nothing less than perfection, and even at our best no amount of good works adds up to that requirement.

Donald Grey Barnhouse illustrated our failure by reference to an old-fashioned scale—the kind in which grocers used to measure out sugar, salt, and other dry foods. A pound weight was put on one side of the scale. The sugar was poured out on the other side until the arms balanced. Barnhouse compared the pound weight to God's righteousness, the standard which his own holy nature demands. That pound of righteousness is placed on one side of the scale, and we are invited to place our "good works" on the other.

The worst elements of society come first—thieves, perverts, murderers, sinners of all kinds. They are not without any human goodness. They have perhaps one or two ounces. But their works do not balance the scale. These people are set aside and thus pass under God's just condemnation.

Next come ordinary folks, people like us. They are better than the "great" sinners. They have perhaps eight ounces of human goodness. That makes them four times as good as the ones who came first. But their goodness, great as it seems to be, does not balance the scale.

Finally, the morally "great" come forward. They are not perfect; their very "greatness" causes them to recognize that fact. But they have twelve or thirteen ounces of good works, and they present them. Will those twelve or thirteen ounces balance God's scale? Not if the pound of righteousness is on the other side! The scale won't balance for them any more than it does for the average folks or great sinners. Therefore, they too are set aside and fall under God's wrath—unless another way of salvation can be found.

"But just here God comes with his message of free salvation. Note well, he does not change his standards one whit. The pound of perfection still stands opposite the empty scales. No one has been able to move the balance. But now God is going to move it for us. . . .

"Since Christ was the Infinite God, he could die for any number of finite creatures. He could take the eternal punishment of an infinite multitude and expiate it in the hour of his death—so that the weight of our sin was counted over upon him, and all of God's righteousness is now available through him. Now God comes to us with the great invitation, 'I want you to be in heaven with me. I love you. It does not make any difference on what plane of life has been your abode.' You stand there on the empty scales with nothing but your few ounces to put in and with no possibility of getting anything more. But God says, 'I love you; I came to die for you. Look to Calvary. Do you see Christ hanging there? It was for you. Look to the empty tomb. Do you see that he has been raised from the dead? It is the proof,' says God, 'that I am forever satisfied with what Christ did there on the cross, and I will take that for your side of the scales, if you will throw away all confidence in your own few ounces.' And thus we come to Christ. . . . We take that righteousness of God and go boldly or tremblingly to the scales and put it over against all the perfection God has demanded and that he must demand. The balance immediately is made. We stand before God justified, for since the scales are tipped, God can never have anything against me forever."[1]

A person who will trust that perfect righteousness of Christ, rather than his or her own righteousness is justified. A person who continues to cling to good works in any degree is not justified. Thus, salvation is "by grace . . . through faith" alone, as Paul says in Ephesians 2:8.

NECESSITY OF GOOD WORKS

Ah, but if that is so, can a person rightly insist on the necessity of works at all? The key word, of course, is "necessity." We can see that good works are by very definition a good thing. We can argue that a Christian will be happier doing good works than not doing them. We can even speak of a certain obligation to do good works. Most people would have no trouble saying that. But how is it that sound Protestant theology insists on the presence of good works as a necessary consequence and evidence of justification? How can we say that if works are not present, a person is not saved?

The answer is that justification, though it aptly describes one important aspect of what it means to be saved, is not the whole of salvation. God justifies, but that is not the only thing he does. He also regenerates. And there is no justification without regeneration, just as there is no regeneration without justification.

Regeneration is the theological term for what Jesus was talking about when he told Nicodemus, "You must be born again" (John 3:7). He was telling him that he needed to have a new start as a result of the life of God being placed within him. It is what Paul was talking about in Ephesians 2, as he described how God "made us alive with Christ even when we were dead in transgressions" (v. 5). It is even what Paul is talking about in our text, for he does not merely say that God commands us to do good works or even urges us to do them. He says rather that God *"created* us in Christ Jesus *to do* good works," adding that these were specifically "prepared in advance for us to do." Clearly, if a person has been created by God specifically to do good works, he will do those good works— even though they have nothing to do with how he was saved in the first place.

In my opinion, this is one of the most neglected (yet most essential) teachings in the evangelical church today. At the beginning of this study I contrasted sound Protestant theology with traditional Roman Catholic theology, showing how Protestants teach "faith equals justification plus works"—the view I have just been expounding—while Catholics teach "faith plus works equal justification." Clearly Catholic theology is wrong. But what are we to say of a theology that has no place for works at all? What are we to say of a teaching that extols justification divorced from sanctification, forgiveness without a corresponding change in life? What would Jesus himself think of such theology? Yet such teaching prevails among Evangelicals today.

When we study Christ's teachings it does not take long to discover that he was not slow to insist on changed behavior. It is true that he taught that salvation would be by his work on the cross. He said, "The Son of Man did not come to be served, but to serve, and to give his life as a ransom for many" (Mark 10:45). This is perfectly consis-

---

[1] Donald Grey Barnhouse, *How God Saves Men* (Philadelphia: The Bible Study Hour, 1955), 33–34.

tent with the doctrine of faith-justification.

But Jesus also said, "If anyone would come after me, he must deny himself and take up his cross daily and follow me" (Luke 9:23).

He said, "Why do you call me, 'Lord, Lord,' and do not do what I say? . . . The one who hears my words and does not put them into practice is like a man who built a house on the ground without a foundation. The moment the torrent struck that house, it collapsed and its destruction was complete" (Luke 6:46, 49).

He told the Jews of his day, "Unless your righteousness surpasses that of the Pharisees and the teachers of the law, you will certainly not enter the kingdom of heaven" (Matt. 5:20).

Moreover, as I am sure you can see even from this short selection of Christ's sayings, it is not only a matter of our demonstrating a genuinely changed behavior and doing good works if we are truly justified. Our good works must also exceed the good works of others. After all, the Christian's good works flow from the character of God within the Christian. Jesus said, "Unless your righteousness *surpasses* that of the Pharisees and the teachers of the law, you will certainly not enter the kingdom of heaven" (Matt. 5:20). This means, "Unless you who call yourselves Christians, who profess to be justified by faith alone and therefore confess that you have nothing whatever to contribute to your own justification—unless you nevertheless conduct yourselves in a way which is utterly superior to the conduct of the very best people who are hoping to save themselves by their works, you will not enter God's kingdom. You are not Christians in the first place."

John H. Gerstner has called this, rightly, I think, "a built-in apologetic."

No one but God could think up a religion like this.

"Whenever you find a person who puts a premium on morality and really specializes in conduct and expects to make it on his record, you invariably find him supposing that he can justify himself by his works. On the other hand, if you find a person who revels in grace, who knows the futility of trying to make it on his own and simply cannot say enough about the blood of Jesus and salvation full and free, he has a built-in tendency to have nothing to do with works in any form. When you get a person who really puts a premium on morality, he almost inevitably falls into the pit of self-salvation. And, on the other hand, when a person sees the principle of grace, he has a built-in temptation to go antinomian. But the Christian religion, while it preaches pure grace, unadulterated grace with no meritorious contribution from us whatever, at the same time requires of us the loftiest conceivable conduct. . . .

"You cannot for one solitary moment say anything other than 'Nothing in my hand I bring, simply to thy cross I cling.' We are justified by faith alone. But we are not justified by a faith that is alone. Therefore, if you really cling to that cross, if you really do what you say you do, you will be abounding in the works of the Lord and will be living out an exceptional pattern of behavior."[2]

GOD WHO WORKS

I know this sounds confusing and even contradictory. But the problem vanishes as soon as we realize that the good works Christians are called upon to do (and must do) are themselves the result of God's prior working in them. That is why in Ephesians 2:10 Paul prefaces his demand for good works by the statement "For we are God's workmanship." It is why, in a similar vein in

---

[2]John H. Gerstner, "Man the Saint," in *Tenth: An Evangelical Quarterly* (July 1977): 43–44.

the very next book of the Bible, he says, "My dear friends, . . . continue to work out your salvation with fear and trembling, for it is God who works in you to will and to act according to his good purpose" (Phil. 2:12–13).

In Ephesians 2:10 Paul calls this work of God a new creation, saying that "we are . . . *created* in Christ Jesus to do good works." Beyond any doubt, Paul has a contrast in mind here between our new creation in Christ and our old creation in Adam, just as he does in Romans 5:12–21. When God made the first man, he made him perfectly furnished to do all good works. But Adam fell, as we know. And since that time, from God's perspective even the best of the good works of Adam and his posterity have been bad "good works."

But now God recreates those men and women whom he is joining to the Lord Jesus Christ. He is bringing into existence something that did not exist before and which now has new and exciting possibilities. Before, the one who was without Christ was, to use St. Augustine's phrasing, *non posse non peccare* ("not able not to sin"). Now he is *posse non peccare* ("able not to sin") and able to do good works.

In this spiritual *re*-creation God gives us a new set of senses. Before, we saw with our eyes physically, but we were spiritually blind. Now we see with spiritual eyes, and everything seems new.

Before, we were spiritually deaf. The word of God was spoken, but it made no sense to us. Or if it did, we resented that word and resisted it. Now we have been given ears to hear, and we hear and respond to Jesus' teaching.

Before, our thinking was darkened. We called the good, bad; and we called the bad, good. Indeed, we reveled in the bad, and we could not understand what was wrong when the supposed "good times" turned out to be bad times and we were left feeling miserable. The things of God's Spirit were "foolishness" to us (1 Cor. 2:14). Now our thinking has been changed; we evaluate things differently, and our minds are being renewed day by day (Rom. 12:1–2).

Before, our hearts were hard. We hated God; we did not even care very much for others. Now our hearts are softened. God appears altogether lovely, and what he loves we love. "We love because he first loved us" (1 John 4:19). Because our hearts have been remade we now give food to the hungry, water to the thirsty, homes to the strangers, clothes to the naked, care to the sick, and comfort to those who are in prison—as Jesus said we must do, if we are to sit with him in glory.

In my study I have a book by a great surgeon, Dr. Paul Brand, who is Chief of the Rehabilitation Branch of the United States Public Health Service Hospital in Carville, Louisiana, a man who has distinguished himself by pioneering research on the care of leprosy. The book is called *Fearfully and Wonderfully Made*. In it Dr. Brand examines the intricate mechanisms of the human body, and marvels at the greatness of a God who can create such wonders. He talks about the body's cells, bones, skin, and complexities of motion. As I read that book I am amazed at man as the pinnacle of God's great and varied creation. But as I marvel, I am aware of a creation that surpasses even that of the human body. It is the re-creation of a man or woman who before was spiritually dead, utterly incapable of doing any good thing that could satisfy God, but who now, as the result of God's working, is able to do truly good "good works."

13

Then and Now

(Ephesians 2:11–13)

Therefore, remember that formerly you who are Gentiles by birth and called "uncircumcised" by those who call themselves "the circumcision" (that done in the body by the hands of men)—remember that at that time you were separate from Christ, excluded from citizenship in Israel and foreigners to the covenants of the promise, without hope and without God in the world. But now in Christ Jesus you who once were far away have been brought near through the blood of Christ.

A number of years ago, when Harry Ironside was in his prime, this well-known Bible teacher (later to become pastor of the Moody Church in Chicago) was on a train going to a preaching assignment in southern California. As he sat on the train a gypsy came and sat beside him. "How do you do, gentleman," she said. "You like to have your fortune told? Cross my palm with a silver quarter, and I will give you your past, present, and future."

"Are you very sure you can do that?" Ironside asked. "You see, I am Scottish, and I wouldn't want to part with silver without getting a full value for it."

The gypsy replied very earnestly, "Oh, yes, gentleman. Please. I will tell you all."

At that point Ironside reached into his pocket and brought out his New Testament. "It is not really necessary for me to have you tell my fortune," he said, "because here I have a book that gives me my past, present, and future. Let me read it to you." He then turned to the second chapter of Ephesians and read the words we have been studying: "As for you, you were dead in your transgressions and sins, in which you used to live when you followed the ways of this world and of the ruler of the kingdom of the air, the spirit who is now at work in those who are disobedient. All of us also lived among them at one time, gratifying the cravings of our sinful nature and following its desires and thoughts. Like the rest, we were by nature objects of wrath."

"That is my past," Ironside said.

The woman tried to get away. "That is plenty!" she protested. "I do not care to hear more."

"But wait," Ironside remonstrated. "There is more. Here is my present: 'But because of his great love for us, God, who is rich in mercy, made us alive with Christ even when we were dead in transgressions—it is by grace you have been saved. And God raised us up with Christ and seated us with him in the heavenly realms in Christ Jesus. . . .'"

"No more!" she protested.

"Here is my future, too," Ironside kept on: "'. . . in order that in the coming ages he might show the incomparable riches of his grace, expressed in his kindness to us in Christ Jesus." By this time the gypsy was on her feet and on her way down the aisle, saying, "I took the wrong man!"[1]

GENTILES AND JEWS

We have already studied Ephesians 2:1–10, of course. So we know how apt Ironside's story is in highlighting the flow of those verses. What I want to point out here is that it is equally apt in tracing the thought of Ephesians 2:11–22. Paul also speaks of a past, present, and future in these verses. The difference is only in the "man" whose fortune he is telling.

In the first half of the chapter Paul spoke of the human race in general and of that portion of the human race that has been saved by the grace of God: "But . . . God, who is rich in mercy, made us alive with Christ." Anyone of whatever nationality, race, sex, or social status who has become a Christian can be so described. In the second half of the chapter too Paul contrasts a past and present (and eventually also a future), but at this point he has in mind gentile Christians in particular. Before their conversion Jews were, like the Gentiles, "dead in . . . transgressions and sins." But the condition of the Gentiles was even worse, Paul argues. Gentiles were "separate from Christ, excluded from citizenship in Israel and foreigners to the covenants of the promise, without hope and without God in the world" (v. 12). In their lost state they did not even have the Jews' unique advantages.

Because the condition of the Gentiles before their conversion can be described in these terms, Paul has a unique way of speaking about their present and future. As to their present: "You who once were far away have been brought near through the blood of Christ" (v. 13). As to their future: "In him you too are being built together to become a dwelling in which God lives by his Spirit" (v. 22).

THE GENTILE PAST

When Paul introduces the contrast between Gentiles and Jews, as he does in verse 11, he seems to make light of the labels the Jews themselves used for this distinction: "uncircumcised" and "the circumcision." He calls this a Jewish designation and refers to circumcision itself as something "done in the body by the hands of men." We know from his writing elsewhere that Paul desired "circumcision of the heart" (Rom. 2:29), that is, an internal change and not merely an external one.

The Jews had focused on superficial external distinctions, but there were real differences too between the condition of lost Gentiles and lost Jews. As Paul states it, the Gentiles were at a disadvantage in five areas:

1. *Separate from Christ.* The first thing Paul mentions is that the Gentiles were "separate from Christ." This could refer to lack of the so-called mystic union of a believer with Jesus, which is accomplished by the Holy Spirit through the channel of human faith. But this is probably not what is involved here. If it were, the same thing would have to be said of the Jew in his unregenerate state and it would therefore not be a thing that could be cited as a particular gentile disadvantage. The clue to what Paul is probably thinking of is the word "Christ," which means "the anointed one" or "Messiah." That is, he is thinking in the same way he was in writing Romans 9:5, when he spoke of Jewish advantages, saying, "Theirs are the patriarchs, and from them is traced the human ancestry of Christ, who is God over all, forever praised." This

[1]H. A. Ironside, *In the Heavenlies: Practical Expository Addresses on the Epistle to the Ephesians* (Neptune, N.J.: Loizeaux Brothers, 1938), 96–98.

means that the Messiah came to Jews and was perceived by Jews. Since they were not Jews, Gentiles were cut off from this advantage.

The Gentiles in their fallen and alienated state were not united to Jesus by saving faith. Of course that was also true of the Jews. But unlike the Jews, the Gentiles had not even had a chance to know Christ. Their religion was totally pagan. They did not even have the expectation of a Savior.

2. *Excluded from citizenship in Israel.* Paul wrote of the spiritual advantages of Jewishness, but the words of Jesus Christ reveal even more clearly what exclusion from citizenship in Israel means. When he was with the Samaritan woman and she had asked him about the proper place to worship— "on this mountain" (Gerazim) or "in Jerusalem"—Jesus had replied, "You Samaritans worship what you do not know; we worship what we do know, for salvation is from the Jews" (John 4:22). This was not a racial slur but a sober fact of salvation history. God had chosen to be known in Israel as he had chosen to be known nowhere else. So in that day, although not now, an individual had to become a Jew, a member of the commonwealth of Israel, to be saved.

Here are two Old Testament examples. The first is found in the book of Ruth. Ruth was a Moabitess, a foreigner, who had been married to the son of a Jewish woman named Naomi. She had met her husband in Moab, where Naomi and her sons had gone during a period of famine in Israel. The sons had died, and when Naomi decided to return to her own land, Ruth, her daughter-in-law, determined to go with her. Ruth had apparently learned from Naomi during the years they were together, and she had come to worship Naomi's God. At first Naomi tried to persuade Ruth to remain in Moab, but Ruth would not. Ruth replied, "Don't urge me to leave you, or to turn back from you. Where you go I will go, and where you stay I will stay. Your people will be my people and your God my God" (Ruth 1:16).

These are beautiful words, but the beauty has kept many from noticing the far more important ordering of thoughts. Ruth wanted to join Naomi in the true worship of Jehovah. But notice, she could not say, "Your God will be my God" until she had first said, "Your people will be my people." In her statement Ruth confessed her need for a change in nationality before there could be a change in her God.

A second example of this truth is from the story of Naaman, the Syrian. Naaman was a general of the most powerful state of his day. He was strong and respected. Yet Naaman was also pitied, for somewhere along the way Naaman had contracted leprosy, and there was no known cure.

Through a young Jewish slave girl who had doubtlessly been captured during one of his raids, Naaman learned of the existence in Israel of Elisha, who he had been told could cure him. He went to Palestine. But when Elisha refused even to come out to meet him and merely sent word that he was to wash himself seven times in the Jordan, all the national pride of the general rose to the surface. He expressed his scorn of the muddy river which could not even begin to compare, he said, with the beautiful rivers of his country. As he cooled down, a servant helped him to change his mind. "It's worth a try," the servant argued. "If Elisha had asked for a ton of gold, you would have given him that. Why not dip in the river? You've come a long way. It will cost you nothing." Naaman did and was cured.

Now follows the significant part of the story. Naaman ordered his servants to fill several sacks with earth and then load them on two mules in order to take the Jewish earth back to Syria. He explained, "For [the word means "because"; it is the key word] your servant will never again make burnt offerings and sacrifices to any other god, but the LORD" (2 Kings 5:17).

We must imagine that the work is done and the caravan of horses with their riders, followed by the mules with their burden of earth, returns to Syria. Word runs ahead that Naaman is returning and that he is cured of leprosy. The travelers arrive. There is a joyous reception. But then, before night comes and Naaman retires, the earth which has been brought from Israel is poured into a frame made to receive it, and Naaman takes his place upon the earth of Palestine to pray to Jehovah—a Gentile who was willing to come as a Jew, relying on the same grace that was shown by the Jews' God when He healed him.

It is interesting that in both these stories Gentiles (Ruth and Naaman) were saved, but they were saved by becoming Jews first. Apart from that prior conversion they were, as Paul says, "excluded from citizenship in Israel" and thus from Jewish blessings.

3. *Foreigners to the covenants of the promise.* Mention of citizenship in the previous phrase leads Paul to think of the Gentiles as being "foreigners." But he moves a step further now, saying, that they were foreigners to God's covenants.

Since Paul writes the word "promise" in its singular form he is apparently thinking of the first and original promise of God to Abraham from which the various covenants made with Israel came. In that original promise God told Abraham, "Leave your country, your people and your father's household and go to the land I will show you. I will make you into a great

nation and I will bless you; I will make your name great, and you will be a blessing. I will bless those who bless you, and whoever curses you I will curse; and all peoples on earth will be blessed through you" (Gen. 12:1–3). The promises of the Old Testament were on the basis of this covenant. The Gentiles had no share in them.

In a certain sense this is still true of unbelievers. D. Martyn Lloyd-Jones writes, "They can read their Bible and it does not move them. They can look at these 'exceeding great and precious promises' and say: To whom does this apply, what is all this about? They are strangers; they are like people from another country; they do not understand the language."[2]

4. *Without hope.* I once heard a preacher say that one of the most dreadful words in the English language is the word "useless." He said that he never wanted it to be spoken of him. I agree that the judgment in that word is terrible. But it is not as terrible as the words Paul next uses to describe the Gentiles before Christ's coming. They were, Paul says, "without hope." Useless may be bad enough, but a useless thing may always find a use, and a useless person may become useful. If there is no hope, all is lost. Without hope there is nothing.

In what ways were Gentiles without hope apart from Christ? The answer is "in all ways," but chiefly in this life and in the life to come. Martyn Lloyd-Jones notes, rightly, I think, that apart from Christ the deeper a man thinks the more pessimistic he becomes. Of course, the frivolous are not pessimistic. They see the glitter, not the tarnish beneath. Those who think—the great philosophers, artists, poets, and writers—all these are increasingly pessimistic without Christ—at least as they

[2]D. Martyn Lloyd-Jones, *God's Way of Reconciliation: Studies in Ephesians, Chapter 2* (Grand Rapids: Baker, 1972), 170.

get older. Without the God of Israel none of us can have any real hope that things will be good or get better. And if this is true of our life in this world, how much truer is it of any good thing beyond the grave. Apart from revelation, apart from the resurrection of Jesus Christ, no one can have any true hope of anything beyond this life but must say, as Satan does in John Milton's great epic *Paradise Lost,* "Our final hope is flat despair" (Book 2, Line 139).

5. *Without God in the world.* Paul's last despair summarizes the dilemma of the Gentile before Christ's coming, just as his first phrase introduced it. At the beginning Paul described the Gentiles as being "separate from Christ." Here he depicts them as being "without God." God is the source of every good thing (James 1:17), including hope. So if we are without God, we are without everything, despite appearances to the contrary.

BUT NOW

These phrases from Ephesians 2:12 are as grim as those with which the apostle Paul began this great chapter: "dead in your transgressions and sins . . . [following] the ways of this world and of the ruler of the kingdom of the air . . . by nature objects of [God's] wrath." But now, just as he had done earlier, Paul indicates a change in the situation as a result of God's intervention. Earlier he had said, "But because of his great love for us, God who is rich in mercy, made us alive with Christ" (v. 4). Now he writes, "But now in Christ Jesus you who once were far away have been brought near through the blood of Christ" (v. 13).

Paul is talking about being brought near to God as a result of Christ's atonement for sin. But he is also referring to God bringing together Jews and Gentiles to form a new unity: the church of Jesus Christ.

To appreciate the gloominess of this

truth we need to see the dismal condition of the Gentiles before they were brought near.

Before, the Gentile was "separate from Christ." He was cut off. Now he is united with Christ, just as Paul said in chapter 1: "You also were included in Christ when you heard the word of truth, the gospel of your salvation" (v. 13). "In him" the Ephesians had all things.

Before, the Gentile was "excluded from citizenship in Israel." Now, as he will say just a few verses later, "You are no longer foreigners and aliens, but fellow citizens with God's people and members of God's household" (2:19). To the Philippians he will write, "But our citizenship is in heaven. And we eagerly await a Savior from there, the Lord Jesus Christ, who, by the power that enables him to bring everything under his control, will transform our lowly bodies so that they will be like his glorious body" (Phil. 3:20–21).

Before, we were "foreigners to the covenants of the promise." Now, as Paul says in chapter 3, "through the gospel the Gentiles are heirs together with Israel, members together of one body, and sharers together in the promise in Christ Jesus" (Eph. 3:6).

Before, we were "without God." Now we are "members of God's household, built on the foundation of the apostles and prophets, with Christ Jesus himself as the chief cornerstone" (Eph. 2:19–20).

This is a tremendous change, which the Ephesians and all who have been brought to faith in Christ have experienced. But we must not take it for granted. Notice that Paul uses the word "remember" twice in this section: "Therefore, *remember* that formerly you who are Gentiles by birth . . . " and "*remember* that at that time you were separate from Christ, excluded from citizenship in Israel and foreigners to the covenants of the promise . . . " (vv. 11–12).

We too must remember. If we forget how God drew us near to him, we can become insensitive to the lost and despairing of God's ability to bring others to himself. Someone was once talking with John Newton, the converted slave trader, whom God brought from a position of utter wretchedness to be a preacher of the gospel. They were talking about despair, and the person asked Newton if he did not despair of the salvation of some person. Newton replied, "I never did despair since God saved me." That is what it means to remember—to remember what we were and what we have become, and then expect to see that same change in others.

14

The Broken Wall

(Ephesians 2:14–18)

For he himself is our peace, who has made the two one and has destroyed the barrier, the dividing wall of hostility, by abolishing in his flesh the law with its commandments and regulations. His purpose was to create in himself one new man out of the two, thus making peace, and in this one body to reconcile both of them to God through the cross, by which he put to death their hostility. He came and preached peace to you who were far away and peace to those who were near. For through him we both have access to the Father by one Spirit.

Every generation has its "buzz words," and one for our day is *alienation*. The popular use of this word probably goes back to Karl Marx, who used it to describe the exclusion of workers from the privileges that go with ownership. According to Marx, workers are alienated both from what we call "the system" and from themselves because of how the system works. Marx said the worker puts part of himself into his product. When the owner sells that product, he alienates the worker from himself and lays the psychological groundwork for class struggle.

Today we talk about alienation more broadly. We speak of political alienation, in which a person is excluded from the democratic process. We speak of alienation in marriage as marriages fall apart. There is hardly a relationship in life to which, at one time or another, we do not apply this idea.

THE WALL OF HOSTILITY

We did not invent alienation, of course. It has been present in the world from the moment Eve ate the forbidden fruit in defiance of God's command and gave some to her husband so that he ate also. But what is to the point here is the way alienation was evident to Paul at the time he wrote his letter to the Ephesians.

In Paul's mind there was a great visible symbol of alienation in the wall that surrounded the inner courtyards of the Jewish temple at Jerusalem, dividing them from the outermost courtyard, called the Court of the Gentiles. The temple of Paul's day had been built by Herod the Great to replace the older, inadequate temple dating from the days of Nehemiah. Much of it was overlaid with gold, and quite naturally it was the glory of the city. It sat on a raised platform on what is today still called the temple mount. The temple was surrounded by courts. The innermost court was called the Court of the Priests, because only male members of the priestly tribe of Levi were to enter it. The next court was the Court of Israel; it could be entered by any male Jew. After this there was the Court of the Women, which any Jew could enter and which was called the Court of the Women because it was as far as a woman could go in this hierarchy.

These courtyards were all on the same level. So although there were great differences between them, they were not as great as the monumental division that came next. From the Court of the Women one descended five steps to a level area in which there was erected a five-foot stone barricade that went around the temple enclosure; then, after another level space, there were fourteen more steps that descended to the Court of the Gentiles. According to the Jewish historian Josephus, the wall dividing Jews from Gentiles was marked at intervals by stone inscriptions stating that no foreigner was permitted to enter the Jewish enclosures upon penalty of death.[1]

In the last century or so several of these inscriptions have been found. One incomplete inscription was discovered as recently as 1935. Another whole inscription was unearthed in 1871 and is now in a museum in Istanbul. It reads: "No foreigner is to enter within the balustrade and embankment around the sanctuary. Whoever is caught will have himself to blame for his death which follows."[2]

That is a serious threat, corresponding to our signs "Trespassers will be prosecuted." Only it is stronger. It means, "Trespassers will be killed."

If Paul was writing his letter to the Ephesians from Rome, as we think he was, he must have had a personal experience of the hostility associated with this wall fresh in his mind. Just a short time before, when he had been in Jerusalem to deliver the offerings of the gentile churches to the Jewish Christians of that city, he had entered the temple enclosure to take a vow and had been set upon by an angry mob and almost killed. Paul was Jewish himself, of course, but the Jews knew of his sympathy with Gentiles and somehow got the idea that he had brought a gentile Christian named Trophimus into the temple enclosure with him. It was as a result of this riot that Paul passed into Roman custody, was taken to Caesarea and eventually, because of his appeal to Caesar, was transported to Rome as a prisoner (cf. Acts 21:27–36).

It was this great visible symbol of Jewish-Gentile enmity that Paul had in mind as he wrote of the work of Christ in removing alienation. In all the ancient world, no wall (whether figurative, like our walls, or literal, like the wall in Jerusalem) was so impassable as the wall between Jew and Gentile. No wall gave greater occasion for scorn or arrogance. But, writes Paul, "He himself [that is, Jesus] is our peace, who has made the two [that is, Jew and Gentile] one and has destroyed the barrier, the dividing wall of hostility, by abolishing in his flesh the law with its commandments and regulations" (vv. 14–15).

ALIENATION FROM GOD

The text goes on to say "His purpose was to create in himself one new man out of the two, thus making peace, and in this one body to reconcile both of them to God through the cross, by which he put to death their hostility" (vv. 15–16). To understand what this means and how Jesus did this we need to understand something further about the Jerusalem temple.

In my description of the temple enclosure I pointed out that the temple was surrounded by a series of concentric courts each designed to discriminate among people on the basis of how near or far they could be to the temple. These successive, concentric courts were all a normal person could see. What I did not mention is that the

---

[1]Josephus, *The Jewish War*, 5.5.2; *Jewish Antiquities*, 25.11.5.

[2]See footnote *d* in *Josephus*, trans. Ralph Marcus, ed. Allen Wikgren, 9 vols. (Cambridge, Mass.: Harvard University Press, 1963), 8:202–3.

greatest barrier of all was not outside in the surrounding enclosures but within the temple itself. Within the temple, separating the Holy Place (which any regularly assigned priest could enter) from the Holy of Holies (which only the high priest could enter, and that only once a year after first making a sacrifice for himself and his family) there was the great veil. It was a curtain about six inches thick, the purpose of which was to seal off the inner temple. In that portion of the temple was the sacred Ark of the Covenant, above which, in the space between the wings of the cherubim mounted on its cover, God was understood to dwell symbolically.

In other words, the entire system of this inner veil and outer walls was meant not merely to show the differences among people, but to show the greatest and most fundamental alienation, the alienation of all people from God. The cause of this alienation, like the cause of all other alienations, is sin.

People do not want to face this. If you can remember back to the years preceding World War II, you may remember that there were many well-meaning people who believed that war could be averted if only the political leaders of the day could sit down and talk to one another like gentlemen. Neville Chamberlain believed this. He met with Adolf Hitler and came away believing that Hitler was basically a reasonable person and a man of his word. He returned from that meeting to declare to the British people that he had achieved "peace in our time!" But he had not. Hitler's response to Chamberlain was to blitz Danzig, Poland, which forced Chamberlain's resignation, made Winston Churchill prime minister, and plunged England into war.

We have a similar situation today. Thousands of equally well-meaning people think that all that is necessary to preserve peace and perhaps even achieve disarmament is for the Western

powers to sit down with Russia and for the leaders of these great nations to agree to be gentlemen. But this will not work. Do not misunderstand me at this point. I am not against negotiating or working out mutually verifiable agreements. Talking is always better than fighting. Agreements are always better than having no agreements at all. But what I am opposing is the idea that this will bring peace. At the best it may mute or delay hostilities. But it will never bring peace, because the enemy of peace is not a lack of negotiations but the fundamental alienation that exists between every individual and God. It is because we are at enmity with God— that is the true meaning of sin—that we are also inevitably at enmity with ourselves, one another, and in a certain sense, with all the world.

PEACE WITH GOD

But see what the Lord Jesus Christ has done! Do you remember that incident from Matthew's account of the death of Jesus in which, at the moment of his death, "the curtain of the temple was torn in two from top to bottom" (Matt. 27:51)? Matthew is the preeminently Jewish Gospel, of course. So his reference to the curtain of the temple is one that would have been understood by every Jewish reader. It is a reference to the veil between the Holy Place and the Holy of Holies, and the fact that it was torn in two from top to bottom indicates in as graphic a way as possible that as the result of Christ's death, sin has been removed as a barrier between man and God, reconciliation has been achieved, and the way is now open for anyone to approach God—if he or she comes through faith in Jesus Christ and His work.

This is precisely what Paul says Christ has done: "His purpose was to create in himself one new man out of the two, thus making peace, and in this one body to *reconcile* both of them to

God through the cross" (vv. 15–16). As a result of this, he says, "Through him we both have access to the Father by one Spirit" (v. 18).

In D. Martyn Lloyd-Jones's discussion of this passage there is a helpful summary of what this powerful word "reconciliation" means. It has five parts, according to this writer: "It means *first* of all a change from a hostile to a friendly relationship. That is the simplest meaning, the most basic meaning. . . .

"In the second place, it does not merely mean a friendship after an estrangement, a mere doing away with the estrangement. It is not merely that it brings people into speaking terms again who formerly passed one another without even looking at each other. It means more; it means really bringing together again, a reuniting, a re-connecting. It carries that meaning.

"In the third place it is a word also that emphasizes the completeness of the action. It means that the enmity is so completely laid aside that complete amity follows. . . . It is not a compromise, the kind of thing that happens so often when a conference has gone on for days and there has been a deadlock and somebody suddenly gets a bright idea and suggests introducing a particular word or formula, which just patches up the problem for the moment. It is not that. It is a complete action; it produces complete amity and concord where there was formerly hostility.

"But in the fourth place, it also means this. It is not merely that the two partners to the trouble or the dispute or the quarrel have decided to come together. This word that the apostle uses implies that it is *one* of the parties that takes the action, and it is the *upper* one that does it. A part of this word indicates an action that comes down from above. It is the Greek word *kata* . . . It is not that the two sides come together as it were voluntarily; it is the one bringing the other into this position of complete amity and accord.

"And finally, in the fifth place, the word carries the meaning that it is a restoration of something that was there before. Now our word 'reconcile,' which is really a transliteration of the Latin word, in and of itself suggests that. Re-concile! They were conciled before, they are now re-conciled, brought back to where they were."[3]

That is what "reconcile" means. It is hard to think of a more comprehensive word for describing what God has done through the work of Jesus Christ on the cross. Before this great work, we were estranged or alienated from God. We were in fellowship with God once—in Adam. But since the Fall of Adam and Eve every man or woman born into the world has been born in a state of enmity against God. From our end the situation is utterly hopeless. We cannot make reconciliation, and, even worse, we do not want to. But God made reconciliation. God the Father sent God the Son, Jesus Christ, to bear the full punishment due to us for our sin. He bore it away in his own body by dying on the cross. Thus, our friendship with God is restored, and the way is open for us to come to God freely, as Paul says.

ONE NEW MAN OF TWO

There is a further benefit. Not only is fellowship with the Father restored, but fellowship between estranged human beings also—if they are in Christ. Notice the progression of thought. I began with human alienation, illustrating it from contemporary life and from the great hostility between Jew and Gentile

[3]D. Martyn Lloyd-Jones, *God's Way of Reconciliation: Studies in Ephesians, Chapter 2* (Grand Rapids: Baker, 1972), 224–25.

in Paul's day. I traced the cause of this alienation to a greater alienation, the hostility between all people and God because of sin. Our third point concerned the solution to the greater alienation, which was the bearing of sin by Jesus Christ on Calvary. His death for sin opened the way to God for all who will come to God by him. Our final point now takes us back to the beginning. For since the greater barrier is down, there is no need for the lesser barriers. In fact, they inevitably fall with the large one.

The reason is that the veil between ourselves and God drops only for those who are in Christ. And if we are in Christ, then there can never be a barrier between us and others who are also in Christ, otherwise Christ would be divided. If we are in him, we are in the same place. We are members of the one body, and peace has been restored between all who are members of it.

We must read the passage with all these ideas in mind, beginning with verse 13: "But now in Christ Jesus you who once were far away have been brought near through the blood of Christ. For he himself is our peace, who has made the two one and has destroyed the barrier, the dividing wall of hostility, by abolishing in his flesh the law with its commandments and regulations. His purpose was to create in himself one new man out of the two, thus making peace, and in this one body to reconcile both of them to God through the cross, by which he put to death their hostility. He came and preached peace to you who were far away and peace to those who were near. For through him we both have access to the Father by one Spirit" (vv. 13–18).

There are two final points.

First, if you are in Christ, then in God's sight you are one with every other believer—whether Jew or Gentile, male or female, bond or free— regardless of any distinction whatever. Therefore, you must act like that. You may not see eye to eye with every other Christian on everything. No one expects you to. But you must not break with them! And you must realize that regardless of your differences of opinion, the unity that you have with them is greater than the unity you will ever have with anyone else in the world, even if the unbeliever is of the same class, race, nationality, sex (or whatever) as you are.

Your duty is to live in harmony with these brothers and sisters in Christ, and to let the world know that you are members of one spiritual family. That in itself should be a large portion of your witness.

Second, if you are not yet "in Christ," you should learn that in the final analysis the solution to your most basic problems is to be found in that relationship. That is, it is to be found in your personal relationship to him. There is an objective side to Christ's work. It is described as his "making peace" between men and "reconcil[ing] both . . . to God through the cross" (vv. 15, 16). It is what Jesus did on Calvary by his death. But there is a subjective side as well. It is the part in which we are joined to him by faith as we hear and respond to the gospel. This is why verse 17 speaks of preaching: "He came and preached peace to you who were far away and peace to those who were near."

So the final question is this: Are you in him? If not, you remain divided from countless other human beings and, what is much worse, from God himself. If you come to him, he will remove the barrier and make you a part of that new humanity that he is uniting in himself.

15

The New Humanity

(Ephesians 2:19–22)

Consequently, you are no longer foreigners and aliens, but fellow citizens with God's people and members of God's household, built on the foundation of the apostles and prophets, with Christ Jesus himself as the chief cornerstone. In him the whole building is joined together and rises to become a holy temple in the Lord. And in him you too are being built together to become a dwelling in which God lives by his Spirit.

For several chapters the apostle has been building toward a consideration of the church, which is the major theme of Ephesians. He has not tackled the theme directly. The word "church" has occurred only once thus far (in 1:22). But this is what he wants to talk about, and everything has been building to a full treatment of it.

Chapter 1 presented the plan of salvation from God's perspective, beginning with God's electing grace in Christ and culminating in the exaltation of Christ as "head over everything for the church, which is his body." Chapter 2 presented the plan from our perspective, showing how we are brought from a state of being spiritually dead to a state of being spiritually alive. But it also ends with the church; for it shows, not merely how we have been made alive in Christ, but how we have been brought into the fellowship of God's redeemed and regenerated people.

This is the point to which the last verses of chapter 2 bring us.

I am sure you remember, when you were a child, being give books of drawings in which various objects were cleverly concealed. The picture might be of a field with trees, grass, and fluffy clouds. Underneath were the words: "Can you find the animals hidden in this picture?" When you looked at the picture carefully, you would find a squirrel hidden in the wavy lines of the clouds, an elephant tucked into the foliage of a tree, fish in the grass, and so on. In a sense, this is what we have in verses 19–22 of this chapter. Paul is not using the word "church," but tucked into these lines are three great biblical images for what the church is and how it functions.

Can you find these images? The first is of the church as a *city-state or kingdom.* Paul refers to it by saying, "Consequently, you are no longer foreigners and aliens, but fellow citizens with God's people" (v. 19). The second picture is of a *family.* Paul slips that in by continuing, " . . . and members of God's household" (v. 19). The third picture is the most carefully developed, a building which turns out to be a *temple:* " . . . built on the foundation of the apostles and prophets, with Christ Jesus himself as the chief cornerstone" (v. 20). And Paul adds, "In him the whole building is joined together and rises to become a holy temple in the Lord" (v. 21).

Later in the letter Paul develops the image of the church as Christ's body (chaps. 4–5), and still later as a well-equipped army (ch. 6).

God's Kingdom

What a rich field of imagery this first picture unfolds! We think at once of the Old Testament theocracy, in which God was the literal head of the earthly Jewish state. Or we think of John the Baptist's preaching: "Repent, for the kingdom of heaven is near" (Matt. 3:2), or of Jesus declaring, "The kingdom of God is within [or, in the midst of] you" (Luke 17:21). We pray for the coming of that kingdom each time we recite the Lord's Prayer: "Your kingdom come, your will be done on earth as it is in heaven" (Matt. 6:10).

In scholarly discussion there has been much debate over whether the kingdom of God is past, present, or future. This debate flows from the texts I have cited, among others. In some cases the kingdom seems to have a past aspect, as in God's rule over Israel. In others it has a present aspect, as in the preaching of John the Baptist, Jesus, and the early Christians. In still other cases the kingdom of God is future; else how could we pray "your kingdom come"?

The solution to this apparent problem is that the kingdom of God actually transcends these temporal concepts and is best dealt with in entirely different terms. Basically the kingdom of God is where God rules. Since God rules over all life and over all worldly kingdoms, there is a sense in which the whole world is God's kingdom. His kingdom prevails. As a result, those who confess God's kingship are comforted in the midst of this world's chaotic conflicts and changes. It is why, although there are always "wars and rumors of wars," we are not to be "alarmed" by them

(Matt. 24:6). The kingdom is also where God rules in individual minds and hearts. Paul described the internal aspects of this kingdom as "righteousness, peace and joy in the Holy Spirit" (Rom. 14:17). In this present time the kingdom comes whenever the righteousness, peace, and joy of Jesus enter an individual life, transform it, and bring spiritual blessing.

Paul does not develop this picture at great length in Ephesians. In fact, he does not even use the word "kingdom." But he introduces his thoughts in such a way that it is clear what he has in mind—the incorporation of gentile believers into the kingdom. In other words, he gets into this image by the things he had said earlier. In these previous verses he had been talking about the hostility that had existed between Jew and Gentile symbolized by the wall around the Jewish portions of the temple in Jerusalem. Paul declares that this wall has been broken down by Christ so that now both Jew and Gentile (and all other elements of human society) are brought near to God on an equal basis and become elements of one great spiritual kingdom, the Christian church.

This is revolutionary thinking—and it has proved itself to be revolutionary historically. When Paul wrote these words the kingdom of Rome was at the height of its territorial expansion and glory. Rome dominated the world. Roman armies kept peace and dispensed justice. Roman roads linked the far-flung reaches of the Empire. Rome had stood for hundreds of years and was thought to be able to stand for thousands of years more. But Paul looked at Rome and saw it, not as one great united Kingdom, but as a force imposed on mutually antagonistic factions: rich and poor, free man and slave, man and woman, Jew and Gentile. And in its place he saw this new humanity, created by God himself, transcending these boundaries. This kingdom was destined to grow and permeate all nations, drawing from all peoples. It is a kingdom that cannot be shaken or destroyed.[1]

GOD'S CHILDREN IN CHRIST

Paul's second picture of the church is a family. He introduces it in the second half of verse 19: " . . . and members of God's household." The Greek word which Paul uses (*oikeios*) can refer to an entire family establishment, including friends who live with the family, servants, and hired workers. But in view of Paul's earlier discussion of our being made alive in Christ, when we had been dead in transgressions and sins, it is most likely that he is thinking of our being born into the "natural" family of God where the ties are of blood and not mere household associations.

No doubt this is why he introduced this image. Wonderful as the relationship of a citizen to a strong, beneficent state may be, it is still a distant, or formal relationship. Family ties are more intimate, the bonds tighter.

To become a member of a family you must be born into it or be adopted into it. Interestingly, the Bible uses both terms to describe what it means to be a Christian. Chiefly it speaks of rebirth. This was Jesus' teaching to the aging Nicodemus: "You must be born again" (John 3:7). Peter wrote about it in his first letter: "For you have been born again, not of perishable seed, but of imperishable, through the living and enduring word of God" (1 Peter 1:23).

This idea highlights the similarity or continuity of natures. The life of the child is not the same life as the life of the father or mother, but it comes from

them and is like theirs. Today we would speak of a genetic relationship in which characteristics of parents are passed to children. This is why there must be holiness in the church. God is holy. So the children of God must be growing in holiness also. If they are not, they show that they are not truly God's children.

Being a member of God's household brings inestimable privileges with it. It brings us into the supportive network of our spiritual brothers and sisters. It gives us a share in the oversight, fellowship, and prayers of the church. It gives us a right to the sacraments and a place in God's plan. More important, it gives us access to God as Father, which means that we can come to him in prayer at any moment of any day with any need or request and have the assurance that he will hear, receive us, and answer our requests out of his own mercy and according to his own pleasing and perfect will.

GOD'S TEMPLE

The most extensive picture of the church in these verses is a temple. Paul speaks of Christians being "built on the foundation of the apostles and prophets, with Christ Jesus himself as the chief cornerstone. In him the whole building is joined together and rises to become a holy temple in the Lord. And in him you too are being built together to become a dwelling in which God lives by his Spirit" (vv. 20–22). As Paul develops it, this image has several important aspects.

1. *The foundation*. The strength and durability of a building rests upon its foundation, and that is true of the church too. This is so important that

---

[1]D. Martyn Lloyd-Jones develops the implications of the church as a kingdom extensively in his commentary, showing how citizens are bound to a common ruler, live under common laws, and share common privileges and responsibilities (*God's Way of Reconciliation: Studies in Ephesians, Chapter 2* [Grand Rapids: Baker, 1972], 290–323). He asks us to make sure we have a birth certificate, showing that we are naturally born citizens of the kingdom and not merely foreigners living in the land on a passport (300–301).

the apostle begins his discussion by reference to this foundation. What is it? Paul says that it is "the apostles and prophets." We remember that 1 Corinthians 3:11 makes this point differently, saying, "No one can lay any foundation other than the one already laid, which is Jesus Christ." But the point is really the same. Jesus *is* the foundation. He said to the apostle Peter, "On this rock [meaning himself] I will build my church" (Matt. 16:18). But it is right to say that the apostles and prophets are the foundation too, in the sense that for us they are their teaching, which is focused on Christ.

The apostles were the appointed and inspired witnesses to Christ in the first generation of the church. Jesus said that he would give the New Testament through them (John 14:26; 15:26–27; 16:13–15), and he did. In this context "prophets" probably refers to that special class of individuals who received and proclaimed direct messages from God and worked along with the apostles in the early days. Paul refers to them again in 3:5, speaking of truths revealed by the Spirit to "God's holy apostles and prophets," and in 4:11, saying that God blessed the church by giving "some to be apostles [and] some to be prophets."

The point is that the basis of the church's unity—to which each of the three pictures of the church attest—is truth or sound doctrine. In our day churchmen are often very concerned about unity, and many have been pouring great energy into what is called the ecumenical movement, an effort to get the many diverse branches of the church together. It can be a good thing. True Christians should be united, and it is sad that we are as divided as we are. But when anyone speaks about unity we must be careful to determine what kind of unity we are talking about. Is it the unity of the lowest common denominator? If that is the case, Christian-

ity quickly loses its uniqueness altogether. Is it the unity of an imposed ecclesiastical structure? The church had that to perfection in the Middle Ages, but those were the worst of all days for Christ's body. No, the only unity that is worth having—the only true unity—is the unity built on the revealed truth of God centering in the person and work of Jesus Christ. Where that is present God blesses the church and enables it to grow "together to become a dwelling in which God lives by his Spirit" (v. 22).

2. *The cornerstone.* In 1 Corinthians 3:11 Paul called Jesus the "foundation." Here he calls him the "cornerstone." A cornerstone was important for two reasons. It was part of the foundation, and it also fixed the angle of the building and became the standard from which the architect traced the walls and arches throughout.

The word also touches upon a rich mine of imagery. We remember that Isaiah, the greatest of the Old Testament prophets, spoke of the coming of Jesus Christ in these terms: "See, I lay a stone in Zion, a tested stone, a precious cornerstone for a sure foundation; the one who trusts will never be dismayed" (Isa. 28:16). The psalmist wrote of a stone which was rejected by the builders of the great temple of Solomon but which was later found and used: "The stone the builders rejected has become the capstone" (Ps. 118:22). Jesus applied this Scripture to himself, quoting Psalm 118 (cf. Matt. 21:42); and Peter tied the texts into one great image, to which he also added a citation of Isaiah 8:14.

In Scripture it says:

> "See, I lay a stone in Zion,
>   a chosen and precious
> cornerstone,
>   and the one who trusts in him
>   will never be put to shame."

Now to you who believe, this stone is precious. But to those who do not believe,

"The stone the builders rejected
has become the capstone."

and,

"A stone that causes men to
stumble
and a rock that makes them fall."
(1 Peter 2:6–8)

Although the leaders of his day rejected the Lord Jesus Christ by crucifying him, God made him the cornerstone of the temple which is the church. This is the Lord's doing (cf. Ps. 118:23). An individual must therefore either be joined to Christ savingly or be broken by him.

3. *Living stones.* Paul does not mention stones specifically in our text, but that is what he is thinking of when he writes, "And in him you too are being built together to become a dwelling in which God lives by his Spirit" (v. 22). Believers are mortared together with Christ, as God the architect through his workmen, the preachers of the gospel, builds his church. Peter said it in the verse just before those I have quoted: "You also, like living stones, are being built into a spiritual house to be a holy priesthood, offering spiritual sacrifices acceptable to God through Jesus Christ" (1 Peter 2:5).

The applications of this part of the picture are so obvious as hardly to need elaboration. Let me suggest a few. First, the stones placed into this great structure are chosen and shaped for their position by God. It is his temple; he is the architect; it is not for us to determine where we will fit in or how. Second, the stones are placed into position in relationship to Jesus Christ. They are attached to him; if they are not, they are not part of this building. Third, the stones are of different shapes and sizes, perhaps even of different

material, and they are employed for different functions. Some serve in one way, some another. Fourth, the stones are linked to one another. From where they are placed they cannot always see this; they cannot always even see the other stones. But they are part of one interlocking whole regardless. Fifth, the stones of the temple are chosen, shaped, and placed, not to draw attention to themselves, but to contribute to a great building in which God alone dwells. Sixth, the placing of each stone is only part of a long work begun thousands of years in the past that will continue until the end of the age when the Lord returns.

What a great process this is! And how mysterious! We are told in 1 Kings 6:7 that when the great temple of Solomon was constructed "only blocks dressed at the quarry were used, and no hammer, chisel or any other iron tool was heard at the temple site while it was being built." To my knowledge, no building in history was ever built in this way. Its construction was almost silent, so holy was the work. Silently, silently the stones were moved and added, and the building rose.

Thus it is with the church. We do not hear what is going on inside human minds and hearts as God the Holy Spirit creates new life and adds those individuals to the temple he is building. But God is working. In the days of the apostles God was adding Gentiles to a temple composed at that time largely of Jewish believers. He was adding Luke, Lydia, Phoebe, Philemon, Onesimus— and the believers at Ephesus, and other Greek and Roman cities. Later he added those we call the early church fathers, then the later church fathers and those to whom they ministered. At the time of the Reformation he added Luther and Calvin and Zwingli and Knox and Cranmer and many others. He is still adding to his temple today.

16

A Mystery Revealed

(Ephesians 3:1–6)

For this reason, I, Paul, the prisoner of Christ Jesus for the sake of you Gentiles—
Surely you have heard about the administration of God's grace that was given to me for
you, that is, the mystery made known to me by revelation, as I have already written briefly.
In reading this, then, you will be able to understand my insight into the mystery of Christ,
which was not made known to men in other generations as it has now been revealed by the
Spirit to God's holy apostles and prophets. This mystery is that through the gospel the
Gentiles are heirs together with Israel, members together of one body, and sharers together
in the promise in Christ Jesus.

One of the great terms of the apostle Paul's vocabulary is "mystery." It is little understood. We are probably most acquainted with it as the result of 1 Corinthians 15:51–52, which is incorporated into Handel's *Messiah* as an aria: "Behold, I show you a mystery: We shall not all sleep, but we shall all be changed, in a moment, in the twinkling of an eye, at the last trump" (KJV). But there are nineteen more uses of "mystery" in Paul's writings, plus seven additional occurrences in the Gospels and Revelation.

Some years ago H. A. Ironside wrote a book in which these "mysteries" were discussed. It had nine chapters, and it covered what Ironside called: "The Mysteries of the Kingdom of Heaven," "The Mystery of the Olive Tree," "The Great Mystery of Christ and the Church," "The Mystery of Piety," "The Mystery of the Rapture of the Saints," and "The Mystery of Lawlessness." He prefaced these chapters with an analy-sis of "mystery" in the Old and New Testaments.[1]

What is a mystery? In contemporary English it is something unknown. But this is not the meaning "mystery" had in Paul's day. In Greek the word *mysterion* (from which we get our word) refers to something known only to the initiated. It is not that the thing itself is unknown. It is known—but only to those to whom it is revealed. The word is used in this way of ancient mystery religions—the mysteries of Mithra, Isis and Osiris, Dionysius, and Eleusis. People in general did not know what went on in these religious cults, but the "mysteries" were revealed to the initiates. When the apostle used the word, it was with similar meaning. He used it to describe something that was unknown before the coming of Christ but is now revealed fully.

THE CHURCH, A MYSTERY

In Ephesians 3 the apostle uses the word "mystery" four times; so the

[1] H. A. Ironside, *The Mysteries of God* (New York: Loizeaux Brothers, n.d.).

88

mystery

chapter is critical for understanding the most important mystery Paul speaks of. Paul anticipates this teaching in chapter 1, speaking of "the mystery of [God's] will," namely, "to bring all things in heaven and on earth together under one head, even Christ" (vv. 9–10). He reviews it with a new slant in chapter 5: "This is a profound mystery—but I am talking about Christ and the church" (v. 32). Nevertheless, it is chiefly in chapter 3 that he develops this doctrine.

Paul writes: "Surely you have heard about the administration of God's grace that was given to me for you, that is, the *mystery* made known to me by revelation, as I have already written briefly. In reading this, then, you will be able to understand my insight into the *mystery* of Christ, which was not made known to men in other generations as it has now been revealed by the Spirit to God's holy apostles and prophets. This *mystery* is that through the gospel the Gentiles are heirs together with Israel, members together of one body, and sharers together in the promise in Christ Jesus" (Eph. 3:2–6).

These verses use the word "mystery" three times, and they are followed by a fourth instance just three verses later: "This *mystery*, which for ages past was kept hidden in God, who created all things. . . . that now, through the church, the manifold wisdom of God should be made known to the rulers and authorities in the heavenly realms, according to his eternal purpose which he accomplished in Christ Jesus our Lord" (vv. 9–11).

What is this mystery? Quite clearly, it is that the Gentiles should be made partakers along with the Jews of God's great blessings in the church.

A person might ask how this is new, seeing that the Old Testament referred to God's purpose to bless the Gentiles. As far back as God's calling of Abraham we read: "All peoples on earth will be blessed through you" (Gen. 12:3). It is true, of course, that God announced his intention of saving Gentiles as well as Jews from the beginning. But before the coming of Christ it was understood that this was to happen only as the Gentiles became Jews through proselytizing. A Gentile could approach the God of Israel, but only as an Israelite. He had to become a member of the covenant people through the rite of circumcision. The new thing revealed to Paul is that this approach is no longer necessary. Christ has broken down that wall, making one new people out of two previously divided people. So now both Jew and Gentile approach God equally on that new basis.

JEW AGAINST GENTILE

Today, removed from the apostolic era by many centuries, as we are, we can hardly appreciate how radical this new disclosure was. But Paul gives us a clue in verse 1, in the sentence he starts but then breaks off to write the long parenthesis (vv. 2–13) we are studying. In that verse he speaks of himself as "the prisoner of Christ Jesus for the sake of you Gentiles—."

This was literally true. What had led to Paul's initial arrest in Jerusalem, which in turn led to his imprisonment there and in Caesarea, his appeal to Caesar, and his transfer to and imprisonment in Rome, where he wrote this letter, was fanatical Jewish opposition to his mission to the Gentiles. The story is told in Acts.

Paul had gone to Jerusalem with his offering from the gentile churches and while there had gone into the temple with some other Jews for purification. Jews from Asia (where Ephesus itself was located) saw him and stirred up the crowd to seize him. They shouted, "Men of Israel, help us! This is the man who teaches all men everywhere against our people and our law and this place. And besides, he has brought

Greeks into the temple area and defiled this holy place" (Acts 21:28).

This latter accusation was untrue. They had seen Trophimus of Ephesus in the city with Paul, and they assumed wrongly that Paul had brought him into the temple. But although this part of the accusation was untrue, the first part had merit. Paul had been teaching that God had broken down the wall of Jewish tradition and was now making one new people through faith in Jesus Christ. In other words, he was accused and arrested for teaching precisely the truths we find in chapter 2 of this Ephesian letter.

The story continues. The Roman centurion responsible for keeping order in the city rescued Paul, and after learning that Paul was a Roman citizen, he permitted him to address the crowd. Paul spoke in Aramaic, their common tongue, which quieted them, and they listened while he gave an account of his life and of God's dealings with him. He told how he had been born in Tarsus but had been raised in Jerusalem, how he had studied under Gamaliel, and how he had persecuted Christians, pursuing them even to Damascus to arrest them, bring them back to Jerusalem, and punish them. Paul spoke of Jesus' appearance to him on the road to Damascus, how he had been blinded by the vision but had been sent into the city where Ananias came to him and was used by God to restore his sight. He told of his early preaching to the Jews of Jerusalem, of their rejection of the message, and finally of the Lord's sending him away.

The crowd listened to every word of this quietly. But when Paul got to the final point and quoted the Lord as saying, "Go; I will send you far away to the Gentiles" (Acts 22:21), at once the crowd broke into a frenzy, shouting,

"Rid the earth of him! He's not fit to live!" (v. 22). Paul's reference to the Gentiles infuriated them. What led to his arrest was his faithful espousal of the gentile cause.

The prejudice was not all on one side, of course, It was particularly intense among the Jews, because for them it was a religious issue and no fanaticism is greater than religious fanaticism. Jews despised Gentiles. Yet, as I suggested, Gentiles also despised Jews and others. The Greek thought that all but Greeks were barbarians. Celsus wrote, in what he undoubtedly thought was a most generous concession, "The barbarians may have some gift for discovering truth, but it takes a Greek to understand."[2] The Romans, who conquered the Greeks, looked on them largely as slaves.

Barriers were absolute in the pre-Christian world. So it really was a great mystery "not made known to men in other generations" but now "revealed by the Spirit to God's holy apostles and prophets . . . that through the gospel the Gentiles are heirs together with Israel, members together of one body, and sharers together in the promise in Christ Jesus" (vv. 5–6).

TOGETHER, TOGETHER, TOGETHER

The chief thing Paul wants to say about the mystery of God's creating one new people in Christ (which he does say in verse 6) is that Jew and Gentile, as well as all other types and conditions of men and women, hold their salvation blessings *jointly* in Christ's church. This is more striking in Greek than in most English versions, because to make his point, Paul assembles (and in the opinion of John Stott, in one case invents) three parallel, composite expressions.[3] In Greek these words each

---

[2] Cited by William Barclay, *The Letters to the Galatians and Ephesians* (Edinburgh: Saint Andrews Press, 1970), 143.

[3] John R. W. Stott, *God's New Society: The Message of Ephesians* (Downers Grove, Ill.: InterVarsity, 1979), 117.

begin with the prefix *syn*, which means "together with." It is added to the words: *"klēronoma*, meaning "heirs"; *soma*, meaning "body" and *metocha*, meaning "partner," "companion," or "one who shares in."

There is no way to capture the precise force of this in English. The King James Version does not do very well at all, although it gives an accurate translation: "fellow heirs, and of the same body, and partakers of his promise." The Revised Standard Version and the New English Bible also translate accurately but obscure the flow. Phillips does better. He says, *"equal* heirs with his chosen people, *equal* members and *equal* partners in God's promise," repeating the word "equal" as an equivalent for *syn*.

In my opinion the New International Version is most effective because it repeats the word "together." It says, "heirs *together* with Israel, members *together* of one body, and sharers *together* in the promise in Christ Jesus." These phrases are worth looking at in detail.

1. *"Heirs together with Israel."* The word "heirs" was an important one for Paul, as his use of it in a number of key passages shows. In Romans 4 he uses it of Abraham, referring to God's promise that he should be "heir of the world" through Christ's righteousness (v. 13). In Galatians he extends it to all believers, saying, "If you belong to Christ, then you are Abraham's seed, and heirs according to the promise" (Gal. 3:29). Titus 3:7 speaks of a future inheritance: "So that, having been justified by his grace, we might become heirs having the hope of eternal life." Galatians 4:1–7 has a more immediate reference, contrasting the heir's position as a child (when he was little more than a slave) with his position as a full-grown son, who has "the full rights" of a son. In Romans 8:17 Paul uses the very word (*sygklēronoma*) that he does in

Ephesians, saying, "Now if we are children, then we are heirs—heirs of God and co-heirs with Christ, if indeed we share in his sufferings in order that we may also share in his glory."

These uses of the words embrace all that a person receives or will receive in salvation. It is the whole of God's blessing, possessed jointly by all believers in and with Christ. So there is no inner circle or outer circle of the saved. The Jews are not first-rate Christians and the Gentiles second, or vice versa. All who are in Christ inherit all God's blessing. And they inherit jointly! They hold it together in the one body of Jesus Christ.

2. *"Members together of one body."* At the end of the preceding chapter Paul compared the church to a kingdom, a family, and a temple. But here he picks up on a theme he introduced at the end of chapter 1: "God placed all things under his feet and appointed him to be head over everything for the church, which is his body, the fullness of him who fills everything in every way" (vv. 22–23).

Paul comes back to this theme again in chapter 4. He mentions that "there is one body," (v. 4) and then he goes on to describe how God has built us all into a single body: "It was he who gave some to be apostles, some to be prophets, some to be evangelists, and some to be pastors and teachers, to prepare God's people for works of service, so that the body of Christ may be built up until we all reach unity in the faith and in the knowledge of the Son of God and become mature, attaining to the whole measure of the fullness of Christ. Then we will no longer be infants, tossed back and forth by the waves, and blown here and there by every wind of teaching and by the cunning and craftiness of men in their deceitful scheming. Instead, speaking the truth in love, we will in all things grow up into him who is the Head, that is, Christ. From him the whole body, joined and held together by every supporting ligament, grows and builds itself up in love, as each part does its work" (vv. 11–16).

This image speaks of a mystical union possessed by God's people in the church. But it also suggests that this is something into which the people of God must grow and toward which they must strive. That is, the unity between Jew and Gentile, bond and free, male and female (and all other human groupings) must be increasingly worked for and realized in this life.

How is this to happen? It is to happen only as we grow in the love and knowledge of the One who has brought us together. As D. Martyn Lloyd-Jones says in his discussion of Ephesians 2, "We are all equally sinners. . . . We are all equally helpless. . . . We have all come to one and the same Savior. . . . We have the same salvation. . . . We have the same Holy Spirit. . . . We have the same Father. . . . We even have the same trials. . . . And finally, we are all marching and going together to the same eternal home."[4] It is a knowledge and appreciation of these things that will draw us together.

3. *"Sharers together in the promise in Christ Jesus."* The Bible has many promises for those who trust God and come to him through faith in the work of Christ. But the word in this phrase is singular, "promise," and for that reason must refer to "the promise of redemption, made to our first parents, repeated to Abraham, and which forms the burden of all the Old Testament predictions (Gal. 3:14, 19, 22, 29)."[5]

To have that, as Paul says the people of God do, is to have a share in the greatest of all possible human blessings. To share it with others from a great variety of races, peoples, and cultures is to participate in the mystery which was revealed to Paul and declared by him.

APOSTLES TO ALL

I close on this note. Wonderful as this mystery may be, it is nevertheless not the same thing as a broad declaration of the so-called universal brotherhood of man and universal fatherhood of God, as the liberals of an earlier generation styled it. This mystery is "in Christ Jesus" and is made known "through the gospel." It is Jesus who has broken down the dividing wall of hostility. It is his messengers who are sent to draw people together—by calling them to Christ.

It can hardly escape notice that it was in connection with his own ministry of making these things known that Paul got into this discussion in the first place. Paul wrote of himself as "the prisoner of Christ Jesus for . . . you Gentiles" (v. 1). He broke off at that point to describe the mystery of the Gentiles being included in the promises originally confined to Israel. But then he was unable to say that without repeated references to himself as one who had received the revelation and was entrusted with declaring it: "Surely you have heard about the administration of God's grace that was given to me for you, that is, the mystery made known to me by revelation, as I have already written briefly" (vv. 2–3); "You will be able to understand my insight into the mystery of Christ, which was not made known to men in other generations as it has now been revealed by the Spirit to God's holy apostles and prophets" (vv. 4–5); "I became a servant of this gospel by the gift of God's grace given me through the working of

[4]D. Martyn Lloyd-Jones, *God's Way of Reconciliation: Studies in Ephesians, Chapter 2* (Grand Rapids: Baker, 1972), 282–88.

[5]Charles Hodge, *A Commentary on the Epistle to the Ephesians* (1856; reprint, Grand Rapids: Baker, 1980), 166.

his power" (v. 7); and "grace was given me: to preach to the Gentiles the unsearchable riches of Christ, and to make plain to everyone the administration of this mystery" (vv. 8–9).

Paul never got over the wonder of the great doctrine of the church, nor that he had been commissioned to make it known to the world. We are not apostles, as Paul was. We have not received fresh revelation. But the revelation is ours no less than it was his, and our responsibility to proclaim it is the same.

17

The Meaning and End of History

(Ephesians 3:7–13)

I became a servant of this gospel by the gift of God's grace given me through the working of his power. Although I am less than the least of all God's people, this grace was given me: to preach to the Gentiles the unsearchable riches of Christ, and to make plain to everyone the administration of this mystery, which for ages past was kept hidden in God, who created all things. His intent was that now, through the church, the manifold wisdom of God should be made known to the rulers and authorities in the heavenly realms, according to his eternal purpose which he accomplished in Christ Jesus our Lord. In him and through faith in him we may approach God with freedom and confidence. I ask you, therefore, not to be discouraged because of my sufferings for you, which are your glory.

Not many people are as forthright in their evaluation of history as Henry Ford, the inventor and industrialist, but there is a feeling in many secular minds that Ford may have been right. In 1919 during his libel suit against the *Chicago Tribune*, Ford said, "History is bunk."[1] On another occasion, when he was asked about history's meaning, Ford said, "History is the succession of one damned thing after another."[2]

SECULAR VIEWS OF HISTORY

Many resist Henry Ford's view, of course, because to live in a world without meaning is to live a life without meaning. One who resisted it strongly was Karl Marx. He had no room for God; he was an atheist. But he took Hegel's historical dialectic, coupled it to Feuerbach's materialism, and produced his own vision of a history that had purpose and was going somewhere.

Feuerbach had taught, with a German pun, that *"der Mench ist was er isst"* ("man is what he eats"), that material factors are everything. Marx accepted this, but added that material forces would produce a class struggle, revolution, and eventually a classless society.

Until relatively recent times most people living in Western societies held a similar, though not necessarily atheistic, view. It was known as a belief in progress. I have always associated that belief with those popular cinematic newsreels produced by the Time/Life company before, during, and for a time after World War II. They were called *The March of Time*. There was stirring "martial" music, the voice of an assured announcer, and a sequence of scenes from around the world that sometimes left the viewer dazzled with all that seemed to be happening in this fast-paced, modern age.

[1] John R. W. Stott, *God's New Society: The Message of Ephesians* (Downers Grove, Ill.: InterVarsity, 1979), 127.

[2] John Warwick Montgomery, *Where Is History Going?* (Minneapolis: Bethany Fellowship, 1969), 15.

What a vision! How inevitable the perfection of all things seemed! Yet it is increasingly difficult to maintain this optimism in the face of two world wars, numerous lesser wars, and epidemics of senseless death and violence that sweep over our planet with increasing frequency.

The two most distinguished modern historians, Germany's Oswald Spengler and England's Arnold Toynbee, both concluded that the overall pattern of history was a recurring cycle of birth, growth, decay, and death—the same pattern the Greeks discerned thousands of years earlier. Spengler and Toynbee do not analyze national and historical movements in the same way. They are not equally pessimistic. But fundamental to their approaches is the shared conviction that nothing is permanent, that all is relative, and that even the best civilizations are destined to pass away. Spengler wrote this conviction into the title of his work, calling it *The Decline of the West.*[3]

THE TURNING POINT

What is history about? Historians study kings, queens, presidents, generals, inventors, nations, wars, battles, peace treaties, and geography—as they struggle to bring meaning to a chaos of events. But in writing to the Ephesians the apostle Paul, who was himself no mean historian, turns to the church as the focal point of world history. This is the point upon which God's purpose is focused, he says. "His intent was that now, through the church, the manifold wisdom of God should be made known to the rulers and authorities in the heavenly realms, according to his eternal purpose which he accomplished in Christ Jesus our Lord" (Eph. 3:10–11).

Paul's view of the historical sig-nificance of the church could not be more in conflict with prevailing secular opinions. John Stott expresses it like this: "Secular history concentrates its attention on kings, queens, and presidents, on politicians and generals, in fact on 'VIPs.' The Bible concentrates rather on a group it calls 'the saints,' often little people, insignificant people, unimportant people, who are however at the same time God's people—and for that reason are both 'unknown (to the world) and yet well-known to God.'

"Secular history concentrates on wars, battles and peace-treaties, followed by yet more wars, battles and peace-treaties. The Bible concentrates rather on the war between good and evil, on the decisive victory won by Jesus Christ over the powers of darkness, on the peace-treaty ratified by his blood, and on the sovereign proclamation of an amnesty for all rebels who will repent and believe.

"Again, secular history concentrates on the changing map of the world, as one nation defeats another and annexes its territory, and on the rise and fall of empires. The Bible concentrates rather on a multi-national community called 'the church,' which has no territorial frontiers, which claims nothing less than the whole world for Christ, and whose empire will never come to an end."[4]

This is the great reality Paul holds before our gaze as he makes known "the administration of [the] mystery, which for ages past was kept hidden in God" but is now revealed (v. 9).

WHAT IS GOD DOING?

It is not only we, the members of the church, who are directed to look at this mystery. "The rulers and authorities in the heavenly realms" are also said to be

---

[3] Oswald Spengler, *The Decline of the West,* trans. Charles Francis Atkinson, 2 vols. (New York: Alfred A. Knopf, 1926, 1928), and Arnold J. Toynbee, *A Study of History,* 12 vols. (London: Oxford University Press, 1934–1961).

[4] Stott, *God's New Society,* 127–28.

looking at the church as the place where God's manifold wisdom is made known (v. 10). What is that "manifold wisdom" these heavenly authorities are to see? What is the purpose of God made known in the worldwide community of God's people? The passage suggests three things.

1. *The bringing together of otherwise divided individuals in Christ.* This point has already been made in the verses that concluded the second chapter of Ephesians and began the third, and it is undoubtedly the chief thing Paul is thinking about. He is writing to Gentiles, who before the coming of Christ and the founding of his church were cut off from Israel's spiritual blessings and were despised by the covenant people, and he is telling them that the period of alienation is now over and that the dividing wall of hostility has been broken down. Gentiles are now one with Jesus within the fellowship of Christ's church.

But there is more in this uniting of people described in the middle portion of the chapter. Earlier Paul had focused on the historical change that took place as the result of Christ's death, in which Jews and Gentiles were brought together. Here he is looking to the distant past and forward to the distant future and is suggesting, I believe, a far greater harmonization.

I say this because of Paul's reference to God as the creator of all things (v. 9). The mere mention of creation makes us think back to those pristine days of earth's history in which the originally perfect world was marred by man's sin. Before the Fall, the harmony between the first man and first woman was analogous to the harmony within the Godhead. It was a unity of mind, purpose, goals, and will. After sin entered, that unity was broken. The man and woman hid, thereby attempting to escape God's presence. It was a dramatization of their rupture with

God. But immediately after this, when God called them forth to meet him and answer questions concerning their conduct, they began to excuse themselves and blame others, thereby disclosing their corresponding alienation on the human level. God asked Adam, "Have you eaten from the tree that I commanded you not to eat from?" (Gen. 3:11).

Adam replied, "The woman you put here with me—she gave me some fruit from the tree, and I ate it" (v. 12). In these words Adam blamed both the woman ("*she* gave me some fruit") and God ("the woman *you* gave me"), and thus displayed that wretched self-righteousness which is a persistent and devastating fact of human history.

In the church God is bringing these otherwise alienated and mutually accusing entities together on a basis that excludes any real cause for alienation. The church is a community of sinners redeemed by Christ and forgiven by God. If salvation were of works, as we might like and even the watching angels might have supposed it would be, the alienation would not have been removed. One person would still feel superior to another, and boasting of moral or spiritual merit would fracture the church and eventually sully heaven. But salvation is not achieved by works. God has achieved it and made it available to us by grace alone. Thus boasting is excluded, and men and women of all races and nations meet as forgiven sinners within the church's fellowship.

This is something the angels might well look upon and marvel at. It is an achievement in which even we may see the goal of human history.

2. *The displaying of Christ by Christian people in the world.* Up to now I have been talking about the church as the focus of world history, the point where its meaning can be found. But it is equally right to speak of Jesus Christ as

the focal point which, of course, is precisely what Paul does. Ephesians 3:9–10 uses the word "mystery" of the church. But an earlier reference is to "the mystery of Christ" (v. 4), and the remaining references are to the "gospel" which is centered in him and has for its object the salvation of the church which is his body.

It is this idea, the idea of the church as Christ's body, which holds the two foci of Paul's thought together. For in Paul's view, the church is the focal point of history only because it is the focal point of Christ's work.

At the beginning of his influential and much discussed book *Christ and Time*, Oscar Cullmann of the University of Basel called attention to the fact that in the Western world we do not reckon time in a continuous forward-moving series that begins at a fixed initial point, but from a center from which time is reckoned both forward and backward. The Jewish calendar begins from what it regards as the date of the creation of the world and moves on from that point. But we begin with the birth of Jesus of Nazareth—fixed within the space of a few years—and then number in two directions: forward, in an increasing succession of years which we identify as A.D. (*anno Domini* "in the year of [our] Lord"), and backward, in a regression of years which we identify as B.C. ("before Christ").

A secular historian might judge that the coming of Jesus was pivotal because of Jesus' obvious influence on later history. But the Christian conviction, symbolized by the division of time, goes beyond this. As Cullmann says, "The modern historian may when pressed find a historically confirmed meaning in the fact that the appearance of Jesus of Nazareth is regarded as a decisive turning point of history. But

the *theological* affirmation which lies at the basis of the Christian chronology goes far beyond the confirmation that Christianity brought with it weighty historical changes. It asserts rather that from this mid-point all history is to be understood and judged."[5]

Christianity affirms that apart from Christ there is no way of determining what history as a whole is all about, nor can we legitimately weigh historical events so that one may be pronounced better or more significant than another. With Christ both these essentials for a true historical outlook are provided.

Moreover, it is in the church alone that this can be seen. When we are talking about Christ there is no way of determining what history as a whole is all about, nor can we legitimately weigh historical events so that one may be pronounced better or more significant than another. With Christ both these essentials for a true historical outlook are provided.

Moreover, it is in the church alone that this can be seen. When we are talking about Christ we are not talking about some vague historical idea or some abstract principle for measuring the meaning of life. We are talking about a person who lives in us and can be known to others as we model him before a watching world. It is not a dead Jesus whom Christians serve, but a living one. Where can people see him except in the church, which gives, as it were, hands and feet, nerves and sinews to his life?

3. *Proof of the principle that suffering for truth and righteousness is the way to glory and the secret of true happiness*. I add this point because the way of Jesus is the way of suffering—he said, "If you belonged to the world, it would love you as its own. As it is, you do not belong to the world, but I have chosen

---

[5] Oscar Cullmann, *Christ and Time: The Primitive Christian Conception of Time and History*, trans. Floyd V. Filson (Philadelphia: Westminster Press, 1950), 19.

you out of the world. That is why the world hates you. . . . If they persecuted me, they will persecute you also" (John 15:19–20)—and because Paul quite naturally alludes to his own sufferings at the close of this section.

Is the meaning of history some promise of Jesus to make you blissfully happy and solve all your problems, to make you materially prosperous, successful, esteemed, and healthy? Hardly! Here in a nutshell is what I think the purpose of history is, as demonstrated in the lives of those who have been saved from sin by Jesus.

When Satan rebelled against God and carried the host of fallen angels, now demons, with him into eternal ruin, God could have crushed the rebellion and annihilated Satan and his hosts forever. That would have been just and reasonable. It might even have been merciful; for if God had gone on to create Adam and Eve, as he had no doubt determined to do beforehand, Satan would not have been there to tempt them, the pair would not have fallen, and sin and death would not have passed upon the race.

But this would not have shown God's "manifold wisdom." It would have shown his power and perhaps even his mercy. But it would not have shown that God's way, the way of truth and righteousness, is the only really good way and the only sure path to happiness.

So instead of annihilating Satan, God took an entirely different path: "I have already determined to create a race called man, and I know in advance, because I know all things, that Satan will seduce him from my righteousness and plunge him into misery. Satan will think he has won. But while Satan is doing that—turning the human race against me and setting individual human beings against one another and even against themselves—I will begin to create a new people who will glory in

doing what is right, even when it is not popular, and who will delight in pleasing me, even when they suffer for it. Satan will say, 'Your people serve you only because you protect them, only because you provide for them materially.' But here and there in a great variety of ways I will allow them to be greatly abused and persecuted, and I will show by their reactions that not only will they continue to praise me in their suffering, and thus bring glory to my name, but that they will even be happier in their sufferings than Satan's people will be with their maximum share of human prestige and possessions."

So God let history unfold like a great drama upon a cosmic stage. The angels are the audience. We are the actors. Satan is there to do everything he can to resist and thwart God's purposes. This drama unfolds across the centuries as Adam and Eve, Noah, Abraham, Moses, David, Isaiah, John the Baptist, Jesus, Peter, Paul, and all the other *dramatis personae* of Christian history, both the great persons and the minor persons, are brought on stage to play the part God has assigned them and speak words that come from hearts that love him. Adam proved that God's way is the best way, and he repented of his sin and trusted in the coming of Jesus. So did Eve and Noah and all the others. All these endured as seeing by faith him who is invisible, and they looked beyond the distresses of this life for their reward.

Now you and I are the players in this drama. Satan is attacking, and the angels are straining forward to look on. Are they seeing the "manifold wisdom" of God in you as you go through your part and speak your lines? They must see it, for it can be seen in you alone. It is there—where you work and play and think and speak—that the meaning and end of history is found.

18

Family Prayers

(Ephesians 3:14–19)

For this reason I kneel before the Father, from whom his whole family in heaven and on earth derives its name. I pray that out of his glorious riches he may strengthen you with power through his Spirit in your inner being, so that Christ may dwell in your hearts through faith. And I pray that you, being rooted and established in love, may have power, together with all the saints, to grasp how wide and long and high and deep is the love of Christ, and to know this love that surpasses knowledge—that you may be filled to the measure of all the fullness of God.

Anybody who has ever thought seriously about prayer has at one time or another wrestled with the question of its value. Sometimes this is because we do not get what we pray for. We pray according to what we think is the will of God, but the answer is denied or delayed. We ask, "What is the purpose of our praying, then? Does prayer work?" Or we struggle with prayer theologically in its relationship to God's decrees. Every Calvinist has at some time been asked, "Why pray if God is going to do what he will do anyhow? Do you really think your prayers will get God to change his mind?"

Our prayers do not get God to change his mind, of course. They would be dangerous if they could. But it is striking that these or any other questions do not seem to have deterred the biblical writers from praying. On the contrary, the more aware they were of God's sovereignty or God's will, the more fervently they petitioned him.

FOR THIS REASON

This is the case with Ephesians 3:14–19, the second of two prayers by Paul for the Ephesian Christians. The prayer begins, "For this reason I kneel before the Father. . . . " That is, Paul is praying to God for a reason. What is this reason?

Is it because Paul was imprisoned and did not want the Ephesians to become discouraged by his suffering for them? This is the way John Calvin saw it. Calvin wrote, "That is what St. Paul is aiming at here, exhorting the Ephesians not to be thrust out of the way, but keep on still truly and constantly in the faith of the gospel, even though they might take offense at seeing him a prisoner."[1]

Is it because of his clear personal interest in the Ephesians' welfare? Harry A. Ironside took this position. "For what cause? Because of his deep interest in the people of God, because of his

---

[1]John Calvin, *Sermons on the Epistle to the Ephesians* (1562; reprint, Carlisle, Pa.: Banner of Truth Trust, 1975), 270–71.

desire that they should enter fully into their privileges in Christ."[2]

John R. W. Stott thinks it is because of the reconciling work of Christ and his own understanding of it by special revelation."[3]

In my opinion, it is none of these. Rather it is Paul's confidence that God has already determined to do these very things for and in the believers for whom he prays. "For this reason" could refer back to any statement in the previous verses, the closer to the end the better. But remember what these verses are about. They tell us how God is establishing his church—a new humanity gathered from the old humanity—in which the manifold wisdom of God is being displayed before the watching angels. God is doing this. God is showing forth his glory in us. Therefore—that is, for this very reason—Paul prays for those in whom he is doing it. He prays that they might be fit vessels, strengthened by God for this important task.

ALL MY CHILDREN

Another way of saying this is to notice that Paul is praying for Christians as God's family and that he is therefore praying with the boldness a family relationship provides. We pray for many persons, of course, even apart from their relationship or lack of relationship to Christ. We pray for kings and all others who are in authority. We pray for the heathen, asking God to bless the testimony of missionaries as they attempt to take the gospel to them. We pray for the lost in our own land.

This is right. But at the same time, we do not pray with the same measure of confidence or in the same way as when we pray for those who are already

Christians. We do not know whom God is going to save. The preaching of the Word hardens some hearts, just as it softens others. But when we pray for Christians we pray for those who have already responded to the gospel, and we know what God is doing in them. God is making them like the Lord Jesus Christ, teaching them to live and serve and even suffer as he did. So we are bold in these prayers. We do not pray, "If it be your will." This is God's will. We pray that God will accomplish it in those for whom we also deeply care.

Moreover, this is to be our prayer for all Christians—not merely for those who are like us or whom we particularly like or favor. When Paul uses the phrase "his whole family" in verse 15, he is doing two very interesting things. In Greek the words are *pasa patria*. Since the word for "Father" in the immediately preceding phrase is *pater*, there is an obvious play on these words which is impossible to capture in English. Our spiritual "family" (*patria*) derives its being and even its very name from its *pater*.

The other interesting word is *pasa*. *Pasa* can mean (and usually does mean) "every," in which case, the phrase *pasa patria* would mean "every family," meaning perhaps "every nation" of the world or "every family within" the one larger family of God's people. Ironside saw it in this last way and referred to the "antediluvian family," the "patriarchal family," the "Old Testament family," the "New Testament family," even the family of "angels."[4] But these meanings are absent from the context. It is not a variety of families that Paul is thinking of here, but one family, the family that derives its very name from God. So *pasa* should be translated

---

[2] H. A. Ironside, *In the Heavenlies: Practical Expository Addresses on the Epistle to the Ephesians* (Neptune, N.J.: Loizeaux Brothers, 1937), 155.

[3] John R. W. Stott, *God's New Society: The Message of Ephesians* (Downers Grove, Ill.: InterVarsity, 1979), 132.

[4] Ibid., 157.

"whole," as the New International Version has it. It is the whole family for whom Paul prays—Jew and Gentile, rich and poor, male and female, young and old, educated and uneducated—everyone, for it is in the family as a whole that God's great purpose of making known his manifold wisdom is fulfilled.

Here is a great lesson in prayer. When we pray we must go beyond our own small interests or the concerns of our own limited circle of Christian friends and instead pray for the church of God at large. We must ask that it be strengthened throughout the whole world, and we must be encouraged by what God is doing through his people everywhere.

A Prayer Ladder

Paul's prayer for the whole family of God shows not only whom we should pray for and why we should pray, but also gives us an outline of what to pray for. John Stott compares it to a "prayer-staircase" consisting of four steps: strength, love, knowledge, and fullness. The idea of a staircase is a good one, but I think there are a few more steps than this. Let me suggest how I look at this progression.

1. *That believers may be strengthened internally through the Holy Spirit.* Paul has been talking about suffering, and this is probably why he begins his prayer with a request that the believers at Ephesus might be strengthened by God's Spirit. None of us show much of the manifold wisdom of God in easy days. It is in suffering that the grace of God is manifested. But who has strength for suffering? We do not choose suffering. We shrink from it. Like Christ in the garden we inevitably draw back and ask that, if it is possible, this cup might pass from us. If we are to show God's wisdom in such times, it must be by God's strength. He must send his angels to minister to us.

Still, it is not only in times of suffering that we need to be strengthened. We need strength every day of our lives and in every circumstance.

Is it temptation? We need strength to resist it and be victorious to the glory of God.

Is it a tough moral choice at work? We need strength to do the right thing so that Jesus, whom we serve, might be honored.

Is it witnessing? We need strength to speak the truth regardless of what the world may think of us for speaking it. When Jesus prayed for God to send the Comforter or Holy Spirit to be with his disciples it was this he chiefly had in mind. The word *paraklētos* ("comforter," "counselor," or "advocate") means "one called alongside to help." The Holy Spirit helps us do the right thing in difficult circumstances.

2. *That believers may be indwelt with Christ by faith.* At first glance this seems like a redundant and unnecessary statement, for what makes believers believers is their having Christ within. If he is not a part of them through faith, they are not Christians. But, of course, Paul means more than this. It is true that all who are truly Christians are indwelt by Jesus Christ, but it is also true that this is something they grow into as Christ takes stronger and fuller possession of every corner of their lives.

The clue to Paul's meaning is found in his choice of the word *katoikeō* rather than the similar word *paroikeō*, both of which are sometimes rendered by the English word "dwell." The second word, which Paul does not use, means to dwell in a place as a stranger. That is, it is the word that would be used of a foreigner (like Abraham) dwelling in a land not actually his own. The first word, *katoikeō*, which Paul does use, means to dwell in the sense of settling down in a place and making a permanent residence there. As Stott points out, it is used for the fullness of the Godhead abiding in Christ and, as here, for Christ's abiding in a believer's heart and life. The prayer is that Christ might settle down in our hearts and control them as the rightful owner.

3. *That believers may be rooted and grounded in love.* Some years ago when I was working for an evangelical magazine I heard the publisher share with one of the editors the worst example of a mixed metaphor he had ever encountered. It was in a business situation, and one of the businessmen had said of something he felt was going wrong: "I smell a rat; I feel him in the air; I'll nip him in the bud." It was an example of how not to use metaphors.

Nobody seems to have warned the apostle Paul about mixed metaphors because he uses one here: "rooted and established in love." The first metaphor is botanical; it compares the believer to a plant rooted in the love of God. The second is architectural; it compares the believer to a building established on love as a foundation. Well, it may be less than perfect English usage, but it is good theology. In the first case, love is pictured as something that nourishes us (which it obviously does), and, in the second case, it is pictured as a solid foundation (which it is).

4. *That believers may be able to grasp the fullest dimensions of Christ's love.* Paul has already prayed that the Christians at Ephesus might be rooted and established in love, that is, that love might fill and support them. But here he thinks of Christ's love for us (rather than of our love for Christ and others) and prays that we might comprehend its greatness. How can this be? A verse later he is going to call it "love that surpasses knowledge." If it surpasses knowledge, how are we to grasp or know it?

There are two answers. First, although we cannot exhaust the love of Christ by our knowledge, we can nevertheless know this love truly. It is the same with the knowledge of God generally. We cannot know exhaustively, but we can know truly. So although, in the same way, we cannot know all of Christ's love for us, we can know that what we perceive as Christ's love is truly love. The love of Christ that we know at the beginning of our Christian life is the same love that we will know (though more fully) at the end.

Second, we are to grow in our awareness of that love, particularly through the routine hardships, sufferings, and persecutions of life. Here is where the matter of the dimensions "wide and long and high and deep" comes in.

In the last century, when Napoleon's armies opened a prison that had been used by the Spanish Inquisition they found the remains of a prisoner who had been incarcerated for his faith. The dungeon was underground. The body had long since decayed. Only a chain fastened around an anklebone cried out his confinement. But this prisoner, long since dead, had left a witness. On the wall of his small, dismal cell this faithful soldier of Christ had scratched a rough cross with four words surrounding it in Spanish. Above the cross was the Spanish word for "height." Below it was the word for "depth." To the left the word "width." To the right, the word "length." Clearly this prisoner wanted to testify to the surpassing greatness of the love of Christ, perceived even in his suffering.

When Paul speaks of width, length, height, and depth, he probably is not thinking of anything special to be associated with each one. Yet it is not wrong to say, as Stott does, that "the love of Christ is 'broad' enough to encompass all mankind (especially Jew and gentiles, the theme of these chapters), 'long' enough to last for eternity, 'deep' enough to reach the most degraded sinner, and 'high' enough to exalt him to heaven."[5]

Another prisoner, his name unknown, also once wrote of God's love:

Could we with ink the oceans fill
And were the skies of parchment
    made,
Were every stalk on earth a quill
And every man a scribe by trade—
To write the love of God above
Would drain the oceans dry;
Nor could the scroll contain the
    whole
Though stretched from sky to sky.

5. *That believers may know this love that surpasses knowledge.* Here is another petition which, like verse 17, seems redundant. But again, it is not so. In verse 18 Paul prayed that the Christians at Ephesus might grasp the full dimensions of the love of Christ, that is, that they might understand it. Here he prays that they might "know" it in the full biblical sense of that word. The chief idea is experience. Paul wanted them to experience the love of Christ, which in its fullest extent surpasses human knowledge.

6. *That believers may be filled to the measure of the fullness of God.* At this point the "prayer-staircase" that we have been ascending reaches its highest, most audacious rung. The phrase "fullness of God" can be either of two grammatical constructions. It can be an objective genitive; in that case, the fullness of God would be the fullness of grace God bestows on us. Or it can be a subjective genitive; in that case, the fullness would be God's own fullness, that which fills himself. Because of the preposition *eis,* which means "unto," it seems that the second is to be preferred. Overwhelming as the petition may be, Paul seems to be praying that we (and all other Christians) may be filled up to or unto all the fullness that is in God himself.

How can this be? Ironside found it so impossible that he changed the meaning to suggest that some of the fullness of God is to be in us like some of the ocean in an empty shell. I think that falls short of the idea. Here is the highest rung of the ladder, the highest step of the stairs. We are to be filled with all God's fullness, an infinite thing. But then, we have all eternity (an infinite time) to be so filled. I think Paul is praying that we will be filled and filled and filled and filled and filled— and so on forever, as God out of his infinite resources increasingly pours himself out into those sinful but now redeemed creatures he has rescued through the work of Christ.

To Him Be Glory

I do not know how God is going to do that, and I will tell you something interesting: even though he talks about it, I do not think Paul understood it either. I say that because of the benediction which immediately follows this prayer. It is "to him who is able to do immeasurably more than all we ask or imagine, according to his power that is at work within us. . . . " When Paul says "we" he includes himself. He is saying that even he, the great apostle, cannot fully understand or even imagine all that God is going to do for us. But Paul does know that God can do it. And not only is God *able* to do it, he is able to do it "immeasurably," which means indefinitely.

My mind stops at that, and I think that is where Paul's mind stopped too. Beyond that top step on the staircase is infinity. It remains only to say, as Paul does, "to him be glory in the church and in Christ Jesus throughout all generations, for ever and ever! Amen" (v. 21).

---

[5]Ibid., 137.

19

A Great Doxology

(Ephesians 3:20–21)

Now to him who is able to do immeasurably more than all we ask or imagine, according to his power that is at work within us, to him be glory in the church and in Christ Jesus throughout all generations, for ever and ever! Amen.

Bible study is a kaleidoscopic experience. The lessons we learn and the experiences we have are multiple. At times the Bible humbles us, making us conscious of our sin. At other times it thrills us as we think of all God has done in Christ for our salvation. Some Bible passages instruct us. Some rebuke us. Some stir us up to great action. In some passages we seem to gain a glimpse into hell. In others, a door is opened into heaven.

The last is the case as we come to the closing verses of Ephesians 3. They are a great doxology, perhaps the greatest in the Bible. In the verses just before this Paul has reached a height beyond which neither reason nor imagination can go. He had been speaking of God's purposes for his redeemed people, and he had expressed the wish that we

should "be filled to the measure of all the fullness of God" (v. 19).

This is beyond comprehension; we cannot even begin to imagine how we can be filled with God's own fullness. We stand on the edge of the infinite. And yet, Paul is still not satisfied. He has prayed that God will do something we cannot even imagine; and now, having exhausted his ability to speak and write along that line, he bursts out in praise to God who, he says, "is able to do immeasurably more than all we ask or imagine, according to his power that is at work within us" (v. 20).

What an amazing doxology! In the last study I spoke of Paul's ascending requests for the Ephesians as a "prayer staircase." But here is another staircase, a "doxology staircase." Ruth Paxson makes this vivid by arranging the doxology as a pyramid (KJV).

Unto him
That is able to do
All that we ask or think
Above all that we ask or think
Abundantly above all that we ask or think
Exceedingly abundantly above all that we ask or think
According to the power that worketh in us

A verse of this scope deserves careful consideration.

The first thing the apostle says about God is that he is able *to do* something. The word for "do" is *poieō*, which actually means "to make, cause, effect, bring about, accomplish, perform, provide, or create," as one Greek dictionary has it. It points to God as a worker, which means, as John Stott says, that "he is neither idle, nor inactive, nor dead."[1]

What a contrast then between this God, the true God, and the so-called gods of the heathen! In Isaiah's day the people of Israel had fallen away from the worship of the true God and were worshiping idols, and God gave Isaiah words for that situation. He described the idols. They are, he said, nothing but pieces of lumber carved up by the worshiper. "They know nothing, they understand nothing; their eyes are plastered over so they cannot see, and their minds closed so they cannot understand" (Isa. 44:18). God calls an idol just "a block of wood" (v. 19). He issues this challenge:

"Present your case," says the LORD.
  "Set forth your arguments," says
    Jacob's King.
"Bring in your idols to tell us
  what is going to happen.
Tell us what the former things
    were,
  so that we may consider them
  and know their final outcome.
Or declare to us the things to come,
  tell us what the future holds,
  so we may know that you are
    gods.
Do something, whether good or bad,
  so that we will be dismayed and
    filled with fear.
But you are less than nothing
  and your works are utterly
    worthless" (Isa. 41:21–24).

According to these verses, the proof of the true God's existence is that he is able to do things. The idols can do nothing, not even evil.

ASK AND RECEIVE

The second thing Paul says about God is that he is able to do what we *ask*. That is, the ability of God to work is not related merely to his own concerns and interests but extends to the concerns and interests of his people. It is a statement about prayer.

Most of us are probably quite cautious in our prayers, unless we have learned to pray through a lifetime of growing in this discipline. So often we hold back in asking, afraid of embarrassing either God or ourselves. But that is not the kind of prayer God commands in the Bible.

To be sure, we do often pray wrongly. James says, "When you ask, you do not receive, because you ask with wrong motives, that you may spend what you get on your pleasures" (James 4:3). But for every verse that warns us about wrong prayers there are others which by example and precept teach us to pray frequently and with confidence. A favorite of mine is 1 John 3:21–22: "Dear friends, if our hearts do not condemn us, we have confidence before God and receive from him anything we ask, because we obey his commands and do what pleases him."

That verse is a great prayer promise. It says that (1) if we are praying with a clear conscience, that is, if we are being honest and open before God, and (2) if we are doing what God in his Word has commanded us to do, and (3) if we are seeking to please God in every possible way, then we can know that what we ask of God we will receive. We can know, to use Paul's words, that God "is

[1]John R. W. Stott, *God's New Society: The Message of Ephesians* (Downers Grove, Ill.: InterVarsity, 1979), 139.

able to (and will) do . . . [what] we ask."

What about our thoughts? Have you ever had the experience of thinking about something you would like to ask God for, but not asking him because you had no real confidence that the thing was God's will for you? I have. There are things I pray for with great confidence. I know it is God's will for me to conquer sin, to bless my preaching of his Word, and many such things. There are other things that I would like to see happen—the type of things God blesses and that I think would please him—but I do not always pray for them, because I have no real confidence that God wants to do them through my life and ministry or that he wants to do them now. So I hold back, only thinking about them and only occasionally mentioning them as possibilities in my prayers.

I do not know whether I am right in this. I may be wrong. I should probably be much bolder in what I pray for. But whether that is the case or not, it is a comfort to come to a verse like this and read that "God is able to do immeasurably more than all we ask *or imagine*." It says that God is able to do those things that I only think about but am afraid to ask for.

ALL WE CAN ASK OR THINK

Paul's doxology would have been great if he had stopped at this point, for it would be wonderful to know that God is able to do what we imagine (or think) as well as what we explicitly ask for. But at this point we are only halfway up this great ascending staircase. The next thing Paul tells us is that God is able to do *all* we can ask or think. It is not a question of God being only fifty percent or even ninety-nine percent able. God "is able to do . . . *all* we ask or imagine, according to his power that is at work within us."

It is God's ability to do *all* we can ask

or imagine that encourages us to stretch forward spiritually and ask for more. My father-in-law was a banker in New York City, and he frequently passed on to me the kind of jokes bankers tell one another. One was about a loan officer who tried to run a gas station in his retirement years. He had been a successful banker, but failed at running a gas station. Whenever a customer came in and asked for ten gallons of gas, he would respond, "Can you get by with five?" Paul tells us that God is not like that. He does not give half of what we ask for (if we ask rightly), but all. Indeed, it is his ability to give all we ask or imagine that encourages us to come with big petitions.

MORE THAN WE ASK

It is greater even than this, for Paul has amplified his doxology to say that God is able to do even *more* than all we might ask or imagine. I put it to you: Is that not your experience of God? Have you not found it to be true that whatever you ask of God (assuming you ask rightly and not with wrong motives, as James warns), God always has something bigger and greater for you— something more than you asked for? It is generally something different, something you would not have anticipated.

That would have been the testimony of all the great biblical characters. I think of Abraham. God called Abraham when he was a pagan living in Ur of the Chaldeans. He told him that he would make him into a great nation, that he would bless him and that he would make him to be a source of blessing to others. I do not know what Abraham would have understood by that at first. In time he probably came to see that the blessing to others would come as a result of the work of the Messiah who would be born in his life. But I suppose that at the beginning he just thought about having a large family which would eventually become a nation similar to those around it. Through most of his life his prayers would have focused on his lack of even one son, and he would have repeatedly asked God to give him children.

How did God answer? We know the story. We know that God did eventually give him a son, a son born to him and Sarah in their old age. And we know that Abraham had other children after that—Genesis 25:2 lists six—and that Abraham's immediate clan grew substantially so that, at the time of the battle against the four kings of the east, Abraham was able to muster 318 trained men of war to pursue them.

But that is only the most obvious of Abraham's blessings. In Abraham's case the "much more" would have included the fact that Isaac, the son of promise, became a type of Jesus Christ and was used to teach Abraham about the future work of Christ, and that the nation promised to Abraham was not limited to his natural descendants, the Jews, but included the entire family of God collected from among all nations throughout all human history. These are the people who have become "as numerous as the stars in the sky and as the sand on the seashore" (Gen. 22:17).

Certainly Abraham would testify that God is able to do more than we can ever ask or think.

Moses would say the same thing. God told Moses that he was going to cause Pharaoh to let the people of Israel leave Egypt, where they had been slaves for four centuries. Moses did not want to go. He had failed once, and did not want to fail again. But when God insisted and when he showed Moses that he would work miracles through him, changing his staff into a serpent and then back again and making his hand leprous and then healing it again, Moses went.

Could Moses have anticipated the full extent of the plagues God brought on Egypt: the turning of the water of the land to blood, the multiplication of frogs, gnats, and flies, the plague on the livestock, the boils, hail, locusts, darkness, and eventually the death of the firstborn? Could he have anticipated the miracles of the Exodus: the parting of the Red Sea, the destruction of the Egyptians, the cloud that accompanied the people during their years of wandering and protected them, the manna, the water from the rock, and other miracles? Could Moses have guessed that God would appear to him again and give him the law or that he would work through him to give us the first five books of the Bible?

Moses would not even have dreamed of these things. He would have testified freely that God is able to do more than we can ask or imagine.

David would speak along the same lines. God called him from following after the sheep. He made him the first great king of Israel, replacing Saul. He blessed him beyond his greatest dreams. At the end of his long and favored life God announced that through his descendant, the Messiah, his house and kingdom would be established forever. David replied, "Who am I, O Sovereign LORD, and what is my family, that you have brought me this far? And as if this were not enough in your sight, O Sovereign LORD, you have also spoken about the future of the house of your servant. . . . What more can David say to you? . . . How great you are, O Sovereign LORD! There is no one like you, and there is no God but you, as we have heard with our own ears" (2 Sam. 7:18–20, 22).

David would have joined others in confessing that God is able to do more than any of us can possibly ask or think, and that he does do it.

Is this not your experience? Life may not have gone exactly as you would have planned it for yourself; you may have had many disappointments. But if you are really trying to obey God and follow after him, can you not say that God's fulfillment of his promises toward you has been more than you have asked?

IMMEASURABLY MORE

There is one more statement in Paul's doxology in which he says that God is not only able to do more than all we can think but that he is able to do *immeasurably* more than we can contemplate. The word translated "immeasurably" (NIV) is another of Paul's coined words: *hyperekperissou*. It occurs only here and in 1 Thessalonians 3:10 in Greek literature. It can be rendered "exceeding abundantly" (KJV), "infinitely more" (PHILLIPS), "far more abundantly" (RSV), "exceeding abundantly beyond" (NASB), and so on.

How can this be? Even though Abraham, Moses, David, and others may not have anticipated the full measure of what God was going to do in their lives, what they experienced *is* measurable. It may take time, but it can be spelled out. Was Paul just carried away in this passage? Was he exaggerating for effect? I do not think so. After all, in the previous chapter, in a complementary passage, Paul wrote that "God raised us up with Christ and seated us with him in the heavenly realms in Christ Jesus, in order that in the coming ages he might show the incomparable riches of his grace, expressed in his kindness to us in Christ Jesus" (Eph. 2:6–7). In this verse Paul uses the word "incomparable" rather than "immeasurable" but his thought is much the same and indicates to my mind how the word in Ephesians 3:20 should be taken. Paul is not thinking of earthly blessings here. He is going beyond these to think of the blessings of God's inexhaustible kindness toward us through Christ in eternity. Since eternity is immeasurable, so

also are the works that God will do for us in the life to come.

In this sense the doxology ends as the prayer ended just a verse before, with reference to our being filled forever to the measure of all the fullness of God, which is immeasurable.

POWER AND GLORY

After a doxology like this we may be so overwhelmed by the promises implied in it that we find ourselves thinking that it cannot possibly apply to us—for others maybe, for Abraham (he was a giant in faith) or Moses or David—but not for normal people like ourselves. Paul does not allow this. He ties it down to our experience by showing that the power of God which is able to do these things is the same power that is already at work in all who are God's children. It is "according to his power that is at work within us."

In other words, although we have not realized the full extent of God's working—and never will, precisely because God is infinite in his workings—what we are yet to experience is nevertheless of the same substance as what we have already known, if we are genuine believers in the Lord Jesus Christ. Our salvation in Christ is a resurrection from the dead, for we were "dead in . . . transgressions and sins" (Eph. 2:1), and it is precisely that resurrecting power of God that we are to go on experiencing. It is by that power and not by our own that these great promises are to be accomplished.

What can be added to this? Nothing but the final, direct ascription of praise to God, which is what Paul does. "To him be glory in the church and in Christ Jesus throughout all generations, for ever and ever!" John Stott says, "The power comes from him; the glory must go to him."[2] And so it shall!

---

[2] Ibid., 140.

20

The Worthy Life

(Ephesians 4:1–3)

As a prisoner for the Lord, then, I urge you to live a life worthy of the calling you have received. Be completely humble and gentle; be patient, bearing with one another in love. Make every effort to keep the unity of the Spirit through the bond of peace.

Years ago when my wife and I were in a Christian education class in seminary, we were given an assignment to design a Sunday school curriculum. It was to have various age levels and an overall theme, tying the various subjects, classes, and age groupings together. Today, years later, there is much about this curriculum that I have forgotten, but the unifying concept is still vivid in my mind. It was based on the principle that "input" (what is taught as content) should equal "output" (the expression of content in practical works of service).

This curriculum was never put into practice; it was only an exercise. I cannot say how successful we might have been in matching each bit of information to some practical expression, but I do know that the principle itself is valid. The apostle Paul followed the same principle in his major epistles. Anyone who has studied Paul's letters knows that they tend to begin with a doctrinal section and that this is customarily followed by a section containing practical advice or application.

The epistle to the Romans fits this pattern. The doctrinal sections are in chapters 1–11. The practical section is chapters 12–15, beginning with the words: "Therefore, I urge you,

brothers, in view of God's mercy, to offer your bodies as living sacrifices, holy and pleasing to God—this is your spiritual act of worship." In Galatians the division is between chapters 1–4, on the one hand, and chapters 5 and 6 on the other. The latter section of Galatians begins: "It is for freedom that Christ has set us free. Stand firm, then, and do not let yourselves be burdened again by a yoke of slavery."

This is the point to which we have now come in our study of Ephesians. With the possible exception of Romans, no New Testament letter contains a stronger or more exhilarating presentation of theology. Chapters 1–3 have spoken of predestination and election, adoption and redemption, the work of the Holy Spirit, rebirth, the work of God in joining people from all nations and all walks of life together in the one holy body of Christ, the church. This is so marvelous a section that Paul ends chapter 3 with a doxology. We want to say with Paul, "To [God] be glory in the church and in Christ Jesus throughout all generations, for ever and ever! Amen" (v. 21). And we do say this, passionately and intently—if we have understood the teaching in these chapters.

109

Yet the letter does not stop. Paul immediately goes on to say, "As a prisoner for the Lord, then, I urge you to live a life worthy of the calling you have received." He is telling us that doctrinal "input" must be matched by an equal, practical "output" of that doctrine in our lives.

SCALES OF LIFE

This important idea is also contained in the word "worthy," which Paul uses in verse 1. "Worthy" means to have worth or value. But it is more than that. It means to have a worth equal to one's position. A worthy opponent is one whose gifts equal one's own. A workman "worthy of his hire" is one whose service merits the wages he receives. In his commentary on Ephesians, D. Martyn Lloyd-Jones describes this as a scale in which the weight on one side always equals the weight on the other, in this case the weight of practice equaling the weight of doctrine: "The Apostle . . . is beseeching them and exhorting them always to give equal weight in their lives to doctrine and practice. They must not put all the weight on doctrine and none on practice; nor all the weight on practice and just a little, if any at all, on doctrine. To do so produces imbalance and lopsidedness. The Ephesians must take great pains to see that the scales are perfectly balanced."[1]

But that is hard to achieve.

There are some Christians who are primarily intellectual in nature. They love books, enjoy study, and delight in the exposition of the Bible's great doctrinal passages. This is a good thing. It is proper to love doctrine and rejoice at what God has done for us in Christ. Paul himself obviously did this; we can tell from the way he has unfolded his doctrines in the first three chapters of this letter. But the intellectual believer

faces a great danger and often has a great weakness as a result of failing to overcome the danger. He loves doctrine so much that he stops with doctrine. He reads the first three chapters of Ephesians and delights in them; but when he comes to chapter 4 he says, "Oh, the rest is just application. I know all about that." Then he skips ahead to the next doctrinal section and neglects what he perhaps most needs to assimilate.

On the other hand, some Christians are primarily oriented to experience. They thrive under the teaching found in the second half of this book. They want to know about spiritual gifts and their own exercise of them. They are excited about Paul's teaching about the family and other such things. This is "where it's at" for them; they find the doctrinal section dry and impractical.

But, you see, each of these is an error. Doctrine without practice leads to bitter orthodoxy; it gives correctness of thought without the practical vitality of the life of Christ. Practice without doctrine leads to aberrations; it gives intensity of feeling, but it is feeling apt to go off in any (and often a wrong) direction. What we need is both, as Paul's letters and the whole of Scripture teach us. We can never attach too much importance to doctrine, for it is out of the doctrines of God, man, and salvation that the direction and impetus for the living of the Christian life spring. At the same time, we can never attach too much importance to practice, for it is the result of doctrine and proof of its divine nature.

CALLING AND CONDUCT

Paul's way of teaching this truth in verse 1 is to urge us to live worthy of our Christian calling. The old versions used the word "vocation" at this point,

---

[1]D. Martyn Lloyd-Jones, *Christian Unity: An Exposition of Ephesians 4:1 to 16* (Grand Rapids: Baker, 1981), 24.

but "calling" is better, at least in contemporary speech. Vocation has come to mean something we choose, while calling is something for which we are chosen. We remember here that the word "church" (Greek, *ekklesia*) means "the called out ones." The emphasis is upon what God has done, which is the point Paul has been elaborating in the opening chapters of Ephesians. Because God has set his hand upon us and called us, changing us from what we were into what we have now become, we are to live as Christians in this world.

Two parts of this calling deserve special notice. First, God has called us "out of darkness into his wonderful light" (1 Peter 2:9). This means that we have been given understanding. Before our calling we were like the blind man in John 9. We could not see Christ, and we were not even fully appreciative of our blind condition since, having never seen, we could never fully value sight. We thought the way to happiness was the world's way. We did not know that we were spiritually bankrupt, emotionally warped, and morally naked. When God called us, opening our eyes to the blessed truths of the gospel, for the first time we understood the nature of God's way and perceived how desirable it is. This is so basic to the experience of salvation that if a person has not had an opening of the eyes to see things differently, we may properly wonder if he has actually been saved. How can a person be urged to live a life worthy of his calling if he has not begun to understand what that calling is?

But there is more than this. The first part of God's calling involves being brought into light from darkness; that is, it involves understanding. The second part involves God's calling us out of death into life, which is what Paul emphasized in Ephesians 2:4: "But because of his great love for us, God, who is rich in mercy, made us alive with

Christ even when we were dead in transgressions—it is by grace you have been saved." This means that God, who has awakened us to a new life also gives us the power to live that life. It is because we are now spiritually alive, where before we were spiritually dead, that we are able to heed Paul's urging and live for God.

LIFE TOGETHER

In the remainder of this letter Paul is going to develop two main themes, both aspects of the worthy life: (1) unity among believers, and (2) the godly life, particularly in regard to relationships. The first will be considered in 4:4–16. The second is from 4:17 to the end. However, in the first three verses of chapter 4 Paul gives a preliminary statement embracing both: "Be completely humble and gentle; be patient, bearing with one another in love. Make every effort to keep the unity of the Spirit through the bond of peace." There are five specific characteristics of the worthy life in these verses.

1. *Humility.* Everyone knows that Christians should be humble. Humility is the opposite of pride or self-assertion. If we are saved "by grace . . . through faith . . . not by works, so that no one can boast" (Eph. 2:8–9), it is evident that Christians cannot be proud. We are to "do nothing out of selfish ambition or vain conceit, but in humility [are to] consider others better than [our]selves," as Paul says in Philippians 2:3.

But it is not easy to do, because our pride is easily wounded by what we consider thoughtless or unfair conduct by others.

In his commentary on Ephesians, Watchman Nee of China tells of a brother in south China who had his rice field on a hill. During the growing season he used a hand-worked water wheel to lift water from the irrigation stream that ran by the base of the hill to his field. His neighbor had two fields below his, and one night he made a hole in the dividing wall and drained out all the Christian's water to fill up his own two fields. The brother was distressed. But he laboriously pumped water up into his own field, only to have the act of stealing repeated. This happened three or four times. At last he consulted his Christian brethren. "What shall I do?" he asked. "I have tried to be patient and not retaliate. Isn't it right for me to confront him?"

The Christians prayed, and then one of them replied. "If we only try to do the right thing, surely we are very poor Christians," he said. "We have to do something more than what is right."

The Christian farmer was impressed with this advice. So the next day he went out and first pumped water for the two fields below his and then, after that, worked throughout the afternoon to fill his own field. From that day on the water stayed in his field, and in time the neighbor, after making inquiries as to what caused him to behave in such a fashion, became a Christian. This is humility. It is refusing to insist on our rights and actually putting our neighbor's interests before our own.

2. *Gentleness.* In the older versions this is called meekness, but for us "gentleness" is probably better, simply because meekness is so generally misunderstood. To most, meekness suggests weakness. But that is not the idea at all. Meekness was the chief characteristic of Moses, according to Numbers 12:3 (where the NIV uses the word "humble"), but Moses was not a weak man. He was a strong man, strong enough to appear before Pharaoh, declaring, "This is what the LORD says: Let my people go" (Exod. 8:1). Similarly, the Lord Jesus was meek or gentle, yet strong. He said of himself, "Come to me, all you who are weary and burdened, and I will give you rest. Take my yoke upon you and learn from me,

for I am gentle and humble in heart, and you will find rest for your souls" (Matt. 11:28–29). He told his disciples, "Blessed are the meek, for they will inherit the earth" (Matt. 5:5).

3. *Patience.* It takes time to learn patience, and unfortunately one of the chief ways we learn it is through suffering. A rather pious individual once came to a preacher and asked him to pray for him that he might have patience. "I do so lack patience," he said, trying to be humble as he said it. "I wish you would pray for me."

"I'll pray for you right now," the preacher replied. So he began to pray: "Lord, please send great tribulation into this brother's life."

The man who had asked for prayer put a hand out and touched the preacher on the arm, trying to stop his prayer. "You must not have heard me right," he said. "I didn't ask you to pray for tribulation. I asked you to pray that I might have patience."

"Oh, I heard what you said," the preacher answered. "But haven't you read Romans 5:3, 'And not only so, but we glory in tribulations also, knowing that tribulation worketh patience'? It means we acquire patience through the things that we suffer. I prayed that God would send tribulations so that you would have patience."

Another valid translation of the word "patience" is "long-suffering," which means "suffering long." It is what God does with us. He suffers long with us; if he did not, there would be no Christianity. Therefore, we ought to suffer long or be patient with each other.

4. *Bearing with one another.* The suffering aspects of patience come out clearly in this next Christlike characteristic, but there is a difference. This one relates specifically to trials we have as a result of uncharitable conduct toward us by other Christians. When the non-Christian neighbor stole the field-water of the Chinese Christian, the Christian

showed patience, gentleness, and humility in the way he dealt with the offense—and won the unbeliever to Christ. But what if that neighbor is a Christian, wronging us in this or some other way? What is to be our attitude to him or her? Paul's answer is that we are to endure the wrong, suffer the slight. Thus, we are to demonstrate a way of life superior to that of the ungodly world and show the special unity which is ours in Jesus Christ.

5. *Unity.* The fifth characteristic is that believers are to "make every effort to keep the unity of the Spirit through the bond of peace" (v. 3). It is evident at this point, in case we had missed it before, that each of these characteristics is related to the others (which the translators show in part by their groupings of them) and that they have all been tending in the direction of this great matter of unity, which is to be Paul's theme for the next thirteen verses. Christians are to be one because, as he will say in just a moment, "There is one body and one Spirit— just as you were called to one hope when you were called—one Lord, one faith, one baptism; one God and Father of all, who is over all and through all and in all" (vv. 4–6).

It is important to say two things about this unity. First, it is "the unity *of the Spirit*," which means that it is a unity the Holy Spirit has already given to those who are in Christ. This is a wonderful and often a very visible thing. Harry Ironside writes about how he once fell sick while in the midst of a series of meetings in Minneapolis and was forced to return home to California by train, which was the best mode of transportation in those days. He could barely stand. So the porter made up a lower berth for him and allowed him to recline there throughout the day. The first morning he opened his Bible and began to read it as part of his devotions. A stout German woman happened by

and stopped when she saw the Bible. "Vat's dat? A Bible?" she asked.

"Yes, a Bible," Ironside replied.

"Vait," she said, "I vill get my Bible and we will haf our Bible reading together."

A short time later a tall gentleman came by and asked, "Vat are you reading?" He was a Norwegian. He said, "I tank I go get my Bible too." Each morning these three met, and others collected. Ironside wrote that once there were twenty-eight people and twenty-eight Bibles and that the conductor would go through the train, saying, "The camp meeting is beginning in car thirteen. All are invited." It was a great experience.

At the end of the trip, as the cars divided up in Sacramento, some to go north and some south, the German woman asked, "What denomination are you?"

Ironside replied, "I belong to the same denomination that David did."

"What was that? I didn't know that David belonged to any denomination."

Ironside said, "David wrote that he was 'a companion of all them that fear God and keep his precepts.' "

The woman said, "Yah, yah, that is a good church to belong to."

This is a real and wonderful unity, as I said. But at the same time, it is often destroyed by false pride, narrow denominationalism, and sinful striving for position. So Paul says, "*Make every effort to keep* the unity of the Spirit through the bond of peace." This is the second important thing to be said about unity. The first is that we have a unity given to us by the Holy Spirit; it corresponds in some measure to the doctrinal truths of Christianity, which is why Paul lapses into doctrine again in verses 4–6. But, second, we are to keep or maintain this unity, which corresponds to the practical or experiential side of Christianity.

21

Unity! Unity!

(Ephesians 4:4–6)

There is one body and one Spirit—just as you were called to one hope when you were called—one Lord, one faith, one baptism; one God and Father of all, who is over all and through all and in all.

Bible numbers do not interest many people today. But this used to be an interesting part of biblical studies, and our contemporary neglect of it is a loss. I have in my study a book by Ethelbert Bullinger, a direct descendant of the great Bullinger of the Swiss Reformation, entitled *Number in Scripture: Its Supernatural Design and Spiritual Significance.* This book has a section of nearly 300 pages in which the significance of specific numbers from one to 666 is analyzed. "One" is the primary symbol of unity. "Two" is the number of differences and divisions. "Three" stands for what is solid, substantial, or entire. "Four" relates to creation; and so on.

I also have part of a seven-volume *Numerical Bible* by F. W. Grant, subtitled "A Revised Translation of the Holy Scriptures With Expository Notes, Arranged, Divided and Briefly Characterized According to the Principles of Their Numerical Structure."

Both of these works date from the late nineteenth century, and the type of study they represent has fallen out of favor, as I said. The significance of biblical numbers was no doubt greatly exaggerated then, but there is still some obvious truth in these emphases. One case in point is Ephesians 4:4–6, which deals with the unity of the church. It is one sentence, to begin with, a fact which may be important in itself. But its chief characteristic is a sevenfold repetition of the word "one": "There is *one* body and *one* Spirit—just as you were called with *one* hope when you were called—*one* Lord, *one* faith, *one* baptism; *one* God and Father of all, who is over all and through all and in all." And there is a fourfold repetition of the word "all." "Seven" is the number of spiritual unity or perfection; and if "four" does actually refer to creation, then there is a suggestion that the created order finds its perfection by being joined to God within the church.

The Swiss New Testament professor Marcus Barth, son of the illustrious Karl Barth, is not given to flights of fanciful scholarship, but he acknowledges that "these figures probably have a symbolic sense," just as these and other numbers do in Revelation.[1]

THE ONE BODY OF CHRIST

Another way of looking at Ephesians 4:4–6 is to see that it is about the

[1] Marcus Barth, *Ephesians: Translation and Commentary on Chapters 4–6* (Garden City, N.Y.: Doubleday, 1960), 463.

114

church (although the word "church" does not appear) and that Paul's concern is to stress the church's unity. This is the point at which this sentence starts: "one body." Body is a metaphor for church.

There are many good metaphors for the church in Scripture, even within this one letter. It is compared to a kingdom, a family, and a temple in chapter 2. In chapter 5 it is compared to a bride. Comparing the church to a body is particularly appropriate in this passage, however, for a body is something that works together, even though it is composed of many diverse parts. Moreover, its unity is organic. That is, it is achieved not by joining a number of diverse parts or pieces in the way one would make a machine, but by growth. The church is not a diesel engine or a watch or an airplane. It is a body. It grows by the multiplication of cells.

In the early days the church was a very small body. It consisted of Adam and his wife Eve, the first people. It grew as others were added. There were Abel and Seth, Enoch, Methuselah, and Noah. Abraham was added, and as his spiritual family increased, there were people like Isaac, Joseph, the twelve fathers of Israel, David, the prophets, and those who believed in God through those ages. The early Christians were members of this body, as were the saints of the Middle Ages and the heroes and martyrs of the Reformation. Those who believe today are also part of it. So are you if you have trusted Christ as your Savior.

In 1 Corinthians 12 Paul develops this image at great length, stressing the mutual interdependence of the body's parts: "The eye cannot say to the hand, 'I don't need you!' And the head cannot say to the feet, 'I don't need you!' On the contrary, those parts of the body that seem to be weaker are indispensable, and the parts that we think are less honorable we treat with special honor. . . . God has combined the members of the body and has given greater honor to the parts that lacked it, so that there should be no division in the body, but that its parts should have equal concern for each other. If one part suffers, every part suffers with it; if one part is honored, every part rejoices with it" (1 Cor. 12:21–26).

Clearly, this is a great argument for preserving the church's unity. It is an argument based on what we are: one body. Therefore, we suffer divisions only at great personal loss, and we should not let them happen.

ONE HOLY SPIRIT

In the second of Paul's seven unities the word "Spirit" is capitalized, and rightly so. Sometimes when the word "spirit" is used, it refers to what we would call the "human spirit," or the "spirit of a thing." That is a valid use of the word, but it is not what is involved here. In Ephesians 4:4 Paul is not saying, "You are all one spirit in the sense that you are one in your enthusiasms and goals." Rather he is saying, "You are one because of the one work of the one Holy Spirit."

When he talks like this Paul is calling our attention to what the Holy Spirit has done in our conversions. Sometimes, when we hear people give testimonies, they focus on the uniqueness of their experience. One will say, "I grew up in a nominal Christian home, but I didn't understand what real Christianity was. When I got to college I was confused and groped around for awhile. Finally, through the witness of a college classmate, I was brought to a Bible study and began to get back into the faith. That's how Jesus reached me."

Another person will say, "I came from a secular background, but God reached me through a tract I found on the seat of an airplane. It got me thinking along spiritual lines. I became a Christian in that way."

When they give testimonies, people tend to emphasize variety. But when Paul says that there is not only one body but "one Spirit," he is undoubtedly asking us to think of the way in which the Holy Spirit works unvaryingly in all who come to Jesus. We have many differences in the small particulars of our conversions. But when we begin to talk about what the Holy Spirit did in our hearts to bring us to faith in Christ, our experiences are identical. There is an *awakening to sin* whereby we become conscious that all is not right between ourselves and God, that we are in violation of his laws, hostile to his holy character, and under his wrath. There is the work of *regeneration,* whereby God in a supernatural way places the new life of Christ within our hearts so that we change. We become different from what we were before. There is the *work of faith* which follows upon that whereby, having been made alive in Christ by the Holy Spirit, we are drawn by that same Spirit to place our faith in Jesus. Following that, there is the work of the Holy Spirit in *sanctification,* which produces the same fruit of the Spirit—"love, joy, peace, patience, kindness, goodness, faithfulness, gentleness and self-control" (Gal. 5:22–23)—in all of us.

When we begin to think along these lines we say, "Isn't it marvelous that, regardless of what background we come from or how we have come to Christ, the one Holy Spirit of God has united us in a much more important common experience?"

OUR COMMON HOPE

The third thing Paul talks about is our hope. Hope has suffered in English speech, so that today it does not mean quite what it meant in earlier, New Testament days. Today hope usually means something uncertain, something

we perhaps hope for wistfully but do not really expect. The biblical idea is quite different. If you have been to a funeral service, you may remember the portion of the service in which we speak of our "sure and certain hope," meaning the resurrection of the dead. "Sure and certain"—that is the biblical idea. It is future, true enough. We have only an earnest of it now, that is, the possession of the Holy Spirit as proof of what is to come. Nevertheless, our hope is not uncertain just because we do not at this precise moment hold it in our hand.

We might wonder at this point why Paul thinks of hope as something that should unite the church of Christ. As a matter of fact, is it not the case that ideas of the future more often then not divide the church rather than unite it? We have people who think there is going to be a Millennium and people who think there will be no Millennium. Some think Christ will come before the Millennium; others think Christ will come after the Millennium, and when you throw in the Tribulation it gets even worse. You have pre-trib, post-trib, and mid-trib. It gets very, very complicated. Some people have divided the church along those lines. They have even made eschatology a test for fellowship.

What Paul is speaking of, of course, is not those details of eschatology which in the course of history have come to divide large bodies of the church, but rather those upon which we are agreed: the return of Christ, the Resurrection, and the Last Judgment.

Furthermore, these are unifying simply because they are future. If we look to the past, we produce the kind of divisions I referred to above. One will say, "I'm a product of the Reformation." Another will say, "I'm a product of the pietist movement." That sort of thing can go on and on. Even if we look to the present, we will have divisions, because we overstress the denominational distinctives we have.

It is entirely different if we look to the future. Jesus is going to come back. We are going to be with him. There is a home for us in heaven. If we look forward to those things, if we anticipate the day when we will stand shoulder to shoulder with people from other denominations, nations, races, and experiences, and if in that day all the things that divide us now will fade away, then that should certainly influence the way in which we think about those divisions now. We will be free to reach out across denominational and other barriers and join hands with those who, like us, believe in Christ and desire to serve him.

OUR LORD JESUS CHRIST

The unities of verse 4—"one body . . . one Spirit . . . one hope"—go together. It is the work of the one Holy Spirit to graft us into the one body and give us that one hope. Verse 5 introduces another set of three: "one Lord, one faith, one baptism." These unities are clustered around the one Lord Jesus Christ, just as the first are clustered around the Holy Spirit.

To hear some Christians talk, you would think there were many Lords. One says, "I follow a Jesus who causes me to do this, which excludes you." Somebody else will say, "I don't follow that Jesus; that's not the Jesus I know." And so it goes. There are not many Lords. There is only one Lord, and that Lord is the Lord Jesus Christ. If we are following him, if we are open to what he is doing, that must be a force for drawing us together.

John T. MacNeil, a great Scottish preacher and evangelist, was a pastor of Tenth Presbyterian Church in Philadelphia for two years in the 1920s. He used to imagine a conversation that might have taken place between the man who had been born blind, whose

story is told in John 9, and the other blind man who was healed by Jesus, whose story is told in Mark 8. The difference between the two stories is that in John 9 Jesus healed the blind man by spitting on the ground and making clay, which he used to anoint the man's eyes. This did not happen in the case of the man whose story is told in Mark.

MacNeil imagined these two getting together to discuss how Jesus healed them. The man who had been healed without the spittle would tell his story, and the man who had been healed with the spittle would tell his. He would say to the other, "But you left out the part about Jesus spitting in the dust and making clay and placing the clay upon your eyes."

"I don't know anything about that," the first would reply.

The man from John would answer, "It has to be that way, because that's the way Jesus gives sight to people. You must have forgotten it. He spit on the ground; he made clay; he put it on your eyes, and he sent you to wash in the pool of Siloam."

"Oh, no," the man from Mark says, "he didn't do that with me. He just spoke and I received my sight."

The first man digs in his heels. "That isn't right," he says. "Jesus heals with clay! If you haven't had that experience, I am beginning to doubt whether you can really see!" Thus originated in the early church the denomination of the "Mudites" and the "Anti-Mudites," two divisions. That is what happens when we get our eyes on the modes of God's working rather than upon the Lord who works.

ONE TRUE FAITH

Paul goes on: not only one Lord but "one faith." "Faith" can be used objectively or subjectively. Subjectively it means our experience of faith; there is no salvation apart from faith. Objectively it means the content of faith or what we believe, the gospel.

I think the latter is what Paul is getting at. He is saying that because we have one Lord we also have one faith. That is, we do not believe diverse doctrines where the core of the gospel is concerned. We believe that God Almighty sent his Son, the Lord Jesus Christ, to become like us and die for our salvation. And it is through faith in his work, not in anything that we have done or can do, but in his work of dying for us that we are saved. That one gospel joins Christian people across all barriers of time, nationality, race, sex, and anything else we can imagine. If we have one faith, then we ought to be able to stand shoulder to shoulder before the world and give united testimony to God's saving work in Jesus Christ.

ONE BAPTISM

It is interesting that Paul should include baptism in his list of unities because opinions about baptism have certainly divided churches. Do you sprinkle? Presbyterians think this is the preferred way. Do you immerse? Baptists think immersion is the only way. What about children—do you baptize them? Paul is not concerned here with modes of baptism, but with what baptism signifies, namely, identification with Christ. That is the unifying thing. Have you been baptized into Christ? I do not care how you were baptized. I do not care whether it was in a baptistery or a stream, whether it was with a little bit of water or in a lot of water. Have you been publicly identified with Jesus Christ? That is the issue. And if that is the issue, then before the world we are identified together with Jesus Christ and must stand together for him.

ONE GOD OF ALL

Verse 6 contains the seventh item, the last of all. The first three have been centered around the Holy Spirit; the second three have been centered around the Lord Jesus Christ. This one concerns God the Father, the first person in the Godhead: "one God and Father of all, who is over all and through all and in all."

This is the good point to ask about the order of these unities. If they are grouped around the Trinity, as they obviously are, why is it that the apostle Paul puts the Holy Spirit first, the Lord Jesus Christ second, and God the Father third? When we talk about the Trinity it is usually the other way around, and Paul himself generally puts it the other way around. We say Father, Son, and Holy Spirit. Here Paul says, Spirit, Son, and Father. Why is this? I think it is because the apostle is arguing from the effect to the cause. He has said in verse 3, "Make every effort to keep the unity of the Spirit through the bond of peace." This refers to the visible unity the Holy Spirit has given the church. So he starts with the one body, which is visible, and with the Holy Spirit himself.

But then we ask, "Where did this effect come from? How did the church get to be the church?" The answer is: through the work of Christ. The church is the company of those who follow Christ. Thus, Paul moves from a discussion of what the Holy Spirit does to what the Lord Jesus Christ has done. And if at that point we say, Yes, but why did the Lord Jesus Christ do that? the answer is that all this flows from the one God who is over all and through all and in all.

John Stott talks about the Trinity as the basis for church unity and sums it up like this: "There can be only one Christian family, only one Christian faith, hope and baptism, and only one Christian body, because there is only one God, Father, Son and Holy Spirit. You can no more multiply churches than you can multiply Gods. Is there only one God? Then he has only one church. Is the unity of God inviolable? Then so is the unity of the church. . . . It is no more possible to split the church than it is possible to split the Godhead."[2]

If any of these points have their proper effect on us, this one at least should strike home. Whatever else you may say about the church, the church is God's church. It is composed of God's people, it is the result of God's work, and it exists for God's glory. So let that be our vision. If it is, we will not find it difficult to keep or make visible the unity that God himself has already worked into the very fabric of our experience together as Christ's body.

---

[2]John R. W. Stott, *God's New Society: The Message of Ephesians* (Downers Grove, Ill.: InterVarsity, 1979), 151.

22

Christ's Gifts to His Church

(Ephesians 4:7–13)

But to each one of us grace has been given as Christ apportioned it. This is why it says:

> *When he ascended on high,*
> *he led captives in his train*
> *and gave gifts to men.*

(What does "he ascended" mean except that he also descended to the lower earthly regions? He who descended is the very one who ascended higher than all the heavens, in order to fill the whole universe.) It was he who gave some to be apostles, some to be prophets, some to be evangelists, and some to be pastors and teachers, to prepare God's people for works of service, so that the body of Christ may be built up until we all reach unity in the faith and in the knowledge of the Son of God and become mature, attaining to the whole measure of the fullness of Christ.

We are dealing with a section of Ephesians in which the apostle is at pains to stress the church's unity. Yet it is a particular kind of unity, unity that admits of great diversity.

What do you think of when you think of the word "unity"? Some people think of a large organizational structure, the dominant model of many in the so-called ecumenical movement. It is a governmental model in which unity comes from the submission of each of the individual parts to authorities. Others think of unity as conformity in which, since we are talking about the church, each Christian is supposed to be the exact boring replica of every other. The unity the Bible speaks of is something quite different.

In verses 4–6 Paul says, "There is one body and one Spirit—just as you were called to one hope when you were called—one Lord, one faith, one baptism; one God and Father of all, who is over all and through all and in all." This unity, a unity of experience and identity, is for *all* Christians, for the one God is Father of *all* and is over *all* and through *all* and in *all*. Yet no sooner has Paul spoken of this unity than he goes on to speak of diversity in the area of gifts. "But to *each* one of us grace has been given as Christ apportioned it. . . . He . . . gave *some* to be apostles, *some* to be prophets, *some* to be evangelists, and *some* to be pastors and teachers (vv. 7, 11). The contrast is between "all" and "each" or "some." All are members of the one body, but some have received one gift and some another.

We find the same truths in 1 Corinthians and Romans. First Corinthians 12:4–6 says, "There are different kinds of gifts, but the same Spirit. There are different kinds of service, but the same

Lord. There are different kinds of working, but the same God works all of them in all men." Then in verse 11, after mentioning several specific gifts, Paul writes, "All these are the work of one and the same Spirit, and he gives them to each one, just as he determines."

Romans 12 says, "Just as each of us has one body with many members, and these members do not all have the same function, so in Christ we who are many form one body, and each member belongs to all the others. We have different gifts, according to the grace given us" (vv. 4–6).

These texts give us a model for church unity which is not that of a well-oiled organization or of identically manufactured objects, but of a body—a body containing diverse but essential and contributing parts. Without the things all Christians share—the common experience of their being joined to Christ through the work of the Holy Spirit—there is no church at all. But on the other hand, without a diversity of gifts the church is not healthy and cannot function completely, any more than a body can function completely without arms or legs.

To Each a Gift

Many commentators consider these verses the heart of the book, for they tell how the church of Jesus Christ is to function. They talk about gifts, and they begin by telling us that these gifts have come from Christ. They are Christ's gifts to his church, and he has not overlooked anyone in the distribution.

Since Paul cites an Old Testament text at this point—Psalm 68:18—it is not at all difficult to know what he has in mind as he describes Jesus apportioning these gifts. Psalm 68 is a psalm of triumph, quite possibly written in celebration of the bringing of the ark of God (which symbolized the presence of God) to Jerusalem. It pictures God as having been victorious over his and Israel's enemies and of now ascending his throne to receive gifts and homage from all men. By citing this psalm Paul puts the Lord Jesus Christ into that role, thereby affirming his deity. On the cross he defeated his and our enemies, and he has now ascended triumphantly to the right hand of the Father from which position he now dispenses the gifts about which this section speaks.[1] The image speaks of Christ's rule, authority, and power in the Christian church.

Two points are worth stressing about Christ's dispensing these gifts. First, if they are given by Jesus, then they are to be used for the purposes for which he gave them, namely, the service and edification of the church. They are not to be used for selfish ends, above all not for drawing attention to the personality or programs of the one using them.

Second, the gifts are given to each Christian—that is, everyone has at least one gift—and for that reason, the church is only fully vigorous and healthy when all are ministering. It has been a failure to see this truth which more than anything else has led in

---

[1] There is a textual problem in Paul's citation of Psalm 68:18 in that the psalm speaks of God *receiving* gifts *from* men while Paul apparently alters the words to speak of Christ *dispensing* gifts *to* men. Some commentators have suggested that Paul just boldly altered the text for his own purposes, but it is hard to be satisfied with that since there was no compelling reason for him to quote the psalm at all. His point does not depend on it. Probably the solution is in the image itself—a victorious king would both receive gifts and dispense them, particularly dispensing the spoils of his conquest—and perhaps also in the broader meaning of the Hebrew word translated "received," which can also be translated "brought." This thought is supported by the fact that two ancient versions of Psalm 68, the Aramaic and Syriac, translate the Hebrew word as "gave." As John Stott observes, "Evidently this was already a traditional interpretation" (*God's New Society: The Message of Ephesians*, 157).

church history to what John Stott calls "the clerical denomination of the laity." As Stott points out, there has developed within the church (for a variety of reasons) a division between "clergy" and "laity" in which the clergy are supposed to lead and do the work of ministry while the people (which is what the word "laity" means) are to follow docilely—and, of course, give money to support the clergy and their work. As an example of this outlook Stott quotes from the 1906 Papal Encyclical *Vehmenter Nos:* "As for the masses, they have no other right than of letting themselves be led, and of following their pastors as a docile flock."[2]

This is not what the church is to be, and where this view prevails, the church and its ministry suffer. They suffer by the loss of the exercise of those gifts given to the laity. Gifts are for use in serving others. The laity serve the church and the world. The clergy serve the laity, particularly in helping them to develop and use their gifts. As Stott says, "Clergy are not hyphenated to the laity as if they were a separate class; they are 'ministers of the people' because they themselves belong to the people they are called to serve."[3]

THESE MANY GIFTS

The second thing these verses teach is the nature or character of the gifts Christ gives. To begin with, there are more gifts than those listed. Christ's gifts to his church (also called the gifts of the Spirit) are listed in four separate chapters of the New Testament and in one of those chapters in two places. So there are five lists in all (Eph. 4:11; 1 Cor. 12:8–10; 1 Cor. 12:28–30; Rom. 12:6–8; and 1 Peter 4:11). The gifts cited in these lists vary. First Peter 4:11, the shortest, contains only two gifts: speaking and service. The lists in 1 Corinthi-

ans 12, the longest, each contain nine, though the two nines are not identical. In all there may be nineteen or twenty gifts mentioned, but this is not an absolute figure. Different words can conceivably be used to describe the same or nearly identical gifts, and there may be others not mentioned.

In the letter to the Ephesians Paul lists apostles, prophets, evangelists, pastors, and teachers.

1. *Apostles and Prophets.* The first gifts are apostles and prophets. Some who have written on the gifts have tried to show how apostles and prophets are present today. They point out that the word "apostle" does not mean only the original band of authoritative spokesmen commissioned by Christ; it can also refer to anyone who is sent forth as a witness, particularly to establish churches. Similarly, "prophet" does not always mean only one who receives a special inspired word from God; it also refers to anyone who speaks boldly in his name (as in 1 Cor. 14).

These points are well taken. But they do not really apply to the use of the words in Ephesians. Here "apostle" and "prophet" must be taken in their most technical sense. Therefore, apostles must refer to those witnesses who were specifically commissioned by Christ to establish the church upon a proper base, and prophets must refer to those who received God's message (as had the prophets of old) and recorded it in the pages of what we call the New Testament. Prophet may also refer to those specially inspired individuals such as Agabus (Acts 21:10–11) who functioned while the New Testament was being written.

Neither one of these gifts exists today. We no longer have apostles or prophets in this sense. But we are not deprived of the benefits of these first

[2] John R. W. Stott, *One People* (London: Falcon, 1969), 9.
[3] Ibid., 47.

and highly significant gifts of God to the Christian community; the apostles did teach authoritatively, and those who spoke from God have left us the New Testament.

2. *Evangelists.* Unlike the first two items, the gift of evangelism has not ceased, and sad is the church or period of church history that has but few who are so gifted. An evangelist is one who possesses a special ability to communicate the gospel of salvation from sin through Jesus Christ. This does not mean that others who are not evangelists are excused from the obligation to tell others about Jesus. We all share that task. The Great Commission declares it. But it does mean that some are especially gifted in this area.

Again, the gift of evangelism is not limited to those who are "professionals," like Billy Graham, Luis Palau, the late Bishop Festo Kivengere, or some others. On the contrary, it is more often the gift of laymen and laywomen. In his study of spiritual gifts in *The Holy Spirit*, Graham points out that the only person in the entire Bible who is actually called an evangelist is Philip, and he was a deacon. Speaking personally, I can say that I have known quite a few people, both men and women, who have had this gift, and none of them was ordained. They were simply people who enjoyed and were particularly effective in speaking about Christ to others.

3. *Pastors and Teachers.* I put these gifts into one category because they may, in fact, actually be one gift. In Ephesians 4:11 the Greek phrasing permits us to join together the words "pastors" and "teachers," so that we could speak of the gift of pastor-teacher.

"Pastor" refers to one who has pastoral oversight of others. It is based on the idea of shepherding and looks to Jesus, who described himself as "the good shepherd" (John 10:11) and is referred to as "that great" (Heb. 13:20) and "Chief Shepherd" of the sheep (1 Peter 5:4). As in the case of evangelists, many have this gift who are not ordained. For example, pastoring should be the gift of an elder, and also of a deacon if he has duties involving spiritual oversight. It is also a valued gift in Sunday school teachers.

The word "teacher" is self-explanatory. What should be said is that it is always a most important gift and may be one of the gifts most needed at the present time. We see the importance of the gift of teaching when we recognize that this is the key thought in Matthew's version of the Great Commission. There Jesus says, "Go and make disciples of all nations, baptizing them in the name of the Father and of the Son and of the Holy Spirit, and [to explain how this specifically is to be done] *teaching* them to obey everything I have commanded you" (Matt. 28:19–20). Clearly, those brought to faith in Christ are to be discipled primarily through teaching.

More may be said. Although there are significant differences between the gifts Paul lists in Ephesians 4:11, which is why they are given different names and are listed individually, it is worth noting that (in this list at least) all the gifts of the Lord to the church involve teaching. The apostles and prophets provided the initial and normative teaching; it is preserved in the New Testament, which parallels the Old. Evangelists proclaim the core of this teaching, centered in the gospel of redemption from sin by Jesus Christ. Pastors and teachers instruct and care for the flock through an even fuller communication of scriptural truth. This is not to say that there are not other gifts that do not particularly involve teaching. But it does mean that the teaching gifts are particularly needed if the church is to mature in the direction Paul describes.

John Stott says, "Nothing is more necessary for the building up of God's church in every age than an ample supply of God-gifted teachers. . . . It is teaching which builds up the church. It is teachers who are needed most."[4]

UNITY IN THE FAITH

If you have been following Ephesians 4:7–13 carefully to this point, it might be natural for you to ask a question. You would see the stress of the apostle on unity and observe his equally important stress on the diversity of Christ's gifts to his church. But you might wonder: "If these gifts really are diverse, how in the light of this diversity is the unity of the church to be maintained? What is to keep everyone from going off in a different direction to do his or her own thing?"

The answer to that question is in the purpose for which the gifts are given. It is, as Paul says, "to prepare God's people for works of service, so that the body of Christ may be built up until we all reach unity in the faith and in the knowledge of the Son of God and become mature, attaining to the whole measure of the fullness of Christ" (vv. 12–13). What is the purpose of Christ's gifts? It is to serve Christ's people, so that the body itself might become increasingly unified in faith and mature in practice.

This can be stated emphatically. If a Christian is using a gift to bring attention to himself rather than to Christ, he is misappropriating it and will answer to his Master in the judgment.

If a Christian is more interested in having others serve him than in his or her serving them, he is dishonoring his Master, who came "not . . . to be served, but to serve, and to give his life as a ransom for many" (Mark 10:45).

If a Christian is using his gift to build his kingdom rather than Christ's and thus divides the church instead of uniting it, he is betraying Christ, who is committed to the unification and maturation of his body.

Let us be done with our little kingdoms as well as with the spirit of complacency that does not care if the church is divided or immature. On the contrary, let us seek out our gifts and ask how we may use them to the building up of Christ's body. Christ does not squander his gifts; each one is essential. He does not withhold his gifts; they are poured out in full measure. He is not indifferent as to how his gifts are used; he has his own wise and lofty purposes in view. He does not give his gifts at cross-purposes; all are to serve and edify the church. He does not abandon those to whom the gifts are given; rather he continues to work through them and in them for the church's well-being. Where the gifts are received in this spirit and are so used, there the unity of the Spirit is maintained, and the body of Christ is built up "until we all reach unity in the faith and in the knowledge of the Son of God and become mature."

---

[4]John R. W. Stott, *God's New Society: The Message of Ephesians* (Downers Grove, Ill.: InterVarsity, 1979), 164.

23

Body Life

(Ephesians 4:11–13)

It was he who gave some to be apostles, some to be prophets, some to be evangelists, and some to be pastors and teachers, to prepare God's people for works of service, so that the body of Christ may be built up until we all reach unity in the faith and in the knowledge of the Son of God and become mature, attaining to the whole measure of the fullness of Christ.

In 1972 an exposition of Ephesians 4 called *Body Life* appeared, written by Ray C. Stedman, pastor of the Peninsula Bible Church of Palo Alto, California.[1] Since then it has had a profound impact on the structure of many churches and has even introduced a new term into contemporary Christian speech. What made the book so successful was its description of how the principles of Ephesians 4 had been put into practice by this one thriving church in California.

Essentially the book is about spiritual gifts, and its underlying premise is that each Christian has at least one gift and that he or she must use it if the church is to be healthy. This was the pattern of the early church, said Stedman: "Whenever anyone, by faith in Jesus Christ, passed from the kingdom and power of Satan into the kingdom of God's love, he was immediately taught that the Holy Spirit of God had not only imparted to him the life of Jesus Christ, but had also equipped him with a spiritual gift or gifts which he was then responsible to discover and exercise."[2]

In Stedman's case, the practice of this principle meant a multiple staff ministry in which the paid teachers of the church saw it as their responsibility to equip the members of the congregation to use the gifts God had given them to do the work of ministry. Of course, this is in perfect accord with Ephesians 4:11–13, which tells how God gives teaching gifts (apostles, prophets, evangelists, pastors, and teachers) "to prepare God's people for works of service, so that the body of Christ may be built up until we all reach unity in the faith and in the knowledge of the Son of God and become mature, attaining to the whole measure of the fullness of Christ."

In our day many churches have discovered these principles, and we have seen an increase in the vitality of the church as a result.

A Superfluous Comma

In older versions of the English Bible there was a small but serious error that may have contributed to the church's blindness at this point or, to state the matter another way, may have resulted from its prejudice. It involves a comma.

[1] Ray C. Stedman, *Body Life* (Glendale, Calif.: Regal, 1972).
[2] Ibid., 39.

In the original King James Version (there has been a change in more recent editions), Ephesians 4:11–12 said, "And he gave some, apostles; and some, prophets; and some, evangelists; and some, pastors and teachers; for the perfecting of the saints, [that is the comma] for the work of the ministry, for the edifying of the body of Christ."

In this version of the text God is said to have given the teaching gifts, which we normally associate with ministers, so that the ministers may do three things: (1) perfect the saints, (2) do the ministry, and (3) edify or build up the body of Christ. That is, the professionals do it all. They have the gifts, and they are to use them to do all the church's work. The members of the church have no other duty than (to quote the 1906 Papal Encyclical *Vehmenter Nos*) "[of] letting themselves be led, and of following their pastors as a docile flock."

But that translation was wrong! Armitage Robinson was probably the first commentator to notice it and insist that it was a mistake.[3] He argued—and virtually all commentators since have agreed with him—that the comma should be eliminated. Without that comma, the passage says something entirely different. Instead of giving three tasks to "ministers," it gives one task to the clergy ("equip the saints") and another to the laity ("do the ministry"). As a result of both fulfilling their proper, God-given function, "the body of Christ may be built up."

Here is the real sequence:

1. Those who have been given the gifts of teaching are to use those gifts to equip or "prepare" the saints, so that, as a first objective,

2. Believers may do the work of "ministry" or "service," and that, as an ultimate objective.

3. The church may be "built up," "reach unity in the faith," and "become mature, attaining to the whole measure of the fullness of Christ."

This translation (the correct one) gives an immediate purpose to God's giving of the teaching gifts: to equip the saints. It gives an ultimate purpose to God's giving of these gifts: to build up the church. But it preserves the essential intermediate step which is an "every-member ministry." It follows that where this intermediate step is not taken, where the clergy try to do the whole work, there the church stagnates and divisions occur.

FALSE MINISTRY PATTERNS

This situation has happened historically. My goal in this chapter is to encourage all who are genuine believers in Christ to seek out their gifts and use them in the church's ministry, but it is worth noting first that there have been many false patterns of ministry in the church in past years as a result of the church's having failed to assimilate these truths. John R. W. Stott, in *One People*, points out that three false answers have been given to the question of the relationship of clergy to other Christians.[4]

The first he calls *clericalism*. It is the view arising out of (or finding expression in) the mistaken translation of Ephesians 4:11–12. In this view the work of the church is to be done by those paid to do it, and the role of the normal member of the church is to follow docilely and, of course, continue to support these works financially.

How did this erroneous picture arise? Historically it resulted from the development of the idea of the priesthood in

---

[3] This is John R. W. Stott's opinion. See *God's New Society: The Message of Ephesians* (Downers Grove, Ill.: InterVarsity, 1979), 166.

[4] John R. W. Stott, *One People* (London: Falcon, 1969), 28–42. Stott discusses the proper pattern on pages 42–47.

the early Roman Catholic Church. In those days the professional ministry of the church was patterned after the Old Testament priestly system with the mass taking the place of the Old Testament blood sacrifices. Only "priests" were authorized to perform the mass, and this meant that a false and debilitating distinction between clergy and laity was drawn.

Those who favor this view would say that it goes back to the days of the apostles. But this is demonstrably false. As reflected in the New Testament, the early church often used the word "minister" or "ministry" as referring to what *all* Christians are and must do, and it never used the word *hiereus* ("priest") of the clergy. As Robert Barclay pointed out in the seventeenth century and Elton Trueblood emphasizes so well in modern times, "the conventional modern distinction between the clergy and laity simply does not occur in the New Testament at all."[5] There are indeed pastors, as distinct from other Christians. But the difference is one of spiritual gifts and service rather than of ministry versus non-ministry. Above all, it is not a matter of "priests" versus those who can only serve a lesser function.

There are, then, historical reasons for the development of clericalism. But these in themselves are not the whole or even the most significant things. We see this when we ask why such developments took place. Was it simply a matter of biblical interpretation? Or did other factors also enter in and perhaps even distort the interpretation?

The causes of clericalism lie deep in the human constitution. Clergy themselves contribute to it. They tend to want to run the show. Sometimes this leads to outright abuse or tyranny. If we need an example, we can find one

in the New Testament in the person of Diotrephes who "love[d] to be first," according to the apostle John who wrote about him (3 John 9–10). A warning against such a pattern is found in a passage in 1 Peter that conveys instruction to church elders: "Be shepherds of God's flock that is under your care, serving as overseers—not because you must, but because you are willing, as God wants you to be; not greedy for money, but eager to serve; not lording it over those entrusted to you, but being examples to the flock" (1 Peter 5:2–3).

The chief biblical example of the right way is the Lord Jesus Christ who, though Lord of all creation, nevertheless put on a servant's garment and performed a servant's job in washing his disciples' feet.

Another reason for the rise of clericalism is the tendency of laypeople to sit back and "let the pastor do it." Stott quotes a remark of Sir John Lawrence to this effect: "What does the layman really want? He wants a building which looks like a church; clergy dressed in the way he approves; services of the kind he's been used to, *and to be left alone.*"[6] Thus do laymen abandon their God-given tasks and the professional clergy pick them up . . . to the church's impoverishment.

The second false answer to the relationship of clergy to laypeople is, understandably enough, *anticlericalism.* If the clergy despise the laity or think them dispensable, it is no surprise that the laity sometime return the compliment by wanting to get rid of the clergy.

This is not always bad. We know of situations in which the church has become so dominated by a corrupt or priestly clergy that a general housecleaning has been called for. Again, we

---

[5] Elton Trueblood, *The Incendiary Fellowship* (New York: Harper & Row, 1967), 39.
[6] Stott, *One People*, 30.

can think of areas of the church's work which are best done by laypeople, for which the clergy are not at all necessary. But these are not grounds for anticlericalism as the normal stance of Christian people. On the contrary, where the church wishes to be biblical it must recognize not only that gifts of teaching and leadership are given to some within the church for its well-being but also that there is ample biblical teaching about the need for such leadership. Judging from Acts and the various Pauline epistles, it was Paul's regular practice to appoint elders in every church and entrust to them the responsibility for the training of the flock for ministry (Acts 14:23; 20:17). In the pastoral epistles the appointment of such leaders is specifically commanded (Titus 1:5), and the qualifications for such leadership are given (1 Tim. 3:1–13; Titus 1:5–9).

Some who have captured the idea of ministry as belonging to the whole church have begun to wonder whether it leaves room for clergy. But properly understood, it does not lead to that conclusion. As Trueblood says, "The earliest Christians were far too realistic to fall into this trap, because they saw that, if the ideal of universal ministry is to be approximated at all, there must be some people who are working at the job of bringing this highly desirable result to pass."[7]

The final false model of the relationship between professional clergy and the laity is what Stott calls *dualism*. In this model clergy and laymen are each to be given their sphere, and neither is to trespass on the territory of the other. This describes the traditional Roman Catholic system in which a "lay status" and a "clerical status" are carefully delineated, but it is also true of certain forms of Protestantism. In such a system the sense of all being part of one

body and serving together in one work evaporates, the church is partitioned, and rivalry enters in instead.

The point I am making, of course, is that the proper pattern is set by Ephesians 4:11–13. For in pointing out that apostles, prophets, evangelists, pastors, and teachers are to equip the saints for the work of ministry, it is saying that the proper relationship of clergy to laypersons is *service,* and that the function of the laity is *service* as well. The clergy serve the laity by teaching and thus preparing them for ministry. The laity serve others by building up the church and by ministering evangelistically to the world.

FINDING YOUR GIFT

In the membership classes at Tenth Presbyterian Church there is a one-week session on the subject "Finding Your Gift," in which a booklet by that title is distributed. The class and booklet are designed to help members in this all-important matter of finding the gift God has given them and then in using it for him. Since this is the chief point I wish to make, I close by drawing from those statements. The booklet asks: How can I discover what my own gifts are? It answers:

First, you can *begin by studying what the Bible has to say about spiritual gifts.* The Bible is God's primary provision for spiritual growth and sanctification. It is in the Bible that God speaks to us. Without a knowledge of what God's Word explicitly teaches in this area we can easily be led to desire experiences which are not his will for us or begin to think of spiritual gifts in secular terms. As we study the Bible's teaching we must be careful to discern God's purpose in giving spiritual gifts. It is for the growth of the body and not merely personal growth or satisfaction, as Paul makes clear in Ephesians.

---

[7]Trueblood, *The Incendiary Fellowship,* 40.

Second, *you must pray.* This is not a matter to be taken lightly or one in which we may feel free to trust our own judgment. We do not know our hearts. We may find ourselves wanting a gift which exalts our sense of self-importance but which God does not have in mind for us. We may find ourselves resisting the gift he actually has in mind. The only way we will get by this hurdle is to lay the entire matter before the Lord in serious, soul-searching prayer and ask him, as he speaks through his Word, to show us the gift he actually has given us.

Third, *you can make a sober assessment of your spiritual strengths and abilities.* If we do not do this on the basis of a careful study of the Word of God and through prayer, we will be misled. But if we have first sought the wisdom and mind of God, we can then go back and look at ourselves through spiritual eyes.

We can ask: What do I like to do? This is not a sure guide to what our gifts are, but it is one indication since God's leading is always toward that for which he has prepared us and which we therefore naturally find enjoyable and satisfying. Stedman writes, "Somewhere the idea has found deep entrenchment in Christian circles that doing what God wants you to do is always unpleasant; that Christians must always make choices between doing what they want to do and being happy, and doing what God wants them to do and being completely miserable. Nothing could be more removed from truth. The exercise of a spiritual gift is always a satisfying, enjoyable experience though sometimes the occasion on which it is exercised may be an unhappy one. Jesus said it was his constant delight to do the will of the one who sent him. The Father's gift awakened his own desire and he went about doing what he intensely enjoyed doing."[8]

Another question we can ask is: What am I good at? If you are asking to fulfill a certain ministry in the church but are constantly failing and feel frustrated, it is likely that you are working in the wrong area and have assessed your gifts wrongly. If God is blessing—if you are seeing spiritual fruit from your efforts—you are probably on the right track and should pursue it even more vigorously. As skill in exercising this gift develops, you will find that the results are even better.

The fourth and final thing you can do is *seek the wisdom of other Christians where your gifts are concerned.* The church does not always function as it should. But where it functions properly one of the things that should happen is that others with the gift of insight or wisdom should be able to sense what your gifts are and point them out in terms of the needs of the particular Christian congregation. Others are almost always more objective about ourselves than we are. We must cultivate the ability to listen to these other members of the family of God and follow their guidance as far as we are able. If others tell us of our gifts, we are at least freed from the presumption of assuming we have gifts which actually we do not have.[9]

---

[8]Stedman, *Body Life*, 54.

[9]Portions of this chapter have already appeared in James Montgomery Boice, *God and History* (Downers Grove, Ill.: InterVarsity, 1981), 133–35, 138–41.

24

Spiritual Adults

(Ephesians 4:14–16)

Then we will no longer be infants, tossed back and forth by the waves, and blown here and there by every wind of teaching and by the cunning and craftiness of men in their deceitful scheming. Instead, speaking the truth in love, we will in all things grow up into him who is the Head, that is, Christ. From him the whole body, joined and held together by every supporting ligament, grows and builds itself up in love, as each part does its work.

Several years ago the elders of Tenth Presbyterian Church spent a great deal of time thinking about a succinct statement of the unique purpose of the church. When it was finished it read like this:

> Tenth Presbyterian Church is committed to developing and maintaining a strong teaching pulpit in center city Philadelphia, an effective network of fellowship groups aimed at meeting individual needs, a program of Christian education to promote the steady growth of our church family to spiritual maturity and, in cooperation with other Christians, an evangelistic outreach to our city and the world beyond.

Then, after this purpose statement was finished, it was passed on to a long-range planning commission, by whom it was expanded into five specific goals:

1. To uphold our tradition of strong expository preaching by skilled men of God from our center city location.

2. To integrate each member of the congregation into smaller fellowship groups where individual needs can be met and each can minister to others.

3. To provide an effective Christian education program to inform, train, and disciple all segments of our congregation.

4. To advance the missionary work of the church in the Philadelphia area and throughout the world, and

5. To serve the social and physical needs of our community.

The next step in this plan will be to compile a list of particular objectives that would accomplish these goals, and then to set up a specific timetable for accomplishing them and a process of measurement afterward to see if they really have been accomplished.

The whole process sounds like a modern approach to church management, but it is as old as Ephesians 4. In that chapter dealing with the church, the apostle Paul states God's purpose for the church and mentions his goals and objectives.

GOD'S PURPOSE FOR GOD'S CHURCH

Without looking at this passage closely, what would you say the purpose of God for his church is? Some answer that question in terms of the missionary mandate. They remember that Jesus instructed his disciples to "go into all the world and preach the good news to all creation" (Mark 16:15). Since this command is repeated with variations in each of the four Gospels and an additional time in the book of Acts it is obviously of great importance. It is neglected at the church's peril. Yet, is this the church's purpose? Those who think so think of the church as a mighty army engaged in a great, worldwide invasion. Their favorite image of the people of God is the church militant.

Others think of the church in terms of its social concern. They remember that Jesus spoke of separating the sheep from the goats on the basis of whether those involved fed the hungry, gave drink to the thirsty, welcomed the stranger, clothed the naked, looked after the sick, and visited the ones who were in prison (Matt. 25:31–46). People who emphasize this ministry generally think of the church as an international social service agency. But is this the proper emphasis? Is this God's greatest purpose for his people?

Still others regard the church as a retreat from the world, and their image of it is a fortress. In the world we have conflict. We take batterings from those who do not own Christ's lordship and are opposed to manifestations or extensions of his rule. To these people the church is a place where we can nurse our wounds and be fired up to fight another day. Is this the proper view? Did God establish the church chiefly to be a refuge from earthly conflicts?

In the verses I am speaking of Paul handles the issue of God's purpose for his church quite differently. No doubt Paul would have had little quarrel with these other emphases. These are things the church is called to do and areas in which it is to function. But "purpose" is a more embracing concept, and when Paul writes about it, as he does here, he thinks of it as God's developing wholeness or maturity in his people. His image is that of a body, Christ's body,

and his concern is that it be built up. See how he puts it. God gave "some to be apostles, some to be prophets, some to be evangelists, and some to be pastors and teachers, to prepare God's people for works of service, *so that the body of Christ may be built up until we all reach unity in the faith and in the knowledge of the Son of God and become mature, attaining to the whole measure of the fullness of Christ"* (vv. 11–13).

Then, after speaking of the opposite possibility, namely, of the church remaining spiritually immature, like children, he says, "Instead, speaking the truth in love, we will in all things grow up into him who is the Head, that is, Christ. From him the whole body, joined and held together by every supporting ligament, grows and builds itself up in love, as each part does its work" (vv. 15–16).

In these verses Paul speaks of maturity once and of building up or growing up four times more. It means that for Paul God's chief purpose for the church is that it might become full-grown and that each of its members might contribute to that maturity by becoming spiritual adults.

Unity to Be Attained

Paul is not just painting the scene with some broad brush of imagery, however. He is also being specific, as a careful examination of these verses shows. Granted that the church is to become spiritually mature. In what does that maturity consist? The first answer Paul gives—the first specific goal under his overriding purpose—is unity, the very point he has been making all along.

Up to this point Paul has been speaking of unity as a given, as something the church has and must maintain. He recognizes that there is diversity within the church, but far more important than the diversity are the things the people of God hold in common. He says,

"There is one body and one Spirit—just as you were called to one hope when you were called—one Lord, one faith, one baptism; one God and Father of all, who is over all and through all and in all" (vv. 4–5). The church possesses these seven great unities. Since that is so, Paul's admonition is: "Make every effort to keep the unity of the Spirit through the bond of peace" (v. 3). A unity like this can only be maintained.

But it is entirely different in verse 13, where Paul speaks of reaching "unity in the faith and in the knowledge of the Son of God." This unity is something to be attained. It does not yet exist but is an expression of the full maturity to which the church and its members should aspire. It has two parts: "Unity in the faith" and "unity . . . in the knowledge of the Son of God."

"Faith" usually means an individual's subjective response to the Word of God and the gospel, and "knowledge" usually refers to the content of what a child of God is to believe. But in this expression—"Unity in the faith and in the knowledge of the Son of God"—it is actually the other way around. "The faith" refers to the theological content of Christianity; it is "the faith that was once for all entrusted to the saints" (Jude 3).

"Knowledge of the Son of God" refers to experiential knowledge of Jesus attained through day-by-day discipleship; it is what Paul refers to in Philippians 3 where he writes of his desire "to know Christ and the power of his resurrection and the fellowship of sharing in his sufferings, becoming like him in his death" (v. 10). Paul means knowledge that goes beyond what can be packed into the head, knowledge that also trickles down into the heart and flows out into the life in obedient and loving service to the Lord.

This twofold knowledge—of the head and of the heart—is what Paul says the mature church should attain. Where possible we should have an outward, visible unity, for Jesus prayed that his church might have a unity on the basis of which unbelievers might be stimulated to faith (John 17:23). But far more important than any outward show of unity is that deep, inward, motivational unity that comes from believers growing in a knowledge of the truth, as we find it in the Bible, and living that truth out experientially in day-by-day fellowship with Jesus Christ. This reality transcends denominational and all other barriers.

CHRISTLIKENESS

The second specific goal under the general heading of maturity is what we would today probably call "Christ-likeness." It is what Paul is speaking of in the phrase "attaining to the whole measure of the fullness of Christ." In other words, it is not only that we are to have an experiential knowledge of Jesus Christ and his ways. In addition we are to become increasingly like him through such fellowship.

This goal has a personal side, namely, that individuals might become Christlike. Ironically the temptation that first came to Adam and Eve in the garden was precisely at this point. The devil had succeeded in getting the man and the woman to doubt God's goodness and then question his word. But the clinching argument was when he said to them, "God knows that when you eat of it [that is, the forbidden tree] your eyes will be opened, and you will be like God, knowing good and evil" (Gen. 3:5). This was a lie, of course, although like all good lies it had a measure of truth mixed with it. It was true that if the man and the woman ate of the tree, they would come to know good and evil. Before this they had known the good but not the evil. The lie was in the fact that they did not become "like God," knowing good and evil. They became *like Satan*, who not only knows what evil is, as God knows, but also practices it.

Here is the irony. Before the Fall the man and the woman actually were like God. That is the meaning of the thrice repeated phrase "in our [his own or God's] image" from the creation account in chapter 1. In their unfallen state our first parents actually were like God, and this is precisely what they lost by succumbing to Satan's temptation. The wonder of the gospel is that this original image, once lost through the Fall, is now progressively restored as individuals are made like Christ within the church's fellowship.

Does anyone feel the need of performance standards for the achieving of this goal? They are in Galatians, where Christlike character, termed "the fruit of the Spirit," is unfolded: "The fruit of the Spirit is love, joy, peace, patience, kindness, goodness, faithfulness, gentleness and self-control" (Gal. 5:22–23). This describes Jesus Christ. It also describes the direction in which individuals grow by the power of Christ's Spirit.

There is another aspect of this that is also worth considering. I have been writing of Christlikeness on the personal level as involving each individual member of the church, and this is important. It is how the church matures. Yet it is also true that in this great passage of Ephesians, dealing with maturity, Paul is thinking not so much of individual believers as of the church as a whole. He is saying that just as there is a growth in maturity for the individual, so also there is a growth in maturity for the church corporately. I think this means that, as the church goes about its business in this world, God works in it to develop one aspect of the character of Jesus Christ in a particular way here and another aspect of the character of Christ in a special way there, so that the entire church in every place is necessary to manifest the full character of the Lord.

Are you aware of that? Do you pray for that? It is what the Lord Jesus Christ wants to see in the people who constitute his body.

GROWING IN TRUTH

The third specific goal of maturity for the church is truth; without truth there is no real maturity. Paul writes in verse 15, "Instead, speaking *the truth* in love, we will in all things grow up into him who is the Head, that is, Christ."

The contrast here is with the nature and conduct of infants described in verse 14: "Then we will no longer be infants, tossed back and forth by the waves, and blown here and there by every wind of teaching and by the cunning and craftiness of men in their deceitful scheming." Children are delightful little creatures to have around, but they do have their limitations. Two are instability and naïveté. Children are notoriously fickle. They will be interested in one thing for five minutes; then they change their minds and focus on something else entirely, and five minutes later they move on to a third concern.

Again, children may be easily fooled. It is easy to deceive them. That is why parents have a special responsibility for the sound education and careful guidance of children; it is part of what it means to be a child. However, it is an unfortunate thing when those same characteristics hang on into adult life, weakening a person's character and limiting his or her usefulness. It is particularly unfortunate when the same marks of immaturity mar a Christian's development. Neither individual Christians nor the church as a whole are to be so weakened. If the church is not to be weakened, it must grow in the truth of God.

This is why Paul began by speaking of teaching gifts: apostles, prophets, evangelists, pastors, and teachers. It is not that these are the only gifts; they are not. Paul lists others elsewhere. But he lists these since they are the ways the church is to grow out of spiritual infancy to maturity. One of the tragedies of our day is that the church is so immature in this area. Consequently, it is always being carried along by the world's fads or being led astray by false theology. The only real cure is teaching followed by teaching and then still more teaching.

Truth Wedded to Love

Yet it is not truth in isolation, as if we only needed to bombard people with facts. Truth is important! But we also need to speak the "truth in love." Love is the fourth and last of these specific expressions of maturity. Indeed, Paul emphasizes love. This is not so evident in our English translations, but in the original text the word "truth" is actually a participle. So a more literal translation than "speaking the truth in love" would be "truthing [it] in love." The combination means both speaking and living the truth in a loving manner. In the combination of these goals, love (the noun) is emphasized.

I was impressed with this emphasis some years ago when I was studying the seventeenth chapter of John in which Jesus prays for his church, highlighting six marks by which the church is to be recognized: joy, holiness, truth, mission, unity, and love (John 17:13–26). Each of these is important. But it struck me that love is most important, which can be seen either by subtracting it from the other marks or by expressing it in every way possible. Subtract love from joy. What do you have? You have the kind of hedonistic reveling found in the secular world, the pursuit of pleasure for its own sake. Joy is distorted.

Take love from sanctification. The result is self-righteousness, the kind of thing that distinguished the scribes and Pharisees of Christ's day but allowed them to be filled with hatred, so that they crucified the Lord Jesus Christ when he came. Sanctification is destroyed.

Take love from truth. The result is bitter orthodoxy. Truth remains, but it is proclaimed in such an unpleasant, harsh manner that it fails to win anybody.

Take love from mission and you have colonialism. In colonialism we work to win people for our denomination or organization, but not for Christ.

Take love from unity and you have ecclesiastical tyranny, in which a church imposes human standards on those within it.

But if instead of subtracting love, you express love—for God the Father, the Lord Jesus Christ, the Bible, one another, and the world—what do you have? You have all the other marks of the church, because they naturally follow. Love for God leads to joy; nothing is more joyful than knowing and loving him. Love for the Lord Jesus Christ leads to holiness; as he said, "If you love me, you will obey what I command" (John 14:15). Love for the Word of God leads to truth; if we love the Bible, we will read it and grow in a knowledge of what the Word contains. Love for the world leads to mission. Love for other believers leads to unity.

When Paul speaks of the church's maturity, as he does in these verses, he does so in terms of bodily growth. And the point of that is that growth is a process. Growth takes time. The church does not become mature overnight any more than we as individuals become mature overnight. But if God is nevertheless working to accomplish this in us, we must trust him to do it and be patient as he works. I am sure you have seen that little pin that quite a few Christians have taken to wearing. It contains just a string of letters

(PBPWMGIFWMY), and it is meant to provoke curiosity. The letters stand for "Please be patient with me, God isn't finished with me yet."

We want everyone to be patient with us. Let us learn to be patient with them, and with the church—as God works in each believer, in all places and at all times to build and perfect Christ's earthly body, of which we are a part.

25

Seeing the World as God Sees It

(Ephesians 4:17–19)

So I tell you this, and insist on it in the Lord, that you must no longer live as the Gentiles do, in the futility of their thinking. They are darkened in their understanding and separated from the life of God because of the ignorance that is in them due to the hardening of their hearts. Having lost all sensitivity, they have given themselves over to sensuality so as to indulge in every kind of impurity, with a continual lust for more.

There is a saying of the ancient classical world that goes, "When in Rome, do as the Romans do." It is an encouragement to conform. If you are among sophisticated people, act sophisticated. If you are among earthy, common types, act earthy and common. If you are among pagans, act like one. Above all, do not stand out—at least not if you want to get on and be successful in the world.

That is foolish advice in most contexts, because it is usually those who stand out who are successful. But what bothers me most about the saying is its wickedness. It is opposed to the way of Christ. In human terms I suppose there is some wisdom in conforming to the ways of others; it gets one liked, it opens doors. But in spiritual terms conformity to the world's ways is fatal. That is why Paul tells us in the next section of Ephesians: "You must no longer live as the Gentiles do" (Eph. 4:17). The Ephesians were Gentiles and had lived as other Gentiles did in the past. But now things had become completely different. They had been called to discipleship and holiness by Christ, and they were to live as he lived. They were to be in the world—as we are in the world—but not of it.

THE HOLY LIFE

Ephesians 4:17 is the beginning of a new section of the epistle, the final one. The theme of these verses will now carry through to the end.

It is generally known that in most of his letters Paul follows a pattern of teaching doctrine first and then following it with applications. (That pattern is also repeated within the practical sections, as he brings in doctrine and applies it again and again.) Romans is a good example. The doctrinal section covers chapters 1–11. This is followed by chapters 12–16, which are practical. The doctrinal section of Galatians is in chapters 3 and 4, after a personal section in chapters 1 and 2, and the practical section closes the book.

The same is true of Ephesians. In the first three chapters Paul discusses the nature and origins of the Christian's salvation, showing that it flows from the grace of God and has as its goal the revelation of the manifold wisdom of God in and through the church. Chapters 4–6, the second half of the book, apply these doctrines to the life of Christians in a secular world.

But the second portion itself falls into two parts: 4:1–16 and 4:17–6:24. The doctrinal section taught that God has called Christians from all nations and all walks of life to be *one* people who must strive for unity. That is what 4:1–16 is all about. However, the doctrinal section also taught that Christians are God's *holy* people who must strive for purity. That is the burden of these closing comments.

This is an extremely important point. Christians are to live holy lives, not just because morality is good in itself (though it is) or because it promotes happiness or success or anything else (though it does), but because of what God has done. Because of what we believe about God's actions toward us through Jesus Christ we should live as God wants and requires us to live. Martyn Lloyd-Jones says, "Our conduct should always be to us something which is inevitable in view of what we believe. . . . If my Christian living is not quite *inevitable* to me, if I am always fighting against it and struggling and trying to get out of it, and wondering why it is so hard and narrow, if I find myself rather envying the people who are still back in the world, there is something *radically* wrong with my Christian life."[1]

Therefore, if I am failing in the Christian life, what should trouble me is not that *I* am failing or that *I* have a problem but that I have failed *God* and his important purposes for me.

THIS PRESENT WORLD SYSTEM

We might think that at this point, having laid his doctrinal foundation in chapters 1–3, Paul might now pass on quickly to positive moralistic instruction: Live a holy life, speak the truth, be kind and loving. He does that eventually. However, before he does, he reminds the Ephesians of some very important truths—in this case the true nature of the world system from which they have been delivered and the reasons it got to be that way.

So far as the nature of this present world system is concerned, Paul describes it in these words: (1) "the futility of their thinking," (2) "darkened in their understanding," and (3) "separated from the life of God" (vv. 17–18). We know that Paul is going to talk about conduct, urging the Ephesians to pursue a different and higher standard of behavior than their pagan neighbors. So what strikes us about this initial description of the world system is its emphasis on the intellectual in non-Christians' lives. We are sometimes given the impression that what a person thinks is not important, so long as he acts properly, or again, that a person can mess up on a practical level and still have his life together intellectually. That is not the way things actually are, according to the apostle. People act as they think, and the reason they are constantly messing up is that they are vain in their thinking and darkened in their understanding as a consequence of being separated from God.

In other words, our problems go back to the mind. It is here and not elsewhere that the unsaved person has his chief flaw. He does not know God; so he cannot think properly. Everything is out of place, and his disordered and sinful conduct reflects his disordered, sinful mind.

This must have been a novel idea to many of Paul's readers. They were Greeks, and the central principle of the Greek world-and-life view was that the best, noblest, and ultimately most worthwhile part of the human being is

---

[1] D. Martyn Lloyd-Jones, *Darkness and Light: An Exposition of Ephesians 4:16–5:17* (Grand Rapids: Baker, 1982), 21.

the intellect. In fact, the Greek made a sharp division between reason and flesh (or substance). The mind is the divine element within the human being. It links us to God and draws us upward. Our flesh is of the earth. It draws us down. For the ancient Greek thinkers salvation consisted mainly in being delivered from the powers of the flesh by human reason. Philosophy was the savior.

But, of course, philosophy did not save the ancients any more than it saves people today, and Paul wanted to impress that upon the Ephesians. Their ability to think was flawed. They thought "mind" was the solution to their problems, but it was actually the chief cause of their failures. It is true that the Greek could pursue a proper logical analysis. He could form syllogisms and paradigms and solve problems. He could master philosophical concepts. But the Greek did not know God. So at some point, though great, all his reasonings and especially his moral conclusions were distorted.

The Greeks were the greatest thinkers of the ancient world; the Romans learned from them. Nevertheless, most of the ancients were either polytheists, who believed in many gods (Zeus, Hera, Poseidon, Aphrodite, and others); pantheists, who believed that god was in everything; or atheists, who believed in no god at all. What folly! Writing of the Roman period that followed and built upon the Greek age intellectually, Edward Gibbon said that the philosophers regarded all religions as equally false, the common people regarded them as equally true, and the rulers regarded them as equally useful.

It is no different today. We live in an age which prides itself on intellectual attainments, just as the Greeks did, but it lacks true spiritual understanding. People protest this conclusion. But this is the way the world is, as God sees it.

HARDNESS OF HEART

The second important truth Paul holds before his readers in this paragraph is the reason the gentile world system has become as it has. It is because of the "hardening of [people's] hearts" (v. 18).

Here is a place where the New International Version and other modern versions help us better than the older King James text. In the Greek language the word the NIV translates as "hardening," but the KJV translates as "blindness," is *pōrōsis*. The noun from which it came was *pōros*, which meant "stone." Usually it referred to a certain kind of marble.

The word was also used medically. *Pōrion* was a "callus." The verb *pōroō* meant to "petrify" or "harden." If it was applied to the joints, it referred to their stiffening, perhaps arthritis. If it was applied to a fracture, it referred to the process by which the broken pieces were united through the growth of new bone or cartilage. Applied to the eyes, it meant blindness. This is what the older translators picked up for the King James Version. And, of course, it is not wrong. A "blind heart" cannot see God. Still, the trouble with "blindness" is that it suggests an inescapable and therefore a morally blameless inability, and this is not the idea.

What Paul is saying is that the unsaved world is actually much to blame. People have willfully hardened themselves against God, and as a result they have become warped in their spiritual understanding. The newer translations help us at this point.

As soon as we see this, we notice that Paul is developing precisely the same line of thought in Ephesians as he did in writing the great first chapter of Romans. Beginning with verse 18 of Romans 1, Paul explains how the wrath of God is revealed against ungodly people, not because they are innocently ignorant of him but because they have willfully closed their eyes to the revelation that God has given to the world.

In Romans 1:18–23 there are four main points, which make a sequence:

1. *God has revealed himself* to people *in nature* so that no one is without blame for failing to seek him out and worship him. He says, "What may be known about God is plain to them, because God has made it plain to them" (v. 19). This does not mean that the revelation of God in nature is a complete or saving revelation, for it is not. There is more to God than what is revealed in nature, and that includes everything pertaining to the work of redemption accomplished by Jesus Christ.

The revelation of God in nature is very limited. Paul refers to it as the revelation of "God's invisible qualities—his eternal power and divine nature" (v. 20). But although limited, it is nevertheless a real revelation and is sufficient in itself to lead a man or woman to worship God properly—if such a person did not have reasons for refusing to do so. It is this revelation that makes the failure of a person to know God a blameworthy offense.

2. In spite of God's revelation of himself in nature, *people have rejected or suppressed the revelation.* Paul says, they "suppress the truth by their wickedness" (v. 18). That is, they try to hide it and deny it. They sense rightly that if they acknowledged the truth about the existence and nature of God, they would have to change their thinking and living. Rather than change, they repress the revelation.

3. Because their ignorance of God is willful and blameworthy and not a natural failure, *God's wrath is upon them* (v. 18). That is, he is not favorable toward them but rather judges them for their sins.

4. The fourth point in this sequence is about how God judges those who willfully ignore him. Paul is thinking here not so much of the final judgment, though there will be one, but that God judges people by an inevitable working out of sin. Saint Augustine once said, "The punishment of sin is sin." That is what Paul has in mind. Therefore, having spoken of the revelation of the wrath of God against men and women for their rejection of the truth, Paul writes of the *consequential darkening of their intellects and their moral lives:* "Although they claimed to be wise, they became fools and exchanged the glory of the immortal God for images made to look like mortal man and birds and animals and reptiles. Therefore God gave them over in the sinful desires of their hearts to sexual impurity . . . to shameful lusts . . . [and] to a depraved mind" (vv. 22–24, 26, 28).

We find an identical sequence of thought in Ephesians 4:17–19, although the Ephesians passage uses different words and is shorter. What is wrong with the world in which the Ephesians (and all other Christians) find themselves is that it has hardened itself against God. The very One who is the Christian's joy and glory is the world's enemy. So we are not on the same team as the world. We do not have the same goals or tasks or loyalties. If we are going to get on with anything like a vigorous Christian life in this world, we need to see that.

PRAYER AND UNDERSTANDING

In the next section of this chapter Paul is going to carry this out in detail: "You must no longer live as the Gentiles do." He will explain exactly what this means. But before we go on to that valuable explanation we need to draw a few conclusions and applications from this study.

First, we must know the world as it really is and not as it likes to think of itself or present itself to others. We live in the world and thus, sometimes almost inevitably, adopt the world's self-assessment. The world thinks it is doing fairly well; it thinks it is getting better and will certainly be even better than it is now some day. We need to realize that this is not the case. This is how the world sees itself, but it is not how God sees it, and it is not the way things actually are. In truth, the world is a dreadful place. It has information, but it lacks true knowledge—the only knowledge that ultimately matters, the knowledge of God—and, lacking that knowledge, it becomes increasingly wicked. We are not to envy it.

Second, we must recognize the spiritual blindness with which the world operates. It is a blindness due to a willful hardening of the heart.

In his commentary on Ephesians, D. Martyn Lloyd-Jones gives an excellent illustration of this point. William Pitt the Younger was one of the great prime ministers of England, a great intellect, and a friend of William Wilberforce, the man who devoted his life to the abolition of slavery throughout the British Empire. Wilberforce had experienced a genuine evangelical conversion, and this had made him the upright man he was. It was because of his Christian convictions that he labored so long and struggled so hard against slavery. Pitt was a nominal Christian, as most Englishmen of that day were, but Christianity did not mean anything to him.

In London in those days there was also a great evangelical clergyman and preacher by the name of Richard Cecil. Wilberforce attended on Cecil's preaching regularly and was delighted with it. It fed his soul and warmed his heart. He wanted his friend, William Pitt, the prime minister, to go with him to hear Cecil. Wilberforce often invited Pitt to attend church with him, but Pitt made excuses. He was always too busy. However, a day came when Pitt told Wilberforce that he could accompany him.

That Sunday morning Cecil was at his best. Wilberforce was uplifted as he had scarcely ever been before; he was glorying in God and prayed for his friend. However, when the service ended and they were going out together, William Pitt turned to his friend Wilberforce and said, "You know, Wilberforce, I have not the slightest idea what that man was talking about."

Many who have witnessed to their non-Christian friends have had that experience and have been saddened by it. This sadness is proper, though surprise is not. This is that blindness and hardness of the heart about which Paul is speaking. A person like this remains blind until God softens the heart and opens the eyes to his truth.

This leads to a final application. We are going to see in this last section of Ephesians that Christians are not to live as the world. That is quite true. But our duty toward the world is not exhausted when we have rejected its values or established a different way of life. We are to pray for the world too. And if prayer for the *world* seems a bit overwhelming, as perhaps it is, then we must pray for specific people we know who need to have their eyes opened. I cannot tell you for certain that God will save that unsaved friend for whom you pray. But I know that the Bible encourages us to pray. It tells us that we do not receive because we do not ask. And I know that historically every great movement of the Spirit of God in what we call revival has been preceded by a long period of fervent, burdened prayer for it by God's people.

We need such a movement of God's Spirit today. Do you believe that? Do you believe it enough to pray for it? It is not enough to denounce the world's sins. It is not even enough to come out from the world and be separate. We must also pray for those we know. And we must make the Word of God known to them, seeing that it is the vehicle by which God habitually turns sinners from darkness to his marvelous light.

26

Jesus, the Great Divide

(Ephesians 4:20–24)

You, however, did not come to know Christ that way. Surely you heard of him and were taught in him in accordance with the truth that is in Jesus. You were taught, with regard to your former way of life, to put off your old self, which is being corrupted by its deceitful desires; to be made new in the attitude of your minds; and to put on the new self, created to be like God in true righteousness and holiness.

Have you ever thought how significant it is that in the Western world we do not reckon time from some fixed point in the past to which we add on year by year but from a midpoint from which we figure both forward and back? The Jewish calendar begins from what it regards as the date of creation and moves on from that point. So does the Chinese calendar. But not the Christian calendar! We begin with an approximation of the year of the birth of Jesus Christ and then number in two directions—backward in a receding series of years, which we call B.C. ("before Christ"), and forward in an increasing accumulation of years, which we call A.D. (*anno Domini*, "in the year of the Lord"). By this strange reckoning we testify that Jesus of Nazareth is the dividing line of history.

Jesus is the great divide in more than a historical sense. He is also a personal dividing point for everyone who has been saved by him. This is what Paul has in mind as he moves in his treatment of practical Christian conduct from the gentile world, as it was (and is) apart from Christ, to the new standards of Christianity. Having described

the world in its darkness, alienation, and futility, Paul now exclaims, "You, however, did not come to know Christ that way" (Eph. 4:20).

This is Paul's introduction to what is going to be an extensive description of the Christian life. So it is important to notice that it begins with a reference to Christ himself and not to anything that might be supposed to come out of the depraved hearts or futile efforts of mere human beings. Some people think that a new life or a new beginning in life can emerge from *self-discovery*. The human potential movement, visible in such organizations as EST, Mind Dynamics, Lifespring, and Scientology, teaches this. Some think that a change can be found through personal *enlightenment*. They seek it through mysticism and the newly resurgent religions of the East. Still others retain belief in the nineteenth-century notion of inevitable *progress*.

Real change comes in none of these ways. The only truly transforming power that has ever come into the world is that of the person and teaching of Jesus Christ, and the only true and lasting changes that ever take place in

141

an individual life take place through believing in and learning from him.

Jesus is the great divide, not only historically but also in countless lives.

THE SCHOOL OF CHRIST

As Paul begins to explain this he uses three verbs, all having to do with education, and he follows them with a reference to "the truth that is in Jesus." Together they create an image of what we might call the school of Jesus Christ. The way these verbs are used is interesting. Marcus Barth calls them "baffling" in his excellent treatment of them and considers them examples of "an extraordinary use of language."[1]

The first verb is *emathete*. The phrase in which it occurs should be rendered literally "you learned Christ" (NIV, "came to know"). The reason this is "extraordinary" is that the idea of learning a person, rather than a mere fact or doctrine, is found nowhere else in the Greek Bible. Nor has it been found in any other pre-biblical document. What does it mean? Well, it probably means more than merely learning about the historical Jesus or becoming acquainted with his doctrines. It is probably to be taken along the lines of Jesus' words when he said in his great prayer to the Father, recorded in John 17, "This is eternal life: that they may know you, the only true God, and Jesus Christ, whom you have sent" (v. 3). It means that Christians are Christians because they have entered into a personal relationship with the living Lord Jesus Christ. It is a learning of him that changes them at the deepest possible level.

The second verb is *ēkousate* and occurs in the phrase "you heard him." The New International Version says, "you heard *of* him," but "of" is not in the text and at this point the NIV is probably in error. The point is not that we have heard *of* Christ but rather that we have heard him speak. How so? How have we heard Jesus? The answer—though this is perhaps also a bit baffling—is that we have heard him in Scripture, particularly as it has been expounded to us by preachers of the gospel. I emphasize preaching because this is the way the Ephesians, to whom Paul is actually writing, must have heard Christ. As Paul preached Jesus, they heard Jesus himself through Paul's exposition.

This is hard for the world to understand. The minds of this world's people are clouded and their eyes blinded, as we saw in the story about William Pitt the Younger and Wilberforce. Yet Christians know exactly what this means. You read the Bible or hear the Word of God preached and, suddenly, sometimes quite unexpectedly, you are aware that Jesus is talking to you personally. This is not mere subjectivity; it is supernatural. For Jesus does speak. He speaks to change the life and thinking of his people.

The third verb is *edidachthete*. It is a heightened form of the common Greek word for instruction and occurs in the phrase "you . . . were taught in him." The puzzling thing about this expression is the words "in him." Normally we would expect the sentence to say "taught *by him*" or "taught *about him*." But it actually says *"in* him," and it probably means that Jesus is the atmosphere within which the teaching takes place. We might say that Jesus is the school, as well as the teacher and the subject of instruction.

Some years ago Marshall McLuhan popularized the phrase "the medium is the message." He used it in reference to forms of communication such as television. In Christ's school we have a case

[1]Marcus Barth, *Ephesians: Translation and Commentary on Chapters 4–6* (Garden City, N.Y.: Doubleday, 1974), 529.

where the Medium really is the Message—and the environment too. Christ is everything. John Stott says in his comments on this passage, "When Jesus Christ is at once the subject, the object, and the environment of the moral instruction being given, we may have confidence that it is truly Christian. For *truth is in Jesus*. The change from his title 'Christ' to his human name 'Jesus' seems to be deliberate. The historical Jesus is himself the embodiment of truth, as he claimed."[2]

Notice that although Paul is speaking of the knowledge of Christ and his ways in the deepest, most personal, and most profound sense, it is nevertheless in terms of *knowing* or *learning of* Christ that he speaks. Why is this? It is because in the previous verse he has described the condition of the secular or gentile world as due chiefly to ignorance. He was pointing out that the depravity of the gentile world was due to its willful ignorance of God. The world has hardened its heart against God and so is alienated from him intellectually and in every other way. It follows, then, that when Paul speaks of the difference Jesus makes he does so in exactly parallel terms. The world is ignorant of God, but Christians have come to know him. The secular mind is hostile to Christ's teaching, but the believer joyfully enrolls in and continually makes progress in Christ's school.

What Is the Difference?

We come to specifics now and ask in concrete terms precisely what difference the coming of Christ and his revelation mean to us. How shall we describe the geography to the right and to the left of this great historical divide? I suggest the following five alternatives.

1. *God and atheism.* I am aware, of course, that there are many religions in the world other than Christianity, and I would even argue that they exist because of the God of Christianity. Not knowing the true God has left a vacuum at the center of the human personality which people everywhere try to fill with religion. But religion itself is empty—"vain" is Paul's word—and it leads to frustration, the kind of thing Edward Gibbon meant when he described the religions of the ancient world either as "equally true" (in the minds of the common people), "equally false" (in the minds of the philosophers), or "equally useful" (in the minds of the magistrates). Mere human debate on this issue leads at best to skepticism and at worst to outright disbelief or atheism. Christ shows that there is a God and that the true God is the God of the Bible.

I am impressed with the fact that in his early apologetic writing this is the place where Francis Schaeffer starts. He starts with the existence of God, and his classic statement of this foundational point is that "God is there, and he is not silent."[3] It is evident why we must start at this point. If God exists and we can know he exists, then everything else follows from that premise. The Bible begins this way: "In the beginning God. . . ." Everything else follows that. If God does not exist or if we cannot know he exists, then nothing follows except chaos.

Jesus shows us that God exists and that this God, the true God, is the God of the Bible. This is the God he himself believed in and about whom he taught. He taught that God is all-powerful, and he declared that after he had died, this God, the God of the Old Testament, the God of Abraham and Isaac and Jacob, would raise him from the dead. This

---

[2]John R. W. Stott, *God's New Society: The Message of Ephesians* (Downers Grove, Ill.: InterVarsity, 1979), 179.

[3]One of Schaeffer's early works is entitled *He Is There and He Is Not Silent*, but the same point is made in *The God Who Is There* and *Escape from Reason*, as well as in other places in his writings.

was a stupendous claim, a seemingly impossible claim. But the God of Jesus stood the test. He did raise Jesus from the dead, and thus both by his teaching and by his resurrection we know that there is a God and that the God proclaimed by Jesus is that God.

2. *Plan or accident.* Is life part of an important, divine plan, or is it just an accident? That is the second issue that hinges on the person of Christ. The proponents of atheistic evolution, of whom there are many in our day, argue that everything that exists, including ourselves, has come about entirely by chance. There has been no guiding Mind or plan. It just happened. One day, for no real reason, certain inorganic compounds (like hydrogen, water, ammonia, and carbon dioxide, which were existing for no real reason) united to form bio-organic compounds (like amino acids and sugars). These bio-organics united to form bio-polymers, which are large molecules such as proteins, and these in turn became the first living cells, like algae. From this point life just progressed upward.

This is an utter absurdity, of course. "Chance" is no thing. It can "form" nothing. So if the choice is between a plan and an accident (or chance), there is really no choice. There must be a plan, and in order for there to be a plan there must be a Planner, who makes it.

The world does not see the absurdity of tracing everything to chance, and therefore in this area as in others Jesus is the point of division.

If there is no plan and everything is the product of mere chance (whatever that may be), then nothing at all has meaning. The world itself is meaningless. History is meaningless. You have no meaning, and neither do I. Everything is just an accident, and whether we live or die, achieve or fail to achieve in this life, is irrelevant. Moreover, since the universe does not care, there is no reason why we should care either.

People do not want to acknowledge this, of course. After all, regardless of their world-and-life view (or even the absence of one), they are all nevertheless made in the image of God and therefore sense that they have meaning anyway.

But my point is that it is only in Jesus Christ that we know this. Otherwise we might as well say, as the ancients did, "Eat, drink, and be merry, for tomorrow we die." This is precisely the manner in which many of our contemporaries are living—and they have empty lives to show for it.

3. *Truth or ignorance.* When I mentioned Francis Schaeffer's statement, "God is there, and he is not silent," it was for the sake of the statement's first part: God is there. Now I return to it for the second part, which tells us not merely that God exists but that we can know he exists and that we can know many other things besides. We can know because of God's authoritative speaking or revelation.

Without the knowledge of God in Jesus Christ the world cannot know anything with real certainty. This must have seemed particularly strange to the Greeks of Paul's day. The Greeks had produced nearly all the great philosophers, and the ancient world prided itself on their wisdom. Still, the best philosophers knew (at least in part) how ignorant they were. Plato said somewhat wistfully, on one occasion, "Perhaps one day there will come forth a Word out of God who will reveal all things and make everything plain." But the Greeks did not know where that Word was—until the early preachers of the gospel told them. They remained ignorant. And our world, which has heard the Word proclaimed but has rejected him, has moved in the direction, not of increasing certainty about absolutes, but of uncertainty.

I have frequently said that in our day people no longer even believe in truth, strictly speaking. They speak of truth, but they mean only what is true for me (but not necessarily for you) or what is true now (but not necessarily tomorrow). This means that in the final analysis there is no truth. A philosophy like this is the opposite of revelation, and the ignorance that results is so deep that it does not even know it is ignorance.

4. *Life or oblivion.* What is in store after death: eternal life or personal oblivion? Here too Jesus Christ's coming into the world has made a difference.

What is the one great fear of men and women apart from Jesus Christ? It is death. People fear death for two reasons.

First, they do not know what stands on the far side of that dark portal, if anything. They are ignorant. Francis Bacon was thinking of this when he said, "Men fear death as children fear the dark."

Second, in spite of their willful ignorance of God, they sense deep in their beings that he is there, that they have offended him, and that beyond the door of death they must give an accounting to him. I think this is what bothered Samuel Johnson when he described his horror at the death of a friend: "At the sign of this last conflict I felt a sensation never known to me before: a confusion of passions, an awful stillness of sorrow, a gloomy terror without a name" (*The Rambler,* no. 54).

But let me say: of all the fears people have in the face of death the least to be feared is oblivion—to die and be no more. The reality of facing God is far worse. To face God apart from Christ is to face judgment. Only in Christ can we pass over the dividing line between the kingdom of wrath and condemnation to that of life and light.

5. *Blessing or cursing* in this life. I have been speaking of the difference Jesus makes for eternity, but I end by saying that Jesus makes all the difference in this life too. Do you remember that great scene in the book of Joshua in which, in obedience to the remembered command of Moses, Joshua gathered the people of Israel at Mount Ebal and Mount Gerizim? The area between the mountains was a natural amphitheater, and the people were to stand on the opposing mountains while the law of God, containing blessings and cursings, was read to them. Mount Ebal was to be the mountain of cursing, and as the curses of God upon all who break his law were read, the people were to say, "Amen." Mount Gerizim was the mountain of blessing. From this mountain the Levites read the blessings of God which were to be upon all who loved him and kept his commandments.

How were the people to keep them? They had no strength to do it. What were they to do if they did break the commandments? How were they to escape the curses of God which hung over them? In the bottom of that amphitheater, between the two mountains, there was an altar which pointed to the atonement to be made one day by Jesus Christ. That is what would deliver them from the curse and keep them in blessing. Christ alone could do it. Christ alone can bring blessing.

I do not fully understand how he does it, but he does. What was our life B.C. (before Christ)? Wrath and disaster. What is it A.D.? It is the way of mercy and blessing. What a Savior!

27

Putting Off and Putting On

(Ephesians 4:25–32)

Therefore each of you must put off falsehood and speak truthfully to his neighbor, for we are all members of one body. "In your anger do not sin": Do not let the sun go down while you are still angry, and do not give the devil a foothold. He who has been stealing must steal no longer, but must work, doing something useful with his own hands, that he may have something to share with those in need.

Do not let any unwholesome talk come out of your mouths, but only what is helpful for building others up according to their needs, that it may benefit those who listen. And do not grieve the Holy Spirit of God, with whom you were sealed for the day of redemption. Get rid of all bitterness, rage and anger, brawling and slander, along with every form of malice. Be kind and compassionate to one another, forgiving each other, just as in Christ God forgave you.

In the fourth chapter of Ephesians Paul is beginning to deal with Christian conduct, the practical application of those great doctrinal teachings declared in the first three chapters. But he has led into it indirectly. First, Paul has reminded the believers at Ephesus of what they were before God saved them. They were hardened against God, darkened and futile in their thinking, separated from God's life, and insensitive to holiness so that they indulged in every kind of sensual vice. Second, he has reminded them that in spite of this dark background they nevertheless had been saved by God and had come to know Jesus Christ, who leads his followers in an entirely different way. His argument was, "Surely you heard of him and were taught in him in accordance with the truth that is in Jesus" (v. 21).

But what is this new way that is in Christ? And how are we to walk in it?

Here Paul lists five specific examples of the new way, prefacing these with an illustration of what it means to walk in this way rather than another.

GRAVECLOTHES AND WEDDING GARMENTS

Paul talks about changing to a new way of life in terms of taking off one set of clothes and putting on another: "You were taught, with regard to your former way of life, to put off your old self, which is being corrupted by its deceitful desires; to be made new in the attitude of your minds; and to put on the new self, created to be like God in true righteousness and holiness" (vv. 22–24).

The image is easy for us to understand. Despite our contemporary tendency to constant casual dress, we still recognize that some kinds of clothes are more suited than others to a particular occasion or activity. John Stott observes, for instance, that we normally

146

wear light, bright clothes for a wedding and dark, somber clothes for a funeral. Again, some people's clothing is determined by their line of work. Doctors and nurses have special clothing. So do members of the armed forces. Prisoners have a type of clothing proscribed for them by the penal system. When they leave prison they exchange this unwelcome type of clothing for normal dress.

In appealing for proper Christian conduct Paul says that Christians are to put off the conduct associated with their former life apart from Christ and put on a new pattern of behavior, just as they might put on a new dress or suit. In most of our Bibles the infinitive verbs of this section ("put off" and "put on") are translated as though they were imperatives, that is, commands: "Put off your old nature" and "Put on your new nature." But John Stott, D. Martyn Lloyd-Jones, and others have pointed out that this cannot be right.[1]

First, in the parallel passage in Colossians 3:9–10, the verbs are aorist participles and are therefore rightly translated "You have taken off our old self with its practices and have put on the new self, which is being renewed in knowledge in the image of its creator." This refers to something that has already happened, not to something to be done.

Second, the use of "therefore" in Ephesians 4:25 indicates that the application is to be found at that point and not earlier. If "put off" and "put on" in verses 22–24 are imperatives, the thought would go: "Put off . . . put on; therefore, put off. . . . " That lacks sense. "Therefore" adds nothing. But if the verbs in verses 22–24 are taken in a past or completed sense, as is the case in Colossians, then it makes sense. Believers are to follow certain Christian standards precisely because God has already made them new creatures in Christ by putting away the old nature and putting on the new.

This is an important point. The apostle is not merely urging a new and higher standard of morality on people. That is an utterly futile thing. We cannot be genuinely better by mere moral suasion. That is not it at all. Rather, Paul is demanding a high form of behavior precisely because something decisive has already taken place. We have already been made new in Christ. That is why we should and must act like it.

We, like Lazarus, have been brought out of death into life by Christ. As part of that spiritual miracle our old graveclothes, which were appropriate for a corpse but not for a living body, have been taken off, and we have been reclothed in wedding garments in preparation for that great wedding supper of the Lamb. From this point on we should act like members of the wedding party.

FIVE EXAMPLES

But what does this mean? How are Christians to act? In a sense, the remainder of Ephesians is written to answer those questions. In this section, verses 25–32, there are five specific examples of what the new, higher standard of Christian conduct should be. Most of them are given both negatively and positively, corresponding to the illustration of putting off one type of conduct and putting on another.

1. *Put off lying and speak truthfully* (v. 25). Paul's first example is an excellent illustration of putting off and putting on. The Greek word translated "falsehood" is actually *to pseudos* ("the lie"). This is the word John uses in reference to the spirit of antichrist (cf. 1 John 2:20–23). Here, Paul may have in mind

[1]John R. W. Stott, *God's New Society: The Message of Ephesians* (Downers Grove, Ill.: InterVarsity, 1979), 180–81; D. Martyn Lloyd-Jones, *Darkness and Light: An Exposition of Ephesians 4:17–5:17* (Grand Rapids: Baker, 1982), 119–24.

the Christian's repudiation of this basic lie as a basis for urging truthful speech upon him. In becoming Christians the believers at Ephesus had repudiated *the* lie and had embraced *the* truth. That is, they had turned from false gods, idols, or Satan to Jesus, who is said to be "truth" (John 14:6). Therefore, because they are already new creatures in respect to this basic truth and falsehood, they should now eschew lying entirely and speak truth always.

Paul has been speaking of truth again and again in this passage. Gentiles do not know the truth; they are darkened in their understanding. Christians do know truth; they have learned it from and in Christ. Moreover, he has said, it is by being made new "in the attitude of [our] minds" that we are to make progress.

This means that if we are to grow as Christians, one of the necessary ingredients is cultivating truthfulness. We can lie quite deliberately, of course. A slander is a lie. A statement deliberately intended to mislead another person is a lie, particularly when the misleading is for our own advantage. But we also lie unintentionally just because we are not in the habit of rigorously cultivating truth.

William Barclay quotes some wise words from Samuel Johnson at this point, spoken while urging parents to teach children to be accurate. He said, "It is more from carelessness about truth than from intentional lying that there is so much falsehood in the world."[2] Whether that sanguine statement is true of the world is questionable, but it probably is true of Christians. All the more reason why we should cultivate accuracy in speaking truth, seeing this as an essential ingredient of our lives.

Paul's reasoning for such a high standard is that "we are all members of one body." We remember that earlier he spoke of the unity and health of the body being established through all "speaking the truth in love" (v. 15).

2. *Put off anger* (vv. 26–27). Paul's second example does not have an expressed positive side, but we are probably to understand it as being a controlled or righteous anger as opposed to an uncontrolled, selfish, or sinful anger. This is because anger itself is not sin. Scores of Old Testament passages speak of the just anger of God against the wicked and even against his own people when they persist in disobedience. Jesus was angry on several occasions (cf. Mark 3:5; Matt. 21:12–13). Indeed, even we can experience righteous anger. That is why Paul introduces this subject by a quotation from Psalm 4:4 ("In your anger do not sin"), which makes a distinction between sinful and sinless wrath.

But our trouble is not usually in that area. It is as wrong not to be angry in a situation demanding anger, such as a gross injustice, as it is to be angry at the wrong time and for the wrong reasons. But we must admit that we are most often angry in precisely that way—at the wrong time and for the wrong reasons. And it is because our own personal feelings, pride, and self-image are wrapped up in our reactions. How do we deal with this?

I suppose there are many things that might be said at this point, but what Paul does say is that we must deal with anger quickly, that is, before the sun sets on our wrath. To allow it to fester and swell and surge about for any extended period is quite dangerous because it gives the devil a foothold, as Paul says. Anger leads to malice and slander, and these lead to many other destructive sins. The only thing to do is

[2] William Barclay, *The Letters to the Galatians and Ephesians* (Edinburgh: Saint Andrews Press, 1970), 183.

to confess the anger and root it out as rapidly as possible.

And even in the case of righteous anger—which we probably have too little of, Christians being sinfully tolerant of gross evil—we should be "slow to become angry" (James 1:19). If we heeded this, we should be angry far less often than we are.

3. *Put off stealing and work for a living instead* (v. 28). Each of these admonitions may be linked in one way or another with the Ten Commandments, but in this case the link is explicit. The eighth commandment says, "You shall not steal" (Exod. 20:15), and this is Paul's precise command here. "He who has been stealing must steal no longer, but must work, doing something useful with his own hands, that he may have something to share with those in need."

There are many different ways that we can steal, of course. We steal from God when we fail to worship him as we ought or when we set our own interests before his legitimate interests. We steal from him when we fail to honor him by our lives or fail to tell others of his love. We steal from an employer when we do not give the best work of which we are capable or when we waste time or consistently leave work early. If we are in business, we can steal by overcharging for what we make or for the service we render. We steal if we sell an inferior product, pretending it is better than it is. We steal by borrowing and not repaying. We steal by damaging another's reputation. We steal from ourselves when we waste the time, talents, or resources God has entrusted to us.

What Paul obviously has chiefly in mind here is taking things or money that do not belong to us, or doing nothing so that others have to take care of us when we are capable of caring for ourselves. Paul's contrast to such a dishonest or indolent attitude is work—"doing something useful" with our own hands.

What is the motivation for such personal industry? Here the difference between a Christian and a non-Christian outlook is most evident. For Paul does not say, as many secular thinkers might say, "Work hard, because that will build self-esteem" or " . . . because then you will be able to buy things you want and enjoy the good life." He says rather, "[because you will then] have something to share with those in need." There are people who have nothing because they will not work for it; they do not deserve handouts. But there are others who, through no fault of their own, genuinely have needs. Who is to help such people? Not the world, not really! The world is out for itself. The poor must be helped by Christian people who work hard precisely so they will have something to give to those in need.

4. *Put off unwholesome talk and instead speak to help others* (v. 29). The contrast between unwholesome talk and helpful talk is stronger and also more obvious in Greek than in English. This is because the word translated "unwholesome" is *sapros*, which literally means "corrupt" or "corrupting." It is used of fruit that is rotting, for example. This is what some talk does, Paul argues. It corrupts things; it rots them away. In contrast to this, Christians should use words to build up other people.

It is hard to read these words without thinking of the apostle James's discussion of the tongue problem in his epistle. The point he makes there, which Paul would echo, is that speech is a powerful tool either for good or for evil. It is like a bit put into the mouth of a horse, he says. It can turn that large animal either one way or another. Or again, it is like a rudder on a ship or a fire. "Consider what a great forest is set on fire by a small spark. The tongue also is a fire, a world of evil among the parts of the body. It corrupts the whole person, sets the whole course of his life on fire, and is itself set on fire by hell" (James 3:5, 6). That is a powerful statement, but it is no exaggeration. Hitler's corrupting speech plunged the entire world into war and caused inestimable suffering and anguish. By contrast, the speech of Jesus Christ has done more to bless more people than any other single thing in all history.

We should learn what good and evil our speech can cause, and we should seek God's help in controlling our evil tongue. How? By allowing God to control our minds.

Frank E. Gaebelein wrote, "Tongue control? It will never be achieved unless there is first of all heart and mind control. . . . When any Christian comes to the point of yielding to the Lord—in full sincerity, cost what it may—control of his thought life, the problem of managing his tongue will be solved, provided that such a surrender goes deeper than the intellect and reaches the emotions and will. For the Bible makes a distinction between mere intellectual knowledge of God and the trust of the heart."[3]

Some commentators have asked why Paul speaks about grieving the Holy Spirit at this point: "And do not grieve the Holy Spirit of God, with whom you were sealed for the day of redemption" (v. 30). That statement might have been inserted anywhere. Why here? Again, it looks like an interruption. Why is it made at all? I think it occurs here because the Holy Spirit is chiefly the Spirit of revelation, first giving the Word of God in written form, in our Bibles, and then blessing the teaching of that Word by faithful persons for the building up of the church. The Holy Spirit blesses human words to edification. So it must grieve him particularly when the speech of Christians, rather than building up the church, as it should, is used to tear down others who are part of that body.

5. *Put off bitterness, rage, and malice and instead show love* (vv. 31–32). The last of Paul's five contrasts is a catchall. On the one hand, he speaks of "bitterness, rage and anger, brawling and slander, along with every form of malice"—six vices. On the other hand, he says, "Be kind and compassionate to one another, forgiving each other, just as in Christ God forgave you"—three virtues.

THREE COMPELLING REASONS

In his treatment of these verses John Stott makes one important observation with which I close: the way in which Paul brings in each person of the Trinity while laying down the Christian's moral obligations.

In the next verse Paul is going to say, "Be imitators of God" (Eph. 5:1). So the first motivation for obeying these instructions is that they are expressions of the character of God. We are to be like this because God is like this. As an introduction to this section Paul has encouraged us "to know Christ" and to grow "in accordance with the truth that is in Jesus" (Eph. 4:20–21). This is a second motivation—on the basis of what we know—and it is reinforced by the fact that Jesus has modeled the Christian graces for us. Third, he has spoken of the Holy Spirit, whose task is to mold us into the image of Jesus Christ and who is grieved if that is not happening. It is as if Paul is saying, "Act like Christians, *for God's sake*. And by God's power as well."

---

[3] Frank E. Gaebelein, *The Practical Epistle of James: Studies in Applied Christianity* (Great Neck, N.Y.: Channel Press, 1955), 80–81.

28

On the Imitation of God

(Ephesians 5:1–2)

Be imitators of God, therefore, as dearly loved children and live a life of love, just as Christ loved us and gave himself up for us as a fragrant offering and sacrifice to God.

The fifth chapter of Ephesians begins with one of the most startling admonitions in the New Testament: "Be imitators of God." It is the only place in the Bible where these words occur, and what makes them so startling is that they point to a standard beyond which there is no other. William Barclay calls this "the highest standard in the world."[1] Alexander Maclaren calls it "the sum of all duty."[2] To Martyn Lloyd-Jones it was "Paul's supreme argument . . . the highest level of all in doctrine and in practice . . . the ultimate ideal."[3]

"Be imitators of God" reminds us of Thomas à Kempis' classic, *Of the Imitation of Christ*. Thomas was born in 1380 at a time when Europe was in turmoil. The church was split by rival popes, one of whom still sat on the throne of St. Peter in Rome while the other exercised a rival rule in Avignon. The Hundred Years War was in progress. The Black Death had ravished city after city. Thomas grew up in the midst of corruption, unrest and disillusion, entered a monastery and, presumably in the 1420s, wrote what has since been called "the most influential book in Christian literature." To be honest, *Of the Imitation of Christ* has never moved me as other books have, but it has been influential, and for more than five hundred years Christians have apparently found no difficulty with the concept of imitating the Jesus of history.

But the imitation of *God the Father* is quite another matter—or at least it seems so. How is it possible to imitate One who is infinitely above us, the sovereign God of the universe?

INCOMMUNICABLE ATTRIBUTES

Part of our problem comes from the nature of God and from what theologians call his noncommunicable attributes. In theological textbooks a distinction is made between God's communicable attributes, in which we share, and God's noncommunicable attributes, in which we do not share. For example, when we talk about God we often begin with the fact that he is self-existent, self-sufficient, and eternal.

Self-existent means that God has no

[1] William Barclay, *The Letters to the Galatians and Ephesians* (Edinburgh: Saint Andrews Press, 1970), 190.

[2] Alexander Maclaren, *Expositions of Holy Scripture*, vol. 10, *2 Timothy, Titus, Philemon, Hebrews, James, Ephesians* (Grand Rapids: Eerdmans, 1959), pt. 2, 270.

[3] D. Martyn Lloyd-Jones, *Darkness and Light: An Exposition of Ephesians 4:17–5:17* (Grand Rapids: Baker, 1982), 291.

origins and consequently is answerable to no one. This sets God utterly apart, for everything else does have origins and is accountable. Human beings are accountable to people (parents and friends), organizations (the church, the state, the company for which one works), and ultimately God. Everyone will face a final judgment.

Self-sufficient means that God has no needs and therefore depends on no one. That is not at all true of us. We need countless things—food, warmth, clothing, homes, companionship, oxygen. If our supply of oxygen is cut off even for a few minutes, we die.

Eternal means that God has always existed and will always exist. That is not true of us either. We have a point before which we did not exist. Moreover, we change as time passes. God does not change. He is always the same in his eternal being.

To these initial attributes, without which God would not be God, we can add such things as omnipotence, omnipresence, omniscience, majesty, and holiness in its fullest sense. We cannot be like God in these characteristics.

Omnipotent means all-powerful. We are not nor will we ever be all-powerful. If we could be, we would be God.

Omnipresent means being everywhere at once. We will never possess this ability. We are finite creatures and will always be finite.

Omniscient means knowing all things. We will never know all things. We will spend all eternity learning.

Majesty and *holiness* also set God off from his creation. They are what make him "wholly other." We are not that. Each of these incommunicable attributes sets God apart from us and delineates an area in which we cannot and never will be like him.

But we are also overwhelmed by God's communicable attributes, that is, those attributes in which we share. They are things like justice, wrath, wisdom, faithfulness, goodness, love, mercy, compassion, tenderness, forgiveness. We can exercise these attributes and indeed we ought to. But when we think of them in reference to God the Father, who is perfect in them, we are necessarily overawed and wonder properly if there is any point in comparing our wisdom to God's wisdom, our goodness to God's goodness, our faithfulness to God's faithfulness, and so on.

That is a healthy comparison, which should humble us, if nothing else. But it is nevertheless true that in our text Paul says that we are to imitate God. We are to imitate God "as dearly loved children." In other words, just as a son should imitate a good father (though he is not a father and cannot imitate his father in many respects) and just as a daughter should imitate a good mother (though she is not a mother and cannot imitate her mother in many respects), so should the children of God imitate God. And they have this going for them: they have the enabling life of God within through the indwelling Holy Spirit. Consequently, just as physical genes should lead a child in the direction of a parent's chief characteristics, so should a Christian's spiritual genes lead in the direction of the moral character of God.

Forgiving Love

When we look at the passage in which the command to imitate God occurs we see at once that it is not just any attribute of God that Paul has in mind for our imitating, though it would be possible to imitate God in more ways than the one he mentions. What Paul chiefly has in mind is the imitation of God's love. Indeed, this is what ties Ephesians 5:1 to the end of chapter 4 and links it also to the following verse. (Ephesians 5:1–2 are part of the preceding paragraph.)

The entire text says, "Be kind and

compassionate to one another, forgiving each other, just as in Christ God forgave you. Be imitators of God, therefore, as dearly loved children and live a life of love, just as Christ loved us and gave himself up for us as a fragrant offering and sacrifice to God." It is in loving that we are to imitate the Creator.

What kind of a love is this? The passage answers this question in several ways, and the first answer is that this love is to be forgiving. Since God the Father forgave us through the work of Christ, we are to forgive one another. This is love's nature.

This link between God's forgiveness of us and our forgiveness of others is important, because it is only through knowing ourselves to be forgiven that we are set free to forgive others lovingly. People are in desperate need of forgiveness. Some years ago I was talking with a friend who is a psychiatrist, and he said, "As far as I am concerned, most of what a psychiatrist does is directly related to forgiveness. People come to him with problems; they feel guilty about their part in them; they are seeking forgiveness. In effect, they confess their sins to the counselor and find that he forgives them. Then a pattern is set up in which they can show their change of heart in tangible ways toward others."

In his book on confession John R. W. Stott quotes the head of a large mental hospital in England as having said, "I could dismiss half my patients tomorrow if they could be assured of forgiveness."[4]

That is what we have in Jesus Christ—forgiveness—and because we find forgiveness there, we can in turn be forgiving. God's forgiveness is not a mere overlooking of sin, as though he said, "Well, boys will be boys (or girls will be girls). We'll overlook it for now;

just don't let it happen again." God takes sin with such seriousness that he deals with it fully at the cross, and it is on that basis—the death of Jesus—that we can know we are forgiven.

Do you know that, really know it? So long as you think you are a pretty good person who does not really need to be forgiven, you will naturally have a very hard time loving and forgiving others. But if you know yourself to have been a sinner under God's just wrath, all that is changed. God says that in his sight even the best of us is vile to the extreme:

It is written,

"There is no one righteous, not
    even one;
  there is no one who understands,
  no one who seeks God.
All have turned away,
  they have together become
    worthless;
there is no one who does good,
  not even one."
"Their throats are open graves;
  their tongues practice deceit."
"The poison of vipers is on their
    lips."
"Their mouths are full of cursing
    and bitterness."
"Their feet are swift to shed blood;
  ruin and misery mark their ways,
and the way of peace they do not
    know."
"There is no fear of God before
    their eyes" (Rom. 3:10–18).

That is the way God sees us. If we see ourselves through his eyes, knowing our vile rebellion against his love and moral standards and yet finding ourselves forgiven on the basis of Christ's death for us, then we will inevitably love and forgive others. For nobody can act as badly toward us as we have acted toward God, and yet he has forgiven us.

If we are not forgiving in our love, we really do not know the extent of God's

[4]John R. W. Stott, *Confess Your Sins* (Philadelphia: Westminster Press, 1964), 73.

forgiveness of us. We still consider ourselves to be better than we are. But if we see ourselves as forgiven sinners, then we will be set free to love others in imitation of God.

GIVING LOVE

The second thing these verses teach about the love of God, which we are to imitate, is that it is a *giving* love—not merely forgiving but also giving. Again, God is the model of such love, and the point at which it is most clearly demonstrated is the cross.

What is it that God chiefly gives us? He has given us all things, of course. Before Adam and Eve were even created God had prepared a wonderful environment to receive them. It was a place of beauty and interest, with meaningful work to do. Sin marred that environment, as we know. But even marred by sin, our experience of God's gifts to us is not entirely unlike the experience of our first parents. God has given us life itself, and he has placed us within an imperfect but nevertheless beautiful and fascinating world. And the work we have to do in it is important. Having said this, however, we have to admit at once that it does not even come close to an expression of the full measure of God's giving love. For that, like God's forgiving love, is seen primarily at the cross:

> For God so loved the world that he gave his one and only Son, that whoever believes in him shall not perish but have eternal life (John 3:16).

> This is love: not that we loved God, but that he loved us and sent his Son as an atoning sacrifice for our sins (1 John 4:10).

> God demonstrates his own love for us in this: While we were still sinners, Christ died for us (Rom. 5:8).

> I have been crucified with Christ and I no longer live, but Christ lives in me. The life I live in the body, I live by faith in the Son of God, who loved me and gave himself for me (Gal. 2:20).

> Greater love has no one than this, that he lay down his life for his friends (John 15:13).

I am particularly interested in Philippians 2:5–8, for those verses tell us that even Jesus did not merely give up *things* to save us; he gave *himself*. He did not give up things which were outward accompaniments of his divinity: his outward glory, the service of the angels, his position at the right hand of God the Father: "Who, being in very nature God, did not consider equality with God something to be grasped, but made himself nothing, taking the very nature of a servant, being made in human likeness."

The heart of the passage is that Jesus gave himself, to the point of even death: "And being found in appearance as a man, he humbled himself and became obedient to death—even death on a cross." The greatest expression of love is not that it gives things or even that it gives up things, but that it gives itself.

In this too we are to be God's imitators. Years ago, Donald Grey Barnhouse was counseling a couple who were having marital difficulties. The husband spoke in frustration at one point, saying, "But I don't understand it. I have given you anything a woman could want. I've given you a nice house. I've given you a car. I've given you all the clothes you can wear. I've given you . . . " The list went on.

At last the man ended and his wife replied sadly, "Yes, John. That much is true. You have given me everything . . . but yourself."

Why don't we give ourselves to other people? It is because we are afraid to, and because we are selfish. We want ourselves for ourselves, and we are afraid that if we give ourselves to others, we will be hurt or disappointed.

Only those who have God are set free from these fears and can give to others out of God's own immensity.

LIVING LOVE

The third thing our text teaches about the love of God which we are to imitate is that it is to be a *living* love: forgiving, giving, but also living. It occurs in verse 2, where Paul says, "and live a life of love, just as Christ loved us and gave himself up for us as a fragrant offering and sacrifice to God."

There are two things that a living love suggests. First, it suggests a *practical* or *active* love. This is what Paul's whole section on practical Christianity involves. For if we ask, "What does it mean to 'live a life of love'?" the answer is in the very thing Paul has been saying. To use the outline of the last chapter, it means: (1) to put off lying and speak truthfully, (2) to put off anger, (3) to put off stealing and work for a living instead, (4) to put off unwholesome talk and instead speak to help others, and (5) to put off bitterness, rage and anger, brawling and slander, along with every form of malice, and instead to be kind, compassionate, and forgiving. That is what it means to live a life of love.

Second, living love suggests love that is made alive by the very life of God and is therefore an *eternal* love, as God is eternal. What a need we have for this today! Our loves are weak and faltering, variable and untrustworthy. What we need in our loves is something of the character of God's love as Paul writes about it in Romans:

Who shall separate us from the love of Christ? Shall trouble or hardship or persecution or famine or nakedness or danger or sword? As it is written: "For your sake we face death all day long; we are considered as sheep to be slaughtered." No, in all these things we are more than conquerors through him who loved us. For I am convinced that neither death nor life, neither angels nor demons, neither the present nor the future, nor any powers, neither height nor depth, nor anything else in all creation, will be able to separate us from the love of God that is in Christ Jesus our Lord (Rom. 8:35–39).

Can you be an imitator of God in such an eternal love as that? The answer, if we look only to ourselves, is no. No, we cannot. Nothing that is natural to us is eternal, or forgiving or giving either, for that matter. But the answer is yes, if we look to God. The very man who wrote Ephesians 4:1 said, "I can do everything through him who gives me strength" (Phil. 4:13).

But we must spend time with God if that is to happen. The word that our text translates "imitate" or "imitator" is *mimētai*, from which we get our English word "mimic." Mimic means to copy closely, to repeat another person's speech, actions, or behavior. That is what we are to do with God. We are to repeat his actions, echo his speech, duplicate his behavior. How can we do that if we do not spend time with him? We cannot, because we will not even know what his behavior is. Oh, Christian, spend time with God! Spend time with God in prayer. Spend time with God in Bible study. Spend time with God in worship. It is only by spending time with God that we become like God. We need men and women who are like God today.

29

Children of Light

(Ephesians 5:3–14)

But among you there must not be even a hint of sexual immorality, or of any kind of impurity, or of greed, because these are improper for God's holy people. Nor should there be obscenity, foolish talk or coarse joking, which are out of place, but rather thanksgiving. For of this you can be sure: No immoral, impure or greedy person—such a man is an idolater—has any inheritance in the kingdom of Christ and of God. Let no one deceive you with empty words, for because of such things God's wrath comes on those who are disobedient. Therefore do not be partners with them.

For you were once darkness, but now you are light in the Lord. Live as children of light (for the fruit of the light consists in all goodness, righteousness and truth) and find out what pleases the Lord. Have nothing to do with the fruitless deeds of darkness, but rather expose them. For it is shameful even to mention what the disobedient do in secret. But everything exposed by the light becomes visible, for it is light that makes everything visible. That is why it is said:

> *Wake up, O sleeper,*
> *rise from the dead,*
> *and Christ will shine on you.*

Not long ago I was in Washington, D.C., for meetings with Christians who work with America's top political leaders. One of them who works with our senators remarked on their disillusionment. The intentions of most are quite good, according to his assessment. But whether they stand on the political right with their conservative programs or on the left with their liberal programs, they are leaning to the view that neither one nor the other is able to solve our country's problems. "Not only don't we solve the problems," one senator said, "our legislation actually makes the problems worse."

The perceived difficulty is a flaw in human nature, which this spokesman described as "greed and lust." These are not Republican vices alone or Democratic vices. They are not vices of the Western bloc any more than they are vices of the Eastern bloc. They are present across the board in all purely human relationships.

John Kenneth Galbraith made the same cynical assessment. He said, "Under communism man exploits man. Under capitalism the situation is exactly the reverse."

In Christianity there really is a reverse, because in Christianity the man who once exploited others becomes a new man—and the woman becomes a new woman. This is what Paul is writing about in Ephesians. He is writing about God's work of making a spiritually alive Christian out of a spiritually dead pagan, and of combining such newly made people into a new society. According to Paul (and Christianity), the hope of the world is not new programs but new people. And new people become new only by the work of that one who alone is ultimately our hope, Jesus Christ. Before, we were people of the dark, just as those around us. Now through him who is the light of the world we have become children of light and so shine in the darkness.

How We Think and Act

The difference is regeneration—which Paul has been writing about in the earlier sections of the letter—and not mere morality, for teaching only a new or higher morality never changes anybody. Not everyone understands Christian morality, but all people know to do better than they actually do. The problem is not with the standard. The problem is ourselves.

Paul's prescription for a higher standard of living is actually quite profound, as a careful reading of Ephesians 4 and 5 shows. It involves three things: (1) what we are, (2) how we think, and (3) the way we act. Each is necessary.

Here is how John R. W. Stott puts it: "Their theme [the theme of these chapters] is the integration of Christian experience (what we are), Christian theology (what we believe) and Christian ethics (how we behave). They emphasize that being, thought and action belong together and must never be separated. For what we are governs how we think, and how we think determines how we act. We are God's new society, a people who have put off the old life and put on the new; that is what he has made us. So we need to recall this by the daily renewal of our

minds, remembering how we 'learned Christ . . . as the truth is in Jesus,' and thinking Christianly about ourselves and our new status. Then we must actively cultivate a Christian life."[1]

Stott points out that holiness is not a condition into which we drift but rather an active working out of what has already been worked into us. This new life is neither automatic nor easy, but it is the only hope for society.

No Hint of Wickedness

At the end of chapter 4 Paul introduced upright Christian living by a contrast between putting off one type of behavior and putting on another. The contrasts were striking and the standards high. In chapter 5 the contrast between the two ways of life is even more striking, and the standards are even higher. Here Paul speaks not merely of exchanging one pattern of behavior for another, something which we might assume would work out gradually, but rather of things that are not even to be hinted at among believers. They are "improper" and "out of place," he says. Indeed, if they are present, they are evidence that the person involved is not even a believer but an "idolater."

Paul mentions six of these intolerable vices in verses 3–7.

1. Sexual immorality. The Greek word translated "sexual immorality" is *porneia*, from which we get our word "pornography." But it does not refer to lewd pictures or films; it refers to sexual intercourse outside marriage. In older versions of the Bible *porneia* was translated "fornication." It would be wrong to suggest that sexual sins are the greatest of all sins, for sins of the flesh are never so great, destructive, or demonic as sins of the spirit. Still Paul is right to place this vice in first position if

---

[1]John R. W. Stott, *God's New Society: The Message of Ephesians* (Downers Grove, Ill.: InterVarsity, 1979), 193.

only because it is so harmful to the individual and society. The positive answer to this view, Christian marriage, is going to be discussed later in the chapter.

2. *Impurity.* This word includes the sexual sins first named, but it probably also goes beyond it to embrace particularly defiling practices. The Greeks, among whom the Ephesians lived, openly approved of such practices as prostitution and homosexuality. In fact, in Athens a great temple to Aphrodite, the goddess of love, was built with the profits from the brothels, which were established in the city with this objective. To the Greeks this was not the least bit strange. Nor was it strange to combine what was regarded as a high moral standard in other areas with homosexuality. Paul says that what was perfectly acceptable in the surrounding society was not even to be hinted at among Christians.

3. *Greed.* If lust and greed are the two great vices of our time, as my friend in Washington suggested, then here is the other one: that intense, acquisitive human desire to have more. D. Martyn Lloyd-Jones says, "This means, of course, avarice, love of money, love of money as money; love of money partly for itself and partly because of what it can do for us, the things we can buy with money, the things we can procure with money, the things we can do if we have money—in fact, the love of all that money can do and achieve—that is what Paul is condemning under the word covetousness."[2]

Jesus was thinking of covetousness when he said, "You cannot serve both God and Money" (Matt. 6:24). It is why Paul says that the immoral, impure, or greedy person "is an idolater" (v. 5).

4. *Obscenity.* Obscenity is a bridge word in this list, referring both to indecent or improper actions, which the earlier terms describe, and to indecent or offensive speech, which comes next. An obscene person is one who has no regard for standards. Nothing commands his respect. Therefore, his actions are consistently disrespectful.

5. *Foolish talk.* This Greek word is easy to remember, for it is made up of the words "moron" and *logos* which means "word": *mōrologia*. It means one who talks like a fool. The concern here is not with intelligence. It is with morals. The word refers to one who makes light of high standards of behavior, thinking that it is somehow funny or sophisticated to tear down anything that is high or praiseworthy or ennobling. It is what television does. Television pretends to be funny, but it is destructive of those values that hold a society together and suppress its worst elements.

6. *Coarse joking.* The last of these terms is closely related to obscenity and foolish talk, but with the emphasis on that kind of coarse, vulgar humor which is the lowest form of wit. As Stott says, "All three refer to a dirty mind expressing itself in dirty conversation."[3]

THANKSGIVING

What is the positive side of this? What are Christians to be or do by contrast? There are several ways of answering this question, and one is by the list of corresponding positive virtues that Paul provides in verse 9 (within the parenthesis in the NIV translation): goodness, righteousness, and truth. These correspond somewhat to sexual immorality and impurity, greed, obscenity, foolish talk, and coarse joking. Each of the positive characteristics flows from the character

---

[2] D. Martyn Lloyd-Jones, *Darkness and Light: An Exposition of Ephesians 4:17–5:17* (Grand Rapids: Baker, 1982), 330.
[3] Ibid., 192.

of Jesus Christ who lives in his people by virtue of the new birth.

But there is another way of speaking of proper Christian behavior in these areas, and that comes from the contrast Paul makes when he says that instead of obscenity, foolish talk, or coarse joking, which are out of place among Christians, there should be "rather thanksgiving." Thanksgiving for what? Well, for all good things, of course. For life, for health, for God himself, for what he has made of us through the work of Christ. . . . All things!

Yet in this context I wonder if John Stott is not right when he suggests that what Paul chiefly has in mind are the things the vices distort and destroy, but which when properly used are great forces for good in society.

The first of these blessings is *sex* of which both immorality and impurity are the distortion. Christians have a bad reputation where sex is concerned because they are thought to be against it. That is understandable from the Christian point of view, for sex has been so vulgarized by pagan society (especially our own) that much of what Christians say on the subject has necessarily been negative. But sex is not something for Christians to deplore, condemning it as evil. It is only the distortions we deplore. On the contrary, sex has been given by God, is itself good, and is therefore something for which we should be thankful, as Paul indicates.

Not long ago I read a marvelous book on marriage by a young Canadian named Mike Mason. It captures something of this wondering thankfulness for sex in Christian marriage: "What can equal the surprise of finding out that the one thing above all others which mankind has been most enterprising and proficient in dragging through the dirt turns out in fact to be the most innocent thing in the world? Is

there any other activity at all which an adult man and woman may engage in together (apart from worship) that is actually more childlike, more clean and pure, more natural and wholesome and unequivocally right than is the act of making love? For if worship is the deepest available form of communion with God (and especially that particular act of worship known as Communion), then surely sex is the deepest communion that is possible between human beings, and as such is something absolutely essential (in more than a biological way) to our survival."[4]

This is what I mean by being thankful. Thankfulness recognizes sex as God's gift and for that very reason seeks to use it to please and honor him.

The second blessing for which we can be thankful is our share of the world's *material possessions*. When distorted such thankfulness turns into greed. Thankfulness means being content with what we have and therefore being free to use our possessions for others. Greed means always wanting to have more.

Someone once asked John D. Rockefeller, then one of the richest men alive, "How much money is enough?" The multimillionaire replied, "Just a little bit more."

If we look at history (or even just around at our contemporaries), we see a constant struggle for increasing mounds of possessions. That is wrong. We must reject it.

But there is another distortion too. "Greed is bad; therefore, things are bad," some Christians (and even non-Christians) argue. So they repudiate things by self-inflicted poverty, a communal lifestyle, holy orders, or just simple living. In anyone case this may be quite proper, even mandatory. Some people who are addicted to things must avoid possessions just as an alcoholic

---

[4]Mike Mason, *The Mystery of Marriage: As Iron Sharpens Iron* (Portland, Oreg.: Multnomah, 1985), 121.

must avoid alcohol. Again, a person may choose to live simply, for the sake of being better able to witness to the poor or to have more to give others.

But neither greed nor abstention is the Christian way. The Christian way is to receive what God gives and to be thankful for it; and if he gives more, to recognize that the increase means an increase of responsibility in how one uses the possessions. The more we have, the larger the percentage we should give to others. Unfortunately, in our covetous society most Christians live just like the world in this area, which is why God probably does not give them more than they already have.

The third blessing is *truth* and the ability to express it by words. It is the ability of words to do this—particularly to communicate truth about God, ourselves, and salvation—that makes the cheapening of words through foolish talk and coarse joking so reprehensible. Again, a buoyant spirit or bright humor is not bad. The God who made monkeys is not humorless. The problem lies rather in our making light of what is eternally important and of using jokes to avoid the commands and warnings of God. I thank God for truth and for the words by which the truth of God may be conveyed to people through preaching.

Enlightened and Enlightening

The bottom line of this discussion is that Christians are to be God's light in the midst of this world's darkness. They are to be an enlightening element, and this is to be so precisely because they have first been enlightened. Paul says in verse 8, "For you were once darkness, but now you are light in the Lord."

The most important thing about this statement is that Paul does not say merely that before their conversion Christians were *in* darkness and that now, since their conversion, they are *in*

the light, though that is true. He says something more profound: before they *were* darkness, now they *are* light. He is pointing to a change in *them*, not merely to a change in their surroundings. Before they were not only in darkness, darkness was in them. And now they not only are *in* light, they *are* light and therefore must shine out as lights to their benighted society. That makes all the difference. If it is only a question of seeking the light or living in the light, then Christianity is no different from any other religion or philosophy, and there is no more hope from it than from any of them. But if becoming a Christian involves a change from darkness to light, then the presence of Christians in the world is itself hope as together we stand against the darkness.

I close with this story. Some years ago the National Religious Broadcasters held their large annual convention in Washington, D.C., and the president of the United States spoke. He said what the broadcasters wanted to hear and closed with a quotation of John 3:16. The conventioneers became ecstatic. They leaped to their feet and applauded until long after the President had left the platform. It seemed as though revival had broken out in the capital. The next speaker was Charles Colson, whose experiences had taught him both the limitations and seductions of political life. He said that he was glad to have heard the President's speech and believed the Bible quotation. "But," he added, "we must remember that the kingdom of God is not going to arrive on Air Force One."

That is profoundly true. In the ultimate sense the kingdom of God is going to arrive only when Jesus Christ sets up his kingdom. But until that time it will arrive only to the extent Christian people—not the highly visible people of the political arena but quite normal and far less visible people like you and me—begin to live like Jesus Christ.

30

Making the Most of Time

(Ephesians 5:15–20)

Be very careful,. then, how you live—not as unwise but as wise, making the most of every opportunity, because the days are evil. Therefore do not be foolish, but understand what the Lord's will is. Do not get drunk on wine, which leads to debauchery. Instead, be filled with the Spirit. Speak to one another with psalms, hymns and spiritual songs. Sing and make music in your heart to the Lord, always giving thanks to God the Father for everything, in the name of our Lord Jesus Christ.

Years ago when I was nearer to the beginning of my ministry than I am now, I spent most of my time trying to amass the facts and acquire the necessary skills for an effective ministry. I suppose that is true of anyone who is entering a new field of work. But as the years went by and I had acquired the necessary facts and skills, I found myself looking for something else: wisdom. I had the facts, but I was concerned how to use them. I had acquired the skills, but I wanted wisdom to apply them rightly. Today, when I pray, I pray for wisdom far more than any other element.

That is a biblical emphasis. Much of the Bible assumes large measures of Christian knowledge and experience but in addition calls for the pursuit of wisdom by those who serve God. The first third of the book of Proverbs pictures Wisdom standing in the streets, crying out for the wise and godly man to pursue her. "The fear of the LORD is the beginning of wisdom, and knowledge of the Holy One is understanding," she declares (Prov. 9:10). In the New Testament Paul de-

plores the so-called wisdom of the Greeks, which is actually foolishness. Instead, he says, "We preach Christ crucified: a stumbling block to Jews and foolishness to Gentiles, but to those whom God has called, both Jews and Greeks, Christ the power of God and the wisdom of God. For the foolishness of God is wiser than man's wisdom, and the weakness of God is stronger than man's strength" (1 Cor. 1:23–25).

There are two parts to this wisdom: (1) its content, centered in the knowledge of God through Jesus Christ, and (2) the application of that content practically. It is this second aspect of wisdom that I have been praying for and that specifically concerns the apostle Paul in this next section of Ephesians.

REDEEMING THE TIME

There are three areas in which Paul thinks of the Christian exercising wisdom, and the first of these is his use of time. "Be very careful, then, how you live—not as unwise but as wise, making the most of every opportunity, because the days are evil" (vv. 15, 16).

In my opinion, most Christians do

161

not consider time as important as it really is. It is one of the two things we have going for us in our calling to serve God: space and time. I call these the warp and woof of history, for they fix us at a particular point in God's vast plan of salvation. Space fixes us as to location. We are in Philadelphia, rather than in New York or Los Angeles or London, to give just one example. What we are going to do for God we must do here. But again, we are not in Philadelphia in the eighteenth century, when the country was just coming into its own and so many of the Christian institutions we know today were getting started, or in the nineteenth century, with its great missionary movements. We are living in the last fifteen years of the twentieth century, and our problems and opportunities are unique. The wise man is the one who recognizes this and applies himself accordingly.

It is almost impossible to overemphasize the importance of time in biblical religion, because the religion of the Bible is a historical religion and history means time. This more than anything else sets Judaism and Christianity off from the religions among which they flourished. In the Old Testament period virtually all the surrounding religions were nature religions. They identified the most high god with some aspect of nature—the sun, moon, wind, rain, or seasons—and in many cases with means or processes of reproduction. The flow of these religions was cyclical—from one new moon or harvest to the next—and history had no real meaning.

In the Greek world there was either a resurgence of these religions, borrowed from the East, a mythologizing of human experience in the cult of the gods, or philosophy. But again, time meant little, and history went nowhere. In contrast, the Old and New Testaments are rooted in history. When God called

Abraham, He made him a promise in history that would also be fulfilled in history. He said, "Leave your country, your people and your father's household and go to the land I will show you. I will make you into a great nation and I will bless you; I will make your name great, and you will be a blessing. I will bless those who bless you, and whoever curses you I will curse; and all peoples on earth will be blessed through you" (Gen. 12:1–3).

In the Old Testament there were many partial fulfillments of this promise, including the Exodus and the eventual invasion and conquest of the land. But the chief fulfillment was in the appearance and work of Jesus Christ. His incarnation was the decisive intervention of God in history, and his time was that which gives all other times their meaning. Paul wrote of the importance of this moment, saying, "But when the time had fully come, God sent his Son, born of a woman, born under law, to redeem those under law, that we might receive the full rights of sons" (Gal. 4:4–5). Nor is this all. Christians also look forward to a culmination of history in the return of Christ when all historical actions will be judged.

Another way of looking at the importance of time when seen from God's perspective is by studying the biblical words for it. There are many of them: *hēmera* ("day"), *hōra* ("hour"), *kairos* ("season"), *chronos* ("time"), *aiōn* ("age") and others, all with unique associations. Of them all the most important is the word *kairos*, the word used in our text in Ephesians.

The significance of this word is best seen by contrasting it with *chronos*. Both *kairos* and *chronos* refer to time and are frequently translated as "time" in our Bibles. But *chronos* refers only to the flow of time, the following of one event upon another; it is the idea involved in our word "chronology." *Kairos* refers to a moment that is especially significant or favorable. It is used this way secularly, as in King Felix's response to Paul's teaching, "When I find it *convenient*, I will send for you" (Acts 24:25). It is used this way chiefly of the coming of Christ. Peter wrote of the prophets searching intently and with greatest care "to find out the *time* and circumstances to which the Spirit of Christ in them was pointing when he predicted the sufferings of Christ and the glories that would follow" (1 Peter 1:11). Jesus used the same word when he said, "My *appointed time* is near" (Matt. 26:18).

What this means is that time is to have this full or meaningful element for the wise Christian. Moreover, he is to redeem it or make the most of it precisely for that reason. Left to themselves "the days are evil." But they can be redeemed from evil for good by Christian people.

A few years after the end of World War II an English historian named Herbert Butterfield wrote a book in which he tried to set the past in perspective and rally Christians to significant ethical behavior. He focused on the biblical perceptions about time: "It has always been realized in the main tradition of Christianity that if the Word was made flesh, matter can never be regarded as evil in itself. In a similar way, if one moment of time could hold so much as this, then you cannot brush time away and say that any moment of it is mere vanity. Every instant of time becomes more momentous than ever—every instant is 'eschatological,' or as one person has put it, like the point in the fairy tale where the clock is just about to strike twelve.

"On this view there can be no case of an absentee God leaving mankind at the mercy of chance in a universe blind, stark and bleak. And a real drama—not a madman's nightmare or a tissue of flimsy dreams—is being enacted on the stage of human history. A real conflict between good and evil is taking place, events do matter, and something is being achieved irrespective of our apparent success or failure."[1]

Making the most of time is to enter into this conflict and make a contribution for good.

WHAT THE LORD'S WILL IS

This leads directly to the second area in which Paul thinks of the Christian exercising true wisdom: in understanding what the will of the Lord is. Usually, when we talk about knowing God's will, we stress knowing Scripture, for God's character and precepts are disclosed there as they are disclosed nowhere else. If we want to know what God's will is, we do not need some special mystical experience or revelation. We can find it by studying the Bible, allowing the Holy Spirit to illuminate it to our understanding and apply it to our heart and circumstances. That is basic, and Paul is probably assuming that in what he says here.

But in this passage I believe Paul is interested in more than knowing God's will as revealed in Scripture. He is concerned with wisdom, which is more than the acquisition of mere facts. He is concerned with our perception of what God is doing in history and with our wise response to it.

If it were only a matter of knowing what God says specifically in Scripture, then the proper exhortation would be to study Scripture. "Learn what God says and live by it," Paul might say. But that is not the way this passage is going. Paul is talking about wisdom and about making the most of that

[1] Herbert Butterfield, *Christianity and History* (New York: Scribner's, 1950), 121. My discussion of time and history is developed in a fuller way in the first three chapters of James Montgomery Boice, *God and History* (Downers Grove, Ill.: InterVarsity, 1981), 15–56, from which some of the material in this chapter has been taken.

specific historical time God gives to us. It is as if he is asking: "What are we to do with our moments? How are we best to spend this day, this hour, this minute? What does God want us to be doing?" Against this background, Paul seems to be encouraging us to perceive what God is doing now and act in accordance with it.

I have a friend who sits on many Christian boards, and he has become somewhat skeptical of movements that promise to do something or other for God. When he speaks of wisdom he says that in his judgment, "Wisdom consists in perceiving where God is going and then jumping on his bandwagon."

I think this is what Paul is saying. The fool, with whom he contrasts the man of understanding, is being led astray into one "promising" program after another and so dissipates both time and energy. The wise man weighs these programs and strives to set a course through them in the direction he perceives God to be leading. This wisdom is particularly necessary for the leadership of churches in our day. The programs available to church leaders for growth, renewal, evangelism, media exposure, fund-raising, and such things are multiple, and not every program can be used. Which should be chosen? Which should be rejected? It takes wisdom to perceive God's direction for a particular church and follow it without deviation.

FILLED WITH THE SPIRIT

The third area in which Paul encourages the wise Christian to excel is in being filled with the Spirit, which he contrasts with getting drunk on wine. There is so much misunderstanding about the Spirit-filled life today that it is necessary to begin with a few definitions.

First, being filled with the Spirit is not the same thing as being "baptized" by the Spirit. Some, having confused the two, have taught the need for a second work of grace, usually accompanied by the gift of speaking in tongues, if a person is to grow or get on in the Christian life. Actually, the baptism of the Spirit refers to the work of the Spirit in regenerating us and uniting us to Christ, which is how we become Christians in the first place. It is rightly called "baptism," because baptism is the sacrament marking the beginning of the Christian life. It is something that happens to every Christian and does not need to be urged upon him.

Being "filled" with the Spirit *is* something that is urged upon Christians, which is what Paul does here. But it does not concern any special miraculous gifts such as speaking in tongues. Rather, it refers to our being so under the Holy Spirit's control and leading that our thought and life are entirely taken up with Jesus Christ, to whom it is the Spirit's chief responsibility to bear witness. In Acts there are ten occasions, at Pentecost and afterward, when an individual or group of individuals is said to have been filled with the Holy Spirit. In each case the common factor is that the persons involved immediately bore testimony to Jesus.[2]

Paul says that the wise man should desire to be so filled with God's Spirit that he might bear a faithful and effective testimony to Jesus Christ. Quite

---

[2]The incidents are (1) the company waiting in the upper room on the day of Pentecost (2:4); (2) Peter before he spoke to the Sanhedrin (4:8); (3) a group of early Christians (4:31); (4) the first deacons (6:3); (5) Stephen (6:5); (6) a second reference to Stephen (7:55); (7) Paul (9:17); (8) a second reference to Paul (13:9); (9) Barnabas (11:24); and (10) the disciples at Antioch (13:52). The one apparent exception is the case of the first deacons, but even this is not actually an exception in that we are not told of a filling of them by the Spirit but only that they gave evidence of having been filled. This may have been known by the fact that they had already been active as witnesses.

obviously, this will be a testimony conveyed by the upright character of his or her life, which is what Paul has been talking about all along. Also, quite obviously, it will be a testimony conveyed by the content and character of his or her speech, which is what the next two verses deal with.

There are three specific things that this verbal side of being filled with the Spirit concerns:

1. *Worship*. Paul has this in mind when he says, "Speak to one another with psalms, hymns and spiritual songs" (v. 19). Actually, it is hard to say precisely what this refers to. On one hand, Paul writes about "speak[ing] to one another," as opposed to singing and making music, which appear in the next sentence. This led John Stott to call what is involved here fellowship. On the other hand, the sentence does speak of "psalms, hymns and spiritual songs" which sounds like worship. Probably the right view is a combination of the two. It is fellowship, but not that of the coffee hour. It is that deeper, closer communion Christians have when they worship God together.

2. *Praise*. When Paul says "Sing and make music in your heart to the Lord" (v. 19), he is writing of music. But since this is "to the Lord," it is clearly the music Christians use to bless God. Paul is probably contrasting the edifying joyous worship of the Christian community, which has praise of God as its aim, with the destructive, noisy revelries of the pagan world, when people are drinking.

3. *Thanksgiving*. Paul had already mentioned thanksgiving once in this section, contrasting it with the six vices of sexual immorality, impurity, greed, obscenity, foolish talk, and coarse joking (vv. 3–4). Now he returns to it again as a proper outworking of the Holy Spirit in the child of God. Spirit-filled believers give "thanks to God the Father for everything, in the name of our Lord Jesus Christ" (v. 20). Shakespeare wrote in *King Lear*, "How sharper than a serpent's tooth it is to have a thankless child!" True! Ingratitude in children wounds and sometimes kills. But how much more unnatural and repugnant is ingratitude in those who have become sons and daughters of the living God. It is so unnatural that a person may wonder if such a one has actually become a Christian in the first place.

Now Is the Time

Earlier I listed a number of biblical words for time and contrasted *kairos*, which deals with the significant moment or opportunity, and *chronos*, which deals only with time's duration. There is another biblical word which I did not mention then but which I turn to now as an appropriate closing: the word *nun*. It means "now," and it occurs in verses which show that the *kairos* in which we live, the pregnant present moment, is eternally significant. "Once you were not a people, but *now* you are the people of God; once you had not received mercy, but *now* you have received mercy" (1 Peter 2:10). "Blessed are you who hunger *now*, for you will be satisfied. Blessed are you who weep *now*, for you will laugh" (Luke 6:21). "*Now* is the time of God's favor, *now* is the day of salvation" (2 Cor. 6:2).

If you and I are going to redeem time, as wise men and women, we had better do it now, because there may be no opportunity tomorrow. If we are to understand the will of God, now is the moment that counts. If we are going to be filled with God's Spirit, now is when we need filling.

Be wise, as Jonathan Edwards was when he wrote in his diary at age twenty: "Resolved, never to lose one moment of time, but to improve it in the most profitable way I possibly can."

31

The First Great Christian Institution

(Ephesians 5:21–33)

Submit to one another out of reverence for Christ.
Wives, submit to your husbands as to the Lord. For the husband is the head of the wife as Christ is the head of the church, his body, of which he is the Savior. Now as the church submits to Christ, so also wives should submit to their husbands in everything.

Husbands, love your wives, just as Christ loved the church and gave himself up for her to make her holy, cleansing her by the washing with water through the word, and to present her to himself as a radiant church, without stain or wrinkle or any other blemish, but holy and blameless. In this same way, husbands ought to love their wives as their own bodies. He who loves his wife loves himself. After all, no one ever hated his own body, but he feeds and cares for it, just as Christ does the church—for we are members of his body. "For this reason a man will leave his father and mother and be united to his wife, and the two will become one flesh." This is a profound mystery—but I am talking about Christ and the church. However, each one of you also must love his wife as he loves himself, and the wife must respect her husband.

The second half of Ephesians (chs. 4–6) deals with the Christian life, which is the pattern Paul follows in most of his epistles: first doctrine, then application. The second half of the second half of Ephesians deals with relationships, which is a way of showing that applied Christianity is never merely a matter of the individual and God but that it always also involves other persons.

I am sure this is why D. Martyn Lloyd-Jones, in his exposition of Ephesians, began a new book of sermons at Ephesians 5:18. He has eight volumes in his series,[1] and the volume that begins at this point is *Life in the Spirit*. It shows that in the writer's opinion the "Spirit-filled" life is not to be measured merely by one's private morality or even by one's private spiritual experience but by how one conducts himself or herself with other persons. In this epistle the apostle highlights three sets of relationships: that of wives to husbands and husbands to wives, that of children to parents and parents to children, and that of slaves (servants, employees) to masters.

THE BASIC INSTITUTION

In this selective but basic list of relationships, the first set and the one dealt with at greatest length concerns marriage.

[1] *God's Ultimate Purpose* (Eph. 1), *God's Way of Reconciliation* (Eph. 2), *The Unsearchable Riches of Christ* (Eph. 3), *Christian Unity* (Eph. 4:1–16), *Darkness and Light* (Eph. 4:17–5:17), *Life in the Spirit* (Eph. 5:18–6:9), *The Christian Warfare* (Eph. 6:10–13) and *The Christian Soldier* (Eph. 6:10–20), all now published by Baker Book House (Grand Rapids).

166

In his excellent book on Christian marriage Dr. Ed Wheat calls marriage "the most valuable institution on earth."[2] It is also the first and foundational institution, which means that all other institutions are in one way or another built upon it.

Marriage is the first human institution because, as the Bible shows, it was the first relationship between human beings that God created. In the first chapter of Genesis we are shown how God created all things and how, after he had created them, he pronounced a blessing upon each, saying, "It is good." It was only after he had created man (but before he had created woman) that God looked at his creation and found fault with it. God said, "It is *not* good for the man to be alone" (Gen. 2:18). As a result of this negative evaluation and as an answer to the man's aloneness, God created the first woman and brought her to the man, thus performing the first marriage ceremony (cf. v. 22).

God said, "Be fruitful and increase in number; fill the earth and subdue it" (Gen. 1:28).

The Lord Jesus Christ said, "At the beginning the Creator 'made them male and female.' . . . Therefore what God has joined together, let man not separate" (Matt. 19:4, 6).

Moreover, marriage is the institution from which all other institutions come, as I indicated. The earliest education was done in the home, as mothers and fathers instructed their children to eat, walk, speak, work, and do many other things. From this basic and natural responsibility have come all formal centers for learning: schools, academies, colleges, universities, and other educational organizations. The earliest health care was developed in the home. Then came hospitals, clinics, and hospices.

The home was the earliest center of human government. From a father's rightful rule in his home there developed patriarchal, monarchical, and later democratic forms of human rule.

Two things follow from this. First, if marriage is allowed to decline (as it is doing in our day), then these other institutions will inevitably decline with it. Second, whoever contributes to the decline of marriage (as many today are doing), sins against God.

One great writer on marriage, Lutheran radio preacher Walter A. Maier, wrote: "Because marriage comes from God above and not from man or beast below, it involves moral, not merely physical, problems. A sin against the commandment of purity is a sin against God, not merely the outraging of convention, the thoughtlessness of youth, the evidence of bad taste. The Savior tells us that, when God's children are joined in wedlock, they are united by God, and beneath the evident strength and courage and love that this divine direction promises there is a penetrating, ominous warning. Those who tamper with God's institution have lighted the fuse to the explosive of retributive justice. Marriage is so holy that of all social sins its violation invokes the most appalling consequences. . . . Throughout history red blotches of warning mark the final record of devastated nations that forgot the divine origin of marriage and its holiness."[3]

SATANIC ASSAULT

In spite of the importance of marriage as the first and foundational human institution and the awesome truth that it was God and not man who invented it, marriage is today under the most ferocious and persistent attack. In fact, this assault is so intense, multifaceted, and insidious that it can hardly be

[2] Ed Wheat, *Love Life for Every Married Couple* (Grand Rapids: Zondervan, 1980), 39.
[3] Walter A. Maier, *For Better, Not for Worse* (St. Louis: Concordia, 1935), 83.

explained by mere human dislike for responsibility or even personal selfishness. It is more than human. It is demonic. It is part of that great spiritual warfare being waged against both God and man by his (and our) great enemy the devil.

In my judgment, that is why Paul's discussion of marriage (as well as his discussion of the relationships between children and parents, and slaves and masters) occurs precisely where it does in Ephesians: between the urgings toward the Spirit-filled life found in Ephesians 5:18–20, and the discussion of the Christian soldier's defense against Satan found in Ephesians 6:10–20. It is on the battleground of our relationships that this battle is fought and a lasting victory for God and his righteousness is either lost or won.

Attacks on marriage come from many sources today. Some—indeed, many obvious and powerful ones—are from the world. We think of changes in the divorce laws which make it relatively easy for disappointed or frustrated persons to achieve "no fault" divorces—as if such could be possible. We think of glossy sex magazines found on thousands of street corners and stores in virtually every town in America. We think of television, which laughs at fidelity and makes light of even the most perverted lifestyles. If I were asked to pick the single most destructive feature of secular American life, I would without any hesitation name television. It destroys the home, beginning with the proper and necessary communication among the members of it. In place of normal, relating individuals, it forms people who think only of themselves—of achieving a "me-first," pleasure-oriented, materialistic, and immediate-gratification lifestyle.

But what worries me most is not television but rather the accelerating adoption of the world's way of thinking about marriage by the church. In this I think we see the devil in his most subtle form.

By this I do not merely mean that Christians often think as the world thinks, being molded by its conversations, books, and mass media. That is true and has perhaps always been true. I mean rather that the world's way of looking at things is being adopted even by leaders in the church. One way of measuring this is by the number of divorces involving prominent Evangelicals. In his book on marriage, *Strike the Original Match*, radio preacher and pastor Charles R. Swindoll tells of a visit he had from a publishing representative. The man said, "Chuck, on my way out here I made six stops, each in a major metropolitan area of our nation. At each place I either heard about or dealt with influential, once-respected Christian statesmen—solid Evangelicals, men committed to the truths of Scripture—who have left their wives."

When Swindoll asked if they had done everything possible to hold their homes together and were now broken by the outcome, the reply was: "Broken? No way! As a matter of fact, most men left their wives for another woman . . . and they are still engaged in the Christian ministry as if nothing ever happened."[4]

Pat Williams, general manager of the Philadelphia 76ers basketball team, who has told of the revitalization of his marriage in the book *Rekindled*, once asked me, "Jim, what is happening? Every week I hear of another Christian leader who has left his wife or a prominent Christian wife who has left her husband." This was in the week a well-known evangelical woman writer and speaker had left her husband to marry a man working for a Christian publisher.

But even this is not the most danger-

---

[4]Charles R. Swindoll, *Strike the Original Match* (Portland, Oreg.: Multnomah, 1980), 15.

ous or subtle thing. What the pastors of Tenth Presbyterian Church have noticed in marriage counseling situations over the last few years is a pernicious attempt to justify divorce and remarriage on supposedly "biblical" grounds. How is this possible in view of the Bible's clear teaching on this issue? Well, it goes like this:

In 1 Corinthians 7:15 Paul says that if an unbelieving person is married to a believing person and if the unbeliever insists on terminating the marriage, then the believer is free to let the unbelieving spouse go. The apostle says, "A believing man or woman is not bound in such circumstances." That is perfectly valid, of course. It is only the apostle's way of saying that it takes two to live together and that if a non-Christian, who is not even attempting to live by biblical standards, wants to leave the marriage, in the final analysis there is no means of stopping him or her. Divorce is inevitable.

However, that concession is then coupled with Christ's teaching about reconciliation (or failure to achieve reconciliation) in Matthew 18:15–17. There Jesus says that if a brother refuses to respond to proper attempts by the church to affect a reconciliation, then the church is to "treat him as [one] would a pagan or a tax collector" (v. 17), that is, as an unbeliever. The argument goes that if in a Christian marriage one party obstinately refuses to be reconciled to the willing spouse after the church has been properly involved in those reconciliation attempts, the obstinate party may then be regarded as a non-Christian and be allowed to depart according to the

principle of 1 Corinthians 7:15, and the Christian may then be allowed to remarry with God's blessing—in spite of God's teaching that he hates divorce (Mal. 2:16) or Jesus' teaching that divorce followed by remarriage is adultery (Matt. 5:32).[5]

What we have found at Tenth Presbyterian Church is that our elders are then put in the position of being manipulated by the one who wants a divorce. They are asked to approach the recalcitrant spouse to effect a change of mind. But if they are unsuccessful, they are then expected to declare that the rebellious one is either an unbeliever or (which is supposed to be the same thing) is acting like one, which allows the person who has made the complaint to get a divorce and remarry. In this way the church is placed on the side of facilitating divorces rather than restraining them.

WINNING THE BATTLE

Fortunately, in recent years there are a number of evangelical writers whom God has raised up to counter this decline and once again proclaim the holiness of marriage from the housetops. I think of Elisabeth Elliot, J. Carl Laney, Ed Wheat, Mike Mason, and Mary Pride.[6] They are declaring, on sound biblical footing, that the way out of the divorce malaise back to happy, permanent marriages is for a couple to openly acknowledge that marriage is an irrevocable covenant and is therefore "until death us do part," as the older vows put it.

Ed Wheat has a whole chapter on this, the longest chapter in his book, entitled "How to Save Your Marriage

---

[5] The chief offender here is Jay E. Adams, who advocates this approach in *The Christian Counselor's Manual* and *Marriage, Divorce and Remarriage in the Bible*, both reprinted by Zondervan Publishing House, Grand Rapids. Adams now calls the remarriage of such divorced persons "desirable."

[6] Elisabeth Elliot, *What God Has Joined . . .* (Westchester, Ill.: Crossway, 1983); J. Carl Laney, *The Divorce Myth* (Minneapolis: Bethany House, 1981); Ed Wheat, *Love Life for Every Married Couple*; Mike Mason, *The Mystery of Marriage* (Portland, Oreg.: Multnomah, 1985); Mary Pride, *The Way Home: Beyond Feminism, Back to Reality* (Westchester, Ill.: Crossway, 1985).

Alone." It is by living an obedient biblical life—in spite of the disobedience of the other person.

Mike Mason has written, "Marriages which are dependent on [romantic] love fall apart, or at best are in for a stormy time of it. But marriages which consistently look back to their vows, to those wild promises made before God, and which trust him to make sense out of them, find a continual source of strength and renewal."[7]

This is the way Paul is approaching the subject in Ephesians. These Christians had been utter pagans not long before the writing of this letter, and there were undoubtedly marriage problems among them, as there are among us. But Paul did not make his commands contingent upon the response of someone else, as if he had said: "Wives, submit to your husbands, *if they are worth submitting to* in your judgment; and husbands, love your wives *if they are worthy of love* in your opinion." His commands are absolute; "submit . . . love . . . care for . . . respect." And the reason given is not the corresponding response of the other person but rather the pattern of the Lord Jesus Christ who acted in this way toward us.

The only thing that will ultimately make marriages between two sinful persons (which we all are) work is unconditional commitment. It is the only thing that will preserve this first and greatest of all human institutions.

Joy of Obedience

Teaching like this runs counter to our culture. What rebellion, what protest it stirs up in the willful Christian's heart! I can hear the objections.

1. *"I believe you, but I just can't do it."* This is what we tell ourselves when we are psychologically defeated and are feeling sorry for ourselves. We acknowledge the standard, but we feel incapable of living up to it. Sometimes we excuse ourselves: "I suppose there are others who can obey God in this area, but I can't. God just didn't give me whatever I need to do it." In the Bible obedience to the commands of God is never made a matter of our supposed ability to obey or, by contrast, our supposed lack of ability to obey. It is simply a matter of obeying.

You may not *feel* that you can do it. Humanly speaking, you actually may be *unable* to do what you are required to do as a Christian. But what of that? The man with the crippled hand may not have felt that he could hold it out in front of him, but when Christ told him to do so he held it out and was cured. Jesus is in the business of making "unable" people able. You never know what you can do until you step out in obedience to the clear commands of God.

2. *"But I won't be happy."* A person is tempted to answer this objection by saying, "Whoever promised you that obeying God would result in your happiness—at least as you are presently defining it?" But a much better answer is the warning that if you do find happiness, it will certainly not be by following the world's ungodly counsel. It will be by following God as he reveals his way to you. This is what Psalm 1 teaches. The happy ("blessed") man is the one "who does not walk in the counsel of the wicked" and whose delight, by contrast, "is in the law of the LORD [in which] he meditates day and night" (vv. 1–2).

A woman who was having marital difficulties told Ed Wheat, "I had to take a stand on this matter of outside influence. Everyone has been anxious to give me advice about my marriage. I refuse to discuss it with people who hold an unbiblical viewpoint, or people

---

[7]Mason, *The Mystery of Marriage*, 95.

who try to turn me against my husband, or people who make me feel sorry for myself and encourage weakness in me. I can't afford to be around worldly friends anymore. . . . I want to be with people who will stand with me and support me when I might falter."[8]

That is what we need in the evangelical church today—not people who will bend the Bible because they do not want to offend the hurting person, but people who will hold their hurting brothers or sisters up to do the right thing, knowing that God honors obedience above all other things and that he is able, even in the most despairing circumstances, to bring love out of hate and life out of death, and give victory.

---

[8]Wheat, *Love Life for Every Married Couple*, 209.

32

Loving Husbands, Happy Wives

(Ephesians 5:21–33)

Submit to one another out of reverence for Christ.
Wives, submit to your husbands as to the Lord. For the husband is the head of the wife as Christ is the head of the church, his body, of which he is the Savior. Now as the church submits to Christ, so also wives should submit to their husbands in everything.

Husbands, love your wives, just as Christ loved the church and gave himself up for her to make her holy, cleansing her by the washing with water through the word, and to present her to himself as a radiant church, without stain or wrinkle or any other blemish, but holy and blameless. In this same way, husbands ought to love their wives as their own bodies. He who loves his wife loves himself. After all, no one ever hated his own body, but he feeds and cares for it, just as Christ does the church—for we are members of his body. "For this reason a man will leave his father and mother and be united to his wife, and the two will become one flesh." This is a profound mystery—but I am talking about Christ and the church. However, each one of you also must love his wife as he loves himself, and the wife must respect her husband.

I title this second study of Ephesians 5:21–33 as I do because of Paul's clear instructions and desire in the passage. But I admit, as I begin, that this or any other title commending marriage is a bit of an embarrassment in our day. That is because many of today's marriages are in dreadful shape, and anything other than pessimistic comments makes people uneasy and even hostile when the subject comes up.

Let me give some examples. My wife and I have been married twenty-five years. A few weeks after our wedding, Linda was with a group of old girl friends, all of whom had been married for a couple years, and she said something about how happy she was to be married. The reply of one friend was a put-down. She retorted, "Who are you trying to convince, us or yourself?"

Recently a friend and I were discussing the upcoming marriage of a certain couple. Both are Christians; they have known each other for a reasonable length of time; they are in early middle age, so they should know their minds in the matter. But my friend's comment—widely heard today—was: "I surely hope it works out." It was a pessimistic assessment with no real cause except the general failure of so many marriages in our time.

I have heard young people say, "I am never going to get married, because I have never known a married person who was happy."

God Calls It "Good"

What is the problem? Part of the problem is that we live in a sinful world where nothing is as perfect as we

172

would like it, and marriage by its very nature opens us up to deep hurts. We are vulnerable in marriage, and we are therefore disappointed and hurt by its failures as we are not equally hurt by shortfalls in other relationships. The chief problem, however, is that we have forgotten God's guidelines for marriage. So we suffer marriage breakdowns just as we would suffer the breakdown of our automobiles if we disregarded the manufacturer's instructions for their maintenance.

The place to begin in any discussion of marriage is with the fact that marriage is God's idea and that it is a good idea. It is a good idea, because it comes from God who never had a bad idea.

I remind you of the creation account in Genesis where marriage is first established and described. Up to this point God had been calling each of his creative acts good. But when he finished creation (except for the creation of the woman), looking at man in his aloneness, God said, "It is not good for the man to be alone. I will make a helper suitable for him" (Gen. 2:18). The one thing in all creation that was not good in God's judgment was the man in his aloneness, without the woman. God's creation of the woman was the completion and perfection of his creative acts. Marriage was the great "good" that topped creation. It follows, then, that marriage *is* good—regardless of what we make of it—and that failed marriages, which we see about us and which seem to be increasing, are the result of our failures rather than God's.

The Duty of Wives

Our real failure is that we do not follow God's directions for marriage. This is what Paul is concerned with in Ephesians, as he gives instructions first to the wife and then to the husband. To the wives he says, "Wives, submit to your husbands as to the Lord. For the husband is the head of the wife as Christ is the head of the church, his body, of which he is the Savior. Now as the church submits to Christ, so also wives should submit to their husbands in everything" (vv. 22–24).

I want to admit at this point that in my frequent teaching about marriage, particularly in the many wedding services I conduct each year, I have tended to move slightly away from what this passage teaches. The passage teaches that wives are to be submissive to their husbands and that husbands are therefore to exercise a certain headship over wives. This is unpalatable teaching, of course, particularly because of the so-called women's liberation movement.

Trying to be sensitive to the legitimate concerns of women's advocates, I have sometimes approached the matter of submission in this fashion. I have pointed out that the instructions given to wives are preceded by a verse which says, "Submit to one another out of reverence for Christ" (v. 21). As a matter of fact, the verb translated "submit" is actually a participle in Greek, which links it to the verbs that come before. They are participles too, and they tell what it means to be "filled with the Spirit": "*speaking* to one another with psalms, hymns and spiritual songs," "*singing* and *making melody* in your hearts to the Lord," and "*giving thanks* to God the Father for everything" (vv. 19–20).

These are things every Spirit-filled Christian should do, and "submitting" is likewise one of those things. Why then does Paul say that wives in particular are to submit to their husbands? I was tending to say, "It is because this is something wives have a particular difficulty doing." Likewise, "Paul tells husbands to love their wives, because this is something husbands have difficulty doing, or at least doing well."

However, this is not a fair treatment of the passage. True, wives do have difficulty submitting to their husbands, and husbands do have trouble properly loving their wives. But to approach the matter of submission this way is greatly to lessen Paul's teaching.

The reason I say this is that submission is the major concern of the apostle, not only in these verses, but in the entire passage leading up to a description of the Christian's spiritual warfare in chapter 6. He offers three examples of submission: (1) the submission of wives to husbands, (2) the submission of children to parents, and (3) the submission of slaves to masters. This is not to say that the submission is identical in each case. Neither wives nor children are slaves, nor are women to be childlike in their marriages. Each of these relationships is unique. Nevertheless, they have this in common—that each involves submission. And it is for this reason that they occur here, after the topical sentence "Submit to one another out of reverence for Christ." They are examples of what Paul means when he talks about submission.

Moreover, this is why the pairs are mentioned in the order they are. We do not usually say "children and parents." We say "parents and children," putting older, more responsible persons first. Similarly, we say "masters and slaves" rather than "slaves and masters." In each case, the order should be reversed in normal presentation. The reasons "wives," "children," and "slaves" occur first in these presentations is that the duty Paul chiefly wishes to emphasize is their submission.

So far as marriage is concerned, Paul is saying that the wife is to assume a subordinate role in the home. This is not a matter of a lack of equality. Whether male or female, child or parent, servant or master, all are made in God's image and are equally valuable to God. Moreover, the subordination involved, particularly that of the wife, is voluntary. No woman need accept the proposal of any man. However, if she does voluntarily accept that proposal and enters into matrimony (and if she is a Christian woman, desiring to be what God declares she is to be), she thereby accepts the headship of her husband over her and promises submission to him. We know that there are thousands of women who rail against this, and there are thousands of men who obviously give them just cause. But a Christian woman will nevertheless desire and seek to live up to God's standard.

Moreover, this is what wives really want. We hear much to the contrary today, particularly from women's liberation spokespersons, and we might therefore think that women want to dominate their husbands—and should, if they have the brains and will to do it. But this is the devil's lie. No good woman (indeed, hardly any woman at all) wants a man she can boss around. She wants a man she can look up to, whose judgment she can respect, and whose leadership she can respond to. If she does not get this in her man, she feels cheated. True, wives are sinners like their husbands. Wives will press their husbands on the question of mastery. They will fight for their own way. But deep inside, what wives really want is a man who will rule them and their home—gently and with love, to be sure—but rule them nevertheless.

According to Paul, the wife is to submit to her husband "as to the Lord." That is, there is an analogy between the way she submits to Jesus Christ as Lord of her life and the way she submits to her husband as lord of her home. This is because God has made the husband to be head of his wife just as he has made Christ to be head of the church, which is his body.

THE DUTY OF HUSBANDS

But just because the wife is to submit to her husband does not give the husband a right to act like a petty tyrant around the house. In fact, he is not to be a tyrant at all. If the wife's standard in the marriage is the very high standard of her love for and submission to Jesus Christ, the man's standard is to be even higher. He is to love his wife as Christ loved the church and gave himself up for her. No woman will have much trouble submitting to a man who loves like that. No good woman will struggle hard against a man who is willing to die for her.

In talking about the husband's duty toward his wife Paul uses five verbs drawn from Christ's actions toward his bride the church.

1. *Christ "loved" the church* (v. 25). "Love" is Paul's key word for Christian husbands, just as "submit" is his key word for Christian wives. It is not a verb to be taken lightly. What does love mean? I like Walter Trobisch's definition: "Let me try to tell you what it really should mean if a fellow says to a girl, 'I love you.' It means: You, you, you. You alone. You shall reign in my heart. You are the one whom I have longed for, without you I am incomplete. I will give everything for you, and I will give up everything for you, myself as well as all that I possess. I will love you alone, and I will work for you alone. And I will wait for you. . . . I will never force you, not even by words. I want to guard you, protect you and keep you from all evil. I want to share with you all my thoughts, my heart and my body—all that I possess. I want to listen to what you have to say. There is nothing I want to undertake without your blessing. I want to remain always at your side."[1]

Love like that blesses and makes homes stable. It is learned only at the feet of Jesus Christ.

Do husbands love like that? Do men even understand that this is what true love is? Not many! Yet this is their standard, and they are responsible for

knowing it and acting upon it. In 1 Peter 3:7, Peter tells husbands that if they do not love like this, God will not even listen to their prayers. "Husbands, in the same way be considerate as you live with your wives, and treat them with respect as the weaker partner and as heirs with you of the gracious gift of life, *so that nothing will hinder your prayers.*" Why should God listen to a man who does not even know how to treat his wife properly?

2. *Christ "gave himself up" for the church* (v. 25). The full measure of Christ's love for the church was his dying for her. We are told in one of the Greek histories that the wife of one of the generals of Cyrus, the ruler of Persia, was accused of treachery and was condemned to die. At first her husband did not know what was taking place. But as soon as he heard about it he rushed to the palace and burst into the throne room. He threw himself on the floor before the king and cried out, "Oh, my Lord Cyrus, take my life instead of hers. Let me die in her place."

Cyrus, who by all historical accounts was a noble and extremely sensitive man, was touched by this offer. He said, "Love like that must not be spoiled by death." Then he gave the husband and wife back to each other and let the wife go free.

As they walked away happily the husband said to his wife, "Did you notice how kindly the king looked at us when he gave you the pardon?"

The wife replied, "I had no eyes for the king. I saw only the man who was willing to die in my place."

That is the picture the Holy Spirit paints for us in this great chapter of Ephesians. The husband is to love his wife as Christ loved the church, giving himself up for her. In fairness, let me say this to husbands. Most of us will

---

[1]Walter Trobisch, *I Loved a Girl* (New York: Harper & Row, 1965), 3–4.

never have a chance to put love to that great and ultimate test, but we do have countless lesser ways to show our love daily. One wife rightly told her husband, "Dear, I know that you are willing to die for me; you have told me that many times. But while you are waiting to die, could you just fill in some of the time helping me dry the dishes?"

3. *Christs goal is "to make [the church] holy"* (v. 26). The verb is *hagios,* and it is translated "sanctify" as well as "make holy." A holy person (or saint) is one who is set apart wholly for God. This is what Jesus desires of his church: that she might be set apart wholly for himself. So also are husbands to love their wives, winning them for themselves. Moreover, since we must think of this in terms of the wives' relationships to God also, it is winning them for devotion to Jesus. In other words, husbands are to have their wives' spiritual development in view.

4. *Christ is "cleansing" his church through the word* (v. 26). This verb carries out the spiritual meaning of the verb "sanctify" or "make holy," and it teaches that God holds husbands responsible for the spiritual growth and maturing of their wives, as well as of their children (cf. Ephesians 6:4).

5. *Christ will "present" the church as a radiant bride without blemish* (v. 27). John Stott calls this the eschatological dimension, that is, the end product, when the church shall appear before God in perfection. "Just so," he says, "a husband should never use his headship to crush or stifle his wife, or frustrate her from being herself. His love for her will lead him to an exactly opposite path. He will give himself up for her, in order that she may develop her full potential under God and so become more completely herself."[2]

I think here of something C. S. Lewis said in one of his writings. He wrote that because we are eternal beings, created with eternal souls, in the ages to come each of us is going to be either some dazzlingly beautiful creature, one that would overwhelm us with awe if we were to see such a creature now, or else an everlasting horror, from which we would all recoil—depending upon our having entered into (or not having entered into) salvation through Jesus Christ. Here is realistic eschatology. And with that in view, I suggest that any husband would be a better husband if he could see his wife as on the way to becoming that dazzling creature, which she will surely be in heaven in her resurrected body, and if he could realize that under God he has a responsible part in her transformation.

Happy Homes

God created marriage in order that, among other things, a Christian man and a Christian woman might find the deepest of all possible fulfillments in each other and be happy. I know there are Christians who will acknowledge this, but who are discouraged by their personal failures and who have concluded that there is now no hope for their marriage. Let me say that for the Christian it is never the case that any given relationship is hopeless. Let me tell you of one marriage resurrection.

Pat Williams, the general manager of the Philadelphia 76ers basketball team, tells in *Rekindled* how, like an unattended fire, his marriage had died out. He is a busy, active man. He had been neglecting his wife Jill. She had complained. But nothing really changed, and the day came (as it does with many) when she told him that it was all over. She was not threatening to move out, but she had no love for him

---

[2]John R. W. Stott, *God's New Society: The Message of Ephesians* (Downers Grove, Ill.: InterVarsity, 1979), 229.

anymore. She was only going through the motions. Pat began to search for what he could do, and in his search he came upon a "Prescription for a Superb Marriage" in Ed Wheat's book *Love Life for Every Married Couple*. It was a simple prescription for what Wheat called the "BEST" of all possible marriages:

> B lessing
> E difying
> S haring
> T ouching

"Blessing" means to speak well of your partner, to show kindness toward your partner, to convey thanks and appreciation for your partner, and to pray to God on your partner's behalf.

"Edifying" mean to build up. Husbands are to build their wives up by praising them. Wives are to build their husbands up by a loving response.

"Sharing" means doing things together—listening, loving, learning, investigating, reporting.

"Touching" refers to nonsexual touching. It is so important in Wheat's prescription that he lists twenty-five specific suggestions for it.

These four rules are actually only ways of doing what the Bible says we are to do to love one another. But that is just the point. They are practical ways of actually *doing* what the Bible says; and because they are ways of doing what the Bible says, they work. They worked with Pat and Jill. It took time, but their marriage was rekindled. Joy returned. Both grew, and the marriage is now a model for many through Pat's book and their testimony.[3]

Loving husbands, happy wives! The words are indeed often an embarrassment, but this is because of our sin. Embarrassment is a confession of failure. But it is also a challenge to heed the Word of God and put God's instructions for a happy marriage into practice.

---

[3]See Pat and Jill Williams with Jerry Jenkins, *Rekindled* (Old Tappan, N.J.: Revell, 1985), and Ed Wheat, *Love Life for Every Married Couple* (Grand Rapids: Zondervan, 1980).

33

Christ and the Church

(Ephesians 5:32)

This is a profound mystery—but I am talking about Christ and the church.

William Barclay is often quite perceptive. This is the case when he points out at the beginning of his treatment of Ephesians 5:22–33 that "no one reading this passage in the twentieth century can fully realize how great it is."[1] As Barclay notes, through the years the Christian view of marriage has come to be accepted, so that although our Western world obviously fails to live up to God's standards for marriage we all nevertheless accept them as proper. But when Paul wrote these verses, the Christian view of marriage was new and radical.

A NEW VIEW OF MARRIAGE?

Of the three ancient cultures into which the Christian Scriptures were written—Hebrew, Greek, and Roman—Hebrew culture had the highest ideal of marriage. This was what we might expect because of the continuity between the two covenants, between God's revelation in the Old Testament and God's revelation in the New. Nevertheless, at the time of the writing of the New Testament the Bible's proper ideal of marriage had been undermined and virtually destroyed. At the time of Christ a Jewish woman was not a person but a thing, much as black people were regarded as things (property) in America before emancipation. A woman had no legal rights whatever, and a wife could be dismissed at will.

It is true that the schools of Shammai and Hillel disagreed on the interpretation of Deuteronomy 24:1, the chief divorce law in Israel. It said that a man could divorce his wife if he found "something indecent about her" (NIV). Shammai said this meant adultery, and adultery alone. Hillel interpreted it as anything that might displease the husband, even spoiling his dinner. This was a major difference, of course. But since either was a recognized possibility, it is easy to see which view prevailed.

Moreover, a woman had no right of divorce, and a man could divorce simply by giving his wife a "bill of divorcement," that is, a simple written statement that he had divorced her. The result was that marriage was in peril in Judaism. As Barclay notes, Jewish girls were refusing to marry at all because of their uncertain position.

If the state of marriage was on perilous ground in Judaism, it was on even worse ground in Greek and Roman cultures. Demosthenes had said, "We have courtesans for our pleasure, con-

---

[1] William Barclay, *The Letters to the Galatians and Ephesians* (Edinburgh: Saint Andrews Press, 1954), 199.

178

cubines for daily cohabitation, and wives for the purpose of having children legitimately and of having a faithful guardian for our household affairs." In Greece a married woman had no part in a man's life. She was not even a true companion to her husband. She was to run his home and care for his children. A Greek husband was expected to find companionship elsewhere.

And what of Rome? Rome was the sewer of the ancient world. For the first five hundred years of the Republic divorce was unheard of. But at the time of Paul, as Seneca said, women were married to be divorced and divorced to be married. Martial tells of a woman who had ten husbands. Juvenal tells of one who had eight husbands in five years. Jerome tells of one Roman matron who was married to her twenty-third husband, and she was his twenty-first wife. Sexual perversions were rampant, and profligacy was widespread.

Barclay says, "It was against that background that Paul writes. When Paul wrote this most lovely passage he was not simply restating the view that every man held. He was calling men and women to a new fidelity and a new purity and a new fellowship in the married life. It is the simple fact of history that no one in this world with the single exception of children . . . owes more to Christ than women. It is impossible to exaggerate the cleansing effect that Christianity had on ordinary everyday home life in the ancient world."[2]

THE TRUE ORDER

Yet the interesting thing about the discussion of marriage in Ephesians 5:22–33 is that, if you had asked Paul if he thought he was unfolding a newer, higher, and purer view of marriage than had been known before, he would have denied it at once. Barclay says that

Paul was "*calling* men and women to a new fidelity and a new purity and a new fellowship in the married life." But Paul, if he could be pressed to acknowledge even this, would have said at best that he was "*re*calling" them to this standard.

The reason is that Paul was conscious of having gotten his ideas of marriage not from some special, new revelation of God but from the Old Testament, indeed, from the very early chapters of Genesis. In Ephesians 5:31 he quotes an Old Testament text specifically, saying, "For this reason a man will leave his father and mother and be united to his wife, and the two will become one flesh." The quotation is from Genesis 2:24. So Paul is saying that his teaching is based on this and other parts of the Old Testament revelation, not on some new revelation or, worse yet, on some insight peculiar to himself or his Christian contemporaries. The true historical order is not a progression from animalistic or merely inadequate views of marriage to higher views. It is rather: first, the high standard; second, a falling away from that standard; third, a recall to that standard through the gospel of Jesus Christ. Paul's view is grounded in the original orders of creation.

In fact, it goes back even further than that. One of my predecessors as pastor of Tenth Presbyterian Church in Philadelphia was Donald Grey Barnhouse, a man who had a remarkable Bible-teaching ministry. Among other things Barnhouse was noted for his gift of sermon illustration. His own explanation of his insight was this. Early in his ministry he read Revelation 13:8 which speaks of Christ having been "slain from [before] the creation of the world." He immediately recognized that if this is so, then in God's mind spiritual things came before all material ones and, as a result,

---

[2] Ibid., 203. Quotations from the ancient sources are from Barclay's discussion (199–203).

everything was created to illustrate some spiritual truth. It did not make any difference what it was—whether the sun and moon, a blade of grass, a snowflake, a lamb, a horse—whatever—God created it to illustrate some spiritual truth that existed in God's mind prior to that creation.

This applies to marriage. When God created marriage it was not simply that God considered marriage to be a good idea, though it certainly is that, or even because God thought it would be a good way to have and rear children. God created marriage to illustrate the relationship between Christ and the church.

The relationship of a husband to a wife in marriage was going to illustrate the relationship of the Lord Jesus Christ to those he would one day redeem from sin's slavery. The relationship of a wife to her husband was going to illustrate the relationship the people of God, the church, would have to Jesus Christ.

This is why the name of Christ occurs again and again throughout this great passage: "Wives, submit to your husbands as to the *Lord*. For the husband is the head of the wife as *Christ* is the head of the church, his body, of which he is the Savior. Now as the church submits to *Christ*, so also wives should submit to their husbands in everything. Husbands, love your wives, just as *Christ* loved the church and gave himself up for her to make her holy, cleansing her by the washing with water through the word, and to present her to himself as a radiant church, without stain or wrinkle or any other blemish, but holy and blameless. In this same way, husbands ought to love their wives as their own bodies. He who loves his wife loves himself. After all, no one ever hated his own body, but he feeds and cares for it, just as *Christ* does the church—for we are members of his body. 'For this reason a man will leave his father and mother and be united to

his wife, and the two will become one flesh.' This is a profound mystery—but I am talking about *Christ* and the church" (vv. 22–32).

Which comes first in the mind of God: the relationship of Christ to the church or marriage, which is the illustration of it? Obviously the relationship of Christ to the church! But if this is so, then several important conclusions follow.

1. *No one will ever be able to understand the truest, deepest meaning of marriage who is not a Christian.* If a husband is to love like Christ, he must know the love of Christ in order to fulfill that commandment. If a wife is to submit to her husband as she submits to Christ, she must first have submitted to Christ to understand it.

2. *No one who is a Christian should ever marry a person who is not a Christian.* Second Corinthians 6:14 says that explicitly: "Do not be yoked together with unbelievers." But even without this text the principle should be evident from the nature of the relationships. If one partner is a Christian and the other is not, a husband and wife cannot possibly have the same ideals for their marriage and the marriage is flawed from the beginning.

3. *No marriage will ever attain its true potential unless those united in the marriage are pursuing it according to God's goal and standards.* In this as in all other areas of life we are to "trust in the LORD with all [our hearts] and lean not on [our] own understanding" (Prov. 3:5). Only when we pursue marriage according to God's standards will God make our paths straight and bring blessing.

TRUE UNION

When Paul writes about Christ and the church he is giving grounds to apply everything about that relationship to everything about the relationship of a man to a woman and a woman to a man in marriage—as the earlier verses in this chapter also suggest. But it is important to note that the point at which Paul actually brings this comparison in is when he is talking about the *union* of two persons in marriage as a result of which they become "one flesh" (v. 31). There are three great mystical unions in the Bible: (1) the union of the three persons of the Godhead, being one God; (2) the union of the two natures of Christ in one person; and (3) the union of the believer with Christ. Marriage illustrates the third of these unions which is why Paul calls it "a profound mystery." It is not incomprehensible, but it is something that taxes even our sanctified understanding.

One thing this means is that a man and woman are to be united to each other in marriage as they can never be united to anyone else, not even to their closest friends or family. Nor is any other closeness in life comparable.

When God made the first man and the first woman he made them in his own image which means, among other things, that he made them a trinity as he is a trinity. God is Father, Son, and Holy Spirit. In a similar way, man is a trinity of body, soul, and spirit. The union of one man with one woman in marriage is to be a union on each of these three levels. It must be if the marriage is to attain to God's design for it and be lasting.

It must be a union of body with body, first of all, which is to say that there must be a valid sexual relationship. For this reason all branches of the Christian church have acknowledged that a marriage has not actually taken place until the sexual union is consummated. If sexual union does not take place or cannot take place, then the marriage can be annulled as invalid. I tell couples that this is a vital part of marriage. According to the Bible, neither the man nor the woman is to defraud the other of the sexual experience. The quickest

way for the marriage to end up in trouble is for the wife to have a headache every night and go to sleep early to avoid sex or for the husband to lose interest in his wife romantically and spend his nights elsewhere. Sex must be a regular expression of the relationship.

On the other hand, if the relationship is based upon nothing but sex—in other words, if it is a marriage of body with body alone and not of soul with soul and spirit with spirit—then the marriage is weak and is headed for the divorce courts. When the glamor wears off, as it always does if there is nothing more to sustain it, the relationship is finished. Such a marriage is based purely on physical attraction and ends in either indifference, divorce, or adultery.

A good marriage is more than a union of body with body. It is also a union of soul with soul. The word "soul" had almost passed out of use in the English language until the blacks of our day revived it; but it is a good word, and we would have been poorer for its loss. It refers to the intellectual and emotional side of a person's nature, involving the characteristics that we associate with the mind. Hence, a marriage that involves a union of souls is a marriage in which a couple share an interest in the same things—the same books, the same shows, the same friends—and seek to establish a meeting of the minds (as it were) both intellectually and emotionally. Such marriages will last longer.

I believe that at this point a special word must be said to Christians who are married. For whenever a minister speaks like this to Christians, many are already racing ahead of him to point three and are concluding that because their marriages are one of spirit with spirit, they do not need to worry very much about a union of their minds or souls. This is not right. Not only do we need to worry about it at times, we also need to work toward it. For an emotional and intellectual union does not in itself come naturally.

What does a young woman have in her mind when she marries a young man? What is her vision of this new husband? It may have something to do with her father and whether she liked him or rebelled against him. It has a little bit of Clark Gable mixed up in it, and perhaps a little of James Bond or Johnny Carson or her minister. What is the vision of the husband? Keith Miller, who wrote the best-selling book *The Taste of New Wine*, said that his vision was probably a combination of Saint Teresa, Elizabeth Taylor, and . . . Betty Crocker.

What happens when a girl with a vision of Clark Gable and a man with a vision of Betty Crocker get married and begin to find out that the other person is not much like their vision? One of two things! Either they center their minds on the difference between the ideal and what they are increasingly finding the other person to be like and they try, either openly or subversively, to push the spouse into the image. Or by the grace of God they increasingly come to accept the other person as he or she is, including his or her standards of how they themselves should be, and then, under God, seek to conform to the best and most uplifting of those standards.

It must be one or the other of those ways. Keith Miller has written, "The soul of a marriage can be a trysting place where two people can come together quietly from the struggles of the world and feel safe, accepted and loved . . . or it can be a battle ground where two egos are locked in a lifelong struggle for supremacy, a battle which is for the most part invisible to the rest of the world."[3]

If we are to have the former in our marriages, then we must work toward it. We must do it by cultivating the interests and the aspirations of the other party.

A true marriage, then, must be a marriage of body with body and of soul with soul. But it must also be a marriage of spirit with spirit. For this reason the only marriages that can approximate the kind of marriage that God intended to exist in this world are Christian marriages.

What does this mean, a marriage of spirit with spirit? Primarily it means that both the husband and the wife must be Christians, for the unsaved person possesses a spirit only in the sense that he supports a vacuum at the center of his life that can only be filled by God. He has a spirit, but the spirit has died—just as Adam's spirit died when he disobeyed God and ran from him. The only persons who possess a live spirit are those who have been touched by the Holy Spirit and have entered into God's family by faith in the Lord Jesus Christ. Only these can be married in the full sense of the word, which means body with body, soul with soul, and spirit with spirit. In this type of union a man and a woman experience the fullest measure of earthly blessing and most fully illustrate the mystical union of Christ and his church.[4]

TRUE AND PERFECT LOVE

Yet when we think of Christ and his relationship to the church, we think not primarily of his mystical union with us (important as that is) but of the simpler and even more wonderful fact that he loved us and gave himself for us. We recognize that this is to be our pattern.

[3] Keith Miller, *The Taste of New Wine* (Waco, Tex.: Word, 1968), 46.
[4] Portions of the discussion of the union of body, soul, and spirit are borrowed from James Montgomery Boice, *The Sermon on the Mount* (Grand Rapids: Zondervan, 1972), 121–24.

In the Old Testament we are told of the marriage of Hosea and Gomer which from the beginning was set forth as an illustration of the way God loves and gives himself for his people in spite of their unfaithful behavior. Gomer was like us. She was married to Hosea, but she was flirtatious and soon left him for another man. Hosea made sure that she had food to eat and clothes to wear— even when she was living with another man. But at last Gomer sank so low that she was sold as a slave in the city of Samaria, and Hosea was told to go and buy her. He bought her for "fifteen shekels of silver and about a homer and a lethek of barley" (Hos. 3:2). At this point Gomer became Hosea's property; he could have killed her if he wished. But he did not kill her. *He loved her!* And now, since she was his again, he promised love for her and claimed her love for himself.

This is a picture of the way the Lord Jesus Christ loves us and of how our marriages are to illustrate that great and prior relationship. We are the adulterous slave, sold on the auction block of sin. He loved us when we did *not* love him. He died for us when we were scorning his love and running from him. Still, he bought us by that greatest of all sacrifices, and we became his. Peter says, "You were redeemed . . . with the precious blood of Christ, a lamb without blemish or defect" (1 Peter 1:18–19). Having become his, we now owe him the fullest measure of love.

Love so amazing, so divine,
Demands my soul, my life, my all.

Never make the mistake of dragging your understanding of the love of God in Christ down to the level of your own weak love. Rather let God draw your love up by the love and power of Christ to his standard. Then Christ shall have his way, and you will be able to testify to the world of his great love.

34

Children and Parents

(Ephesians 6:1–4)

Children, obey your parents in the Lord, for this is right. "Honor your father and mother"—which is the first commandment with a promise—"that it may go well with you and that you may enjoy long life on the earth."

Fathers, do not exasperate your children; instead, bring them up in the training and instruction of the Lord.

It is a conviction of mine that no man has a right to tell other people how to raise their children until he has children of his own and has tried to raise them. As a corollary, I am convinced that no *wise* man will give advice even then until his own children have grown up and turned out well.

Unfortunately, a preacher cannot teach the sixth chapter of Ephesians without dealing with the relations of parents to children and children to parents, since Paul introduces the subject. And a pastor who is concerned for his people will not want to ignore relationships simply because they are troublesome. I sometimes jokingly tell parents that they can get by with two children, because they are matched in numbers and the parents are bigger. But when you have three, one is always getting away from you. In a sense that is what is happening in a broader way today. We can handle one or two problems. But the home is beset by so many problems today that success at being good parents seems to be getting away from us.

Norman Corwin wrote in an article for *Reader's Digest* entitled "Perfect Home": "One child makes a home a course in liberal education for both himself and parents; two children make it a private school; three or more make it a campus."[1] But many parents today are not sure that they are up to being professors in this university, and even then they are unsure of what should be offered in the curriculum.

A NEW POSITION FOR CHILDREN

Paul introduces the subject with the duty of children toward their parents. It is another example of submission by Christians to Christians, going back to his thematic statement in Ephesians 5:21: "Submit to one another out of reverence for Christ." He began with wives submitting to husbands. Here he deals with children submitting to parents, and later he will address slaves and masters.

But before we deal directly with Paul's teaching on children, it is worth noting that nothing in all history has done so much for the elevation and development of children as Christianity. In our study of the preceding

[1] Quoted by Howard G. Hendricks, *Heaven Help the Home!* (Wheaton, Ill.: Victor, 1973), 40.

passage, Ephesians 5:22–33, I pointed out the great advance for women produced by Christianity. But that elevation, great as it was, is overshadowed by the improvement in the status of children. William Barclay, whom I quoted in regard to women, notes correctly that under the Roman law of *patria potestas* ("the father's power"), "A Roman father had absolute power over his family. He could sell them as slaves; he could make them work in his fields, even in chains; he could take the law into his own hands, for law was in his own hands, and he could punish as he liked; he could even inflict the death penalty on his child. Further, the power of the Roman father extended over the child's whole life, so long as the father lived. A Roman son never came of age."[2]

There was also the matter of child repudiation, leading to exposure of the newborn. When a baby was born it was placed before its father. If the father stooped and lifted the child, the child was accepted and was raised as his. If he turned away, the child was rejected and was literally discarded. Such rejected children were either left to die, or they were picked up by those who trafficked in infants. These people raised children to be slaves or to stock the brothels. One Roman father wrote to his wife from Alexandria: "If—good luck to you!—you have a child, if it is a boy, let it live; if it is a girl, throw it out."[3]

Against such pagan cruelty the new relations of parents to children and children to parents brought by the Christian gospel stand forth like sunshine after a dismal storm.

The Duty of Children

In writing to families, Paul begins with children because of his purpose in providing examples of submission, as I said. As he develops this duty, the apostle stresses two matters.

1. *Obedience.* Obedience is the fundamental relationship of children to parents. As we are to see, it is not an absolute obedience (as, for example, if a parent should command a child to do a wicked or un-Christian thing), and it ought always to be obedience rendered in the context of a loving parent-child relationship. Nevertheless, it is a true obedience, guided, but not abolished, by love.

What Paul has in mind as he speaks of the obligation of a child to obey his or her parents is natural law, that is, the law of relationships written upon the human conscience by God apart from special revelation. Children are to obey, "for this is right." This is not confined to Christian ethics. It is recognized and taught by all the world's cultures, both ancient and contemporary. Children owe obedience to parents. It is true that this duty has often been greatly distorted and abused, in Christian as well as in non-Christian circles, but it is an abiding obligation nonetheless.

The obligation is not merely on the side of the child, who must obey, but also on the side of the parent, who must enforce the obedience. This is because the parent stands as God in relationship to the child. To teach the child to obey the parent is to teach the child to obey God. To allow the child to defy and disobey the parent is to teach the child to defy and disobey God with all the obvious consequences.

In his discussion of this point John R. W. Stott points out that in the traditional Christian handling of the Ten Commandments the rule "Honor your father and your mother" (Exod. 20:12), the fifth of the ten, is placed in the second table of the law which deals

---

[2] William Barclay, *The Letters to the Galatians and Ephesians* (Edinburgh: Saint Andrews Press, 1954), 208.

[3] Ibid., 209.

with human relationships, while in the Jewish handling of the Ten Commandments it is placed in the first table, which deals with our relationship to God. Stott argues that this, rather than the Christian division, is "surely right."[4] It is because obedience to parents is part of our relationship to God and because disobedience to parents is at heart a spiritual rebellion.

Stott points out that this is why under Jewish law the most extreme penalty, death, was proscribed for anyone who cursed his or her parents or was incorrigible in relationship to them (cf. Lev. 20:9; Deut. 21:18–21).

2. *Honor.* The second duty Paul imposes on children in relationship to parents is honor, a duty which, he is careful to show, *is* based on divine revelation and not merely on natural law. Indeed, it is the fifth of the Ten Commandments, which I have already cited: "Honor your father and your mother, so that you may live long in the land the LORD your God is giving you" (Exod. 20:12).

That is a difficult area, of course, for not all parents live in such a way that their children can properly honor them, especially if the child has become a Christian and the parents are not Christians. What is a child to do, for example, if his or her father is an irresponsible alcoholic or profligate or if the mother is immoral, undisciplined, and excessively worldly? Can a child properly honor such a parent? Should he? To link this duty to the preceding, should a child obey the commands of such non-Christian parents?

The answer is that a child, while he is a child, owes obedience to a parent in all areas except those that contradict the revealed law of God. In this, the child's position is the same as that of a Christian wife in relationship to a non-Christian husband or a Christian citizen who finds himself in conflict with an anti-Christian government. The principle is: "If you owe taxes, pay taxes; if revenue, then revenue; if respect, then respect; if honor, then honor" (Rom. 13:7). All owe obedience and respect to those over them, *but not at the expense of the obedience we owe to God.*

Stott suggests, to give an example, that if a non-Christian parent forbids a Christian child to be baptized, this is a matter in which the child can justly obey the parent. For although Jesus commanded baptism, he did not specify precisely when it was to be done, and it is possible to postpone baptism to a later time. On the other hand, if the parent should command the child not to worship and follow the Lord Jesus Christ in his or her heart, this the child could not obey. For to abandon following after Christ would be to abandon Christianity.

If you are having difficulty in this regard, I suggest that you study your parents and pick out those areas in which you can properly honor them. I remember doing this with my father at a very critical point in my growing up, although my father was not at all a bad father in the sense I have been speaking of and never discouraged, but rather encouraged, my Christian commitment. The difficulty was twofold: first, my father was a busy doctor who was very seldom home and, second, when he was home it was difficult to talk to him. My father does not communicate easily on a personal level. In fact, I cannot remember ever having had a meaningful and constructive conversation with my father.

But I determined to examine his life for areas in which I could particularly honor and admire him, and I discovered that there were many such areas. I

---

[4]John R. W. Stott, *God's New Society: The Message of Ephesians* (Downers Grove, Ill.: InterVarsity, 1979), 239.

learned that my father was extremely hardworking and conscientious. Indeed, that was why he was away from home so much. So although his being away created problems, there were advantages also. The fact that he could pay for an extended and thorough education for me was one of them. Second, I discovered that he was extremely generous. My father never flaunted his giving to Christian and other charitable causes; in fact, he hardly mentioned it, although my father was quite open in talking about money. When I learned what he did, some of the resentments I had in other areas dissipated.

Let me encourage you to do this, as Paul encourages children in this paragraph. I notice three inducements. First, obedience and honor are *right* relationships; they are grounded in natural law. Second, they are a *Christian duty;* they are to be exercised "in the Lord" and are part of the Ten Commandments. Third, they are enforced by a *promise,* namely, that it will "go well with" those who practice them and they will "enjoy long life on the earth." This last promise is not a blanket assurance that every individual who honors his or her parents will live longer than every individual who does not. But it is a general promise that God's material and physical blessing rests on those who work at being Christians in these relationships.

THE DUTY OF PARENTS

It should be obvious from what I have already said that the duty placed upon children involves a correspondingly great responsibility for their parents, which is what Paul turns to next. For if children are to obey their parents, parents must give them proper directions to obey. And if they are to honor

their parents, their parents must be worthy of that honor.

It is important that Paul gives instructions to fathers specifically. This does not exclude mothers, of course. It includes them in the same way the word "brothers" or "brethren" is used to include all Christians in other passages, and because Paul is speaking of "parents" (both "fathers and mothers") in the first three verses. For this reason the Good News Bible actually translates "fathers" (*pateres*) as "parents" in verse 4. Nevertheless, it is significant, as I say, that Paul addresses fathers specifically for the simple reason that the responsibility for managing a home and raising children is primarily theirs.

They are not responsible entirely for what their children become, as I hope to show, for a part of what children become is their own responsibility. But fathers are responsible for treating them in a non-exasperating way and for bringing them up in the instruction of the Lord.

Paul's words to fathers have two parts, one negative and the other positive. The negative part involves restraint. Fathers are not to "exasperate" their children but are rather to exercise their authority as fathers in a balanced way. In the parallel passage in Colossians Paul tells fathers, "Do not embitter your children, or they will become discouraged" (Col. 3:21). That is, although there is a proper and necessary place for discipline, that discipline must nevertheless "never be arbitrary (for children have a built-in sense of justice) or unkind. Otherwise, they will 'become discouraged.' Conversely, almost nothing causes a child's personality to blossom and gifts to develop like the positive encouragement of loving, understanding parents."[5]

Barclay tells of the testimony of the distinguished painter Benjamin West in

[5] Ibid., 246.

this respect. He was young, and one day his mother went out, leaving him in charge of his younger sister Sally. In his sister's absence he discovered some bottles of colored ink and decided to paint his mother's portrait. He made an awful mess. But when his mother came back she said nothing about the terrible ink stains. Instead she picked up the piece of paper on which he had been working and exclaimed, "Why, it's Sally!" Then she stooped and kissed him. Benjamin West used to say, "My mother's kiss made me a painter."

Martin Luther said, "Spare the rod and spoil the child—that is true. But beside the rod keep an apple to give him when he has done well."[6]

On the positive side Paul speaks to fathers about training, saying, "instead, bring them [your children] up in the training and instruction of the Lord." How are fathers to do this unless they know what the Word of God teaches? How are they to teach with wisdom unless they have themselves learned in Christ's school? Obviously fathers will fail at this great task unless they are themselves growing with God. They must be studying the Bible. They must be seeking to live by it and practice it in their own daily lives. Parents (and especially fathers) must be models. Howard Hendricks says, "Children are not looking for perfect parents; but they are looking for honest parents. An honest, progressing parent is a highly infectious person."[7]

Yet I must say a word on the matter of the child's own responsibility, as I promised. Children are their own people, and they have their own set of responsibilities both before God and others. Consequently, although they may be taught wisely and raised morally and that instruction be supported by parental example, they nevertheless

sometimes do go astray, and *that is not necessarily the parents' fault.*

The first example of child-rearing in the Bible should teach us that. We know that Adam and Eve were a sinful man and woman after the Fall, as we all are. But they were undoubtedly model parents nonetheless. They were highly intelligent and knew God intimately. Moreover, they are numbered in the godly line of the age before the Flood, the line which contained such outstanding spiritual giants as Enoch, Methuselah, and Noah. There is no question but that they raised their children to know and honor God. Yet in spite of this their first child, Cain, turned out to be a murderer. Why? The Bible says it was the result of the outworkings of his own sinful heart.

So I say to parents: If your child has abandoned the Lord and is living a worldly life, it is not necessarily your fault. It may be, but not necessarily. Do not abandon hope. God has called many such children. Your duty is to continue to live as Christians and pray for your child regularly. The Bible says, "The prayer of a righteous man is powerful and effective" (James 5:16).

On the other side, I want to say a word to children who have not had godly parents. The fact that your parents did not teach you about the Lord or lead a consistently godly life is unfortunate for them and a handicap for you, but it is not an excuse for your failing to be what God would have you be as his followers. I spoke of Cain, an ungodly son of godly parents. But when I think of Cain I inevitably also think of Joseph, who is a great contrast. Joseph's father was not particularly spiritual, and he was raised in a family environment that was not conducive to any high standards of behavior. His brothers were spiteful, profligate, and

[6]Barclay, *The Letters to the Galatians and Ephesians*, 211–12.
[7]Hendricks, *Heaven Help the Home!* 58.

violent. Joseph was carried away to Egypt. He had no outward spiritual support. Yet he had determined in his youth to follow God, and he did it even through adversity. He was never turned aside by outward circumstances.

FAITH OF OUR FATHERS

Sometimes those who are properly raised go astray, and sometimes those who are spiritually disadvantaged are models of Christian life and character. But these are exceptions, and the normal pattern is the communication of faith from generation to generation within the context of a genuinely Christian home. It is hard for children to learn to obey their parents. It is hard for parents to bring their children up in the training and instruction of the Lord.

But difficult is not impossible, and by the grace of God Christian parents and children have been managing just those difficulties for centuries. They can manage it in our own time too. Howard Hendricks's book, from which I have quoted several times, is called *Heaven Help the Home!* It is a clever, provocative title, but by the addition of an *s* it also becomes a true statement. *Heaven* (that is, God) *helps the home!* God is in the business of building homes, and he is on our side if we are truly trying to obey him and follow his directions.

The world is against us. The world wants absolute autonomy and will attempt to destroy any established structure to get it. It will try to destroy our families. It will try to get us on its side. But it need not succeed. We can live as Jesus tells us to live, and God can and will bless our homes.

35

Slaves and Masters

(Ephesians 6:5–9)

Slaves, obey your earthly masters with respect and fear, and with sincerity of heart, just as you would obey Christ. Obey them not only to win their favor when their eye is on you, but like slaves of Christ, doing the will of God from your heart. Serve wholeheartedly, as if you were serving the Lord, not men, because you know that the Lord will reward everyone for whatever good he does, whether he is slave or free.

And masters, treat your slaves, in the same way. Do not threaten them, since you know that he who is both their Master and yours is in heaven, and there is no favoritism with him.

Years ago, Dr. C. Everett Koop, later the surgeon general of the United States, gave an address to the Christian Medical Fellowship of England on the topic "Christian Medicine: A Compromise with Mediocrity?"[1] The address asked whether Christian doctors are poorer doctors because of their Christianity or if their Christian commitment has made them even more strongly committed to high standards of medicine. The address encouraged doctors to be better doctors than they otherwise would be because they serve Christ.

Koop's concern was the concern of the apostle as he wrote about the duty of slaves and masters in Ephesians. It is important to see this, because if we do not see it—if instead we are expecting Paul to be answering questions about the legitimacy or illegitimacy of slavery, for example—we will misunderstand his teaching and miss what he really has to say to us. Slavery was part of the

social and economic fabric of the ancient world. It has been estimated that in the Roman Empire at this time there were about sixty million slaves. That means about half of the population was enslaved to the other half.

Sometimes a slave's situation was quite good. Yet there was often terrible cruelty and abuse. A slave could be whipped, branded, mutilated, or killed. Barclay says, "The terror of the slave was that he was absolutely at the caprice of his master."[2] This terrible institution was eventually changed by Christianity, just as Christianity also bettered the status of women and children as time passed. But it is the nature of a Christian's work, not slavery, that is Paul's chief concern in this passage.

CHRISTIANITY AND SLAVERY

Yet that is not the whole story. I say this because the discussion of the duties of slaves and masters in Ephesians 6:5–

---

[1] C. Everett Koop, *Christian Medicine: A Compromise with Mediocrity?* (London: Tyndale Press, 1962).

[2] William Barclay, *The Letters to the Galatians and Ephesians* (Edinburgh: Saint Andrews Press, 1954), 213.

9 is the last of three examples of the submission of one class of persons to another which Paul introduces by the topical sentence: "Submit to one another out of reverence for Christ" (Eph. 5:21). Since Paul is presenting these as parallel examples, we cannot help wondering if he is thereby suggesting that slavery has the same permanent validity as marriage relationships or home relationships. Or, since we would all say that slavery has been rightly abolished in our time, should we infer that each of these relationships is also just temporary? Although Paul is not dealing with the rightness or wrongness of slavery itself, as I said, the very way in which he speaks of slaves inevitably raises this question.

To put the matter even more stringently, what do we say to those who condemn Paul because, when he had the chance, as here, he did not denounce slavery outright?

The first thing we must say is that although Paul did not condemn slavery here, he did not condone it. That makes his treatment of slavery entirely different from his treatment of marriage and the home. In the first case Paul grounded the relationship between spouses in the relationship of Christ to the church. Marriage is an outgrowth of this eternally prior relationship. In the second case, he grounded the duty of children to parents in natural law ("for this is right") and revelation ("the first commandment with a promise"). This is not the case with his discussion of slaves' duties to masters or masters' responsibilities to slaves. Nothing in the passage affirms slavery as a naturally valid or divinely mandated institution.

Second, Paul's discussion of the duties of Christian slaves and the responsibilities of Christian masters transforms the institution, even if it falls short of calling for outright abolition. In the ancient world the slave was a thing. Aristotle, the most brilliant of the Greeks, wrote that there could never be friendship between master and slave, for master and slave have nothing in common: "a slave is a living tool, just as a tool is an inanimate slave."[3]

Paul's words are entirely different. He calls the slave a "slave of Christ," one who wants to do "the will of God" (v. 6), and who will receive a "reward" for "whatever good he does" (v. 8). Likewise, the master is responsible to God for how he treats the slave, who is ultimately God's rather than his own property (v. 9). This is another way of saying that the slave, no less than the master, has been made in God's image. As such, he possesses inestimable worth and great dignity. He is to be treated properly. In such a framework slavery, even though it remained slavery, could never be the same institution as for non-Christians.

Third, it was this transformation (which came from viewing all persons as made in God's image) that ultimately destroyed slavery and continues to transform work relationships today.

R. C. Sproul was speaking to the executives of a large corporation, and they were uneasy about his linking religion and business. Eventually he caught the understanding and the enthusiasm of the board chairman. This man said, "Let me see if I can connect what you're saying. What I hear is that our business life is affected by how we treat people. How we treat people is a matter of ethics. Ethics are determined by our philosophy. Our philosophy reflects our theology. So respecting people is really a theological matter."[4]

That was absolutely on target, and it is an outline of the way Christianity has

---

[3] Ibid.
[4] R. C. Sproul, *The Search for Dignity* (Ventura, Calif.: Regal Books, 1983), 93.

transformed the world, including the abolition of slavery. Christianity is a new theology. Theology changes philosophy. Philosophy effects ethics. And these transformed ethics determine how we treat people at home, school, church, and in the marketplace. Because Christianity brought a new, true theology, it inevitably uplifted man—and continues to do so.

This is a continuing transformation, and we must all be involved in it. That is our ultimate answer to the critic who asks, "Why didn't Paul condemn slavery? And why did the Christian church take so many centuries to abolish it?" The answer is really a counter-question, "Why are you not treating other people as God has treated you?"

You see, the problem is not why somebody else did not do what he or she should have done quicker, but rather why you and I are not doing what we know we should be doing now. In the ancient world slaves were often very unjustly treated. But workers are often treated unjustly today. It is true that in most lands workers cannot be killed for poor performance. This is due in part to a pervasive Christian ethic. But workers can be scorned just as thoroughly, wounded just as deeply, threatened just as harshly, and despised just as cruelly. We are often part of those injustices. That is why these verses continue to speak just as insistently to us as they did to those who lived in the first century.

THE DUTY OF EMPLOYEES

When I turn to Paul's specific teaching about slaves, I speak of the duty of *employees*—not because being a working person is the same thing as being a slave or to make light of slavery, but because it is in the arena of employee-employer relationships that these principles need to be applied today. What

does an employee owe an employer? The text lists a number of items.

1. *Obedience.* This is the word Paul used to describe the responsibility children have to parents (v. 1), and I do not doubt that he chose it here deliberately. In terms of the work to be done, employees stand in the same relationship to employers as children to parents. It is the employer's job to determine what must be done and (in many cases) how it should be done. It is the employee's job to obey his employer in these areas.

Now this does not mean that the employee is free to disobey God, even if his employer tells him to, or that he is forbidden to make suggestions. But it does mean that he should willingly do all honest work assigned without assuming he knows better than his boss or bosses.

Recently my wife and I had carpet installed in our new home. The foreman of the crew sent to install it had been given a plan by the man who had sold the carpet, and two days had been apportioned for this work. The foreman was outraged. How could the salesman be so foolish! Anyone could see that this was a three-day job! Besides, the salesman had planned the job wrong. He had not said that there were stairs to climb, a piano to be moved, and so on. Several hours were lost in this way as the foreman tried (I thought) to show his crew how important he was. But when they all finally did get down to work, the carpet fit as planned and the work was completed in two days—in spite of the time lost in such complaining.

2. *Respect.* Paul's second thought is that slaves owe their masters "respect and fear." This is not a begrudging respect or a craven, scraping fear, of course, for these same words are used of the Christian's relationship to God. They denote a proper respect and reverence. This may be difficult at times,

particularly if the employer is unwise or arbitrary. But it is made easier by the thought that the employee ultimately serves Christ, even in a difficult situation. This Godward relationship is the key to the entire paragraph. For slaves are to obey their earthly masters as they "would obey Christ," strive to win their favor "like slaves of Christ," and serve them as "serving the Lord."

3. *Sincerity.* "Sincerity" is an interesting word. It comes from two Latin words: *sine* ("without") and *cere* ("wax"). Its meaning comes from the fact that in the ancient world, where the making of pottery was an important industry, dishonest potters would sometimes cover up cracks or flaws in their pottery by filling them with wax. In normal usage this might not be detected. But it could be seen if the pottery was held up to the light before it was purchased. Then the wax would show up as a lighter hue. Good pottery was sometimes stamped with the words *sine cere* ("without wax") as proof of its good quality. In the Greek language there was a corresponding word that means "sun tested."

I should say, however, that the word Paul actually uses in this sentence is *aplotēti*, which has the idea of generosity or liberality as well as sincerity. It suggests that the employee should not hold back from his best but should actually pour himself out liberally in honest service.

4. *Loyalty.* It is not easy to say in one English word what Paul conveys by the sentence "obey them not only to win their favor when their eye is on you, but like slaves of Christ, doing the will of God from your heart," but it is easy to visualize what he has in mind. He is thinking of a slave who will work hard only when the master is looking, like a secretary who types fast when the

office manager is around but who talks most of the rest of the time, or a manager who is "out to lunch" except when the boss is pressing him for something. By contrast, Paul recommends a steady, faithful service that comes from having the heart in the right place, which is why I speak of loyalty. It involves loyalty to the employer and to the company and a desire to see the work done.

5. *Good will.* The New International Version uses the word "wholehearted" at this point. The New English Bible says "cheerful." But I prefer the words "good will," which occur in the Authorized and Revised Standard versions. As John Stott says, employees should work as if their "heart and soul" are in it.[5] This term comes last because it aptly summarizes the preceding.

REWARDS

There is one more thing we need to notice before we move on to Paul's commands for masters, and that is the matter of rewards. As motivation for faithful and exemplary behavior Paul says, "Serve wholeheartedly . . . , *because* you know that *the Lord will reward everyone* for whatever good he does, whether he is slave or free" (vv. 7–8).

When Paul wrote these words he was thinking of a heavenly reward only, since slaves were not normally rewarded in earthly terms. But the interesting thing is that rewards, whether earthly or heavenly, do matter and that he is not afraid to introduce this as a motivation. Put in economic terms, this means that a system that guarantees workers a due reward for labor is closer to God's own way of operating than a system that does not. And it will work better! For this reason (and others), I believe that capitalism is a better system than communism—though this does not

---

[5]John R. W. Stott, *God's New Society: The Message of Ephesians* (Downers Grove, Ill.: InterVarsity, 1979), 253.

mean that Christianity necessarily puts a stamp of approval (or disapproval) on either. For this same reason I also approve of profit-sharing and other plans that draw employees into the economic well-being of their company.

THE DUTY OF EMPLOYERS

Having described the duty of slaves to masters (or, in our terms, employees to employers) at length, Paul now treats the corresponding duty of those who are in charge. This is dealt with more briefly because, as I have pointed out, he is interested in examples of submission chiefly: wives to husbands, children to parents, and slaves to masters. However, everything Paul said to employees also applies to employers since, as he argues, masters are to treat their slaves "in the same way" (v. 9).

"In the same way" does not mean that masters are to obey slaves just as slaves obey masters, because that would reduce the idea of obedience to chaos. But it does mean that masters are to treat slaves as they themselves might want to be treated. All are God's children. So in the final analysis both are to be serving God and are to be rewarded or judged by that Master.

In R. C. Sproul's book *The Search for Dignity,* there is discussion of a phrase that the author heard when researching the life of Wayne Alderson, a pioneer in management-labor relations. The term was "dropping his head." It occurred in a sentence like: "The supervisor comes in and drops his head." At first Sproul did not know what this meant. But one day he was in a hospital observing nonverbal communication between doctors, nurses, and other members of the staff that in a subtle way indicated the individual's status. He noticed how the nurses perked up when the doctor entered, for example. Obviously the doctors were on top of the pyramid.

While Sproul was watching this and thinking about it he saw a man coming up the corridor pushing a cart of soiled laundry. He was a member of the lowest caste of the hospital, a housekeeper. Yet he was cheerful. He was obviously happily relating to the others. As he came up, a nurse who had been very alert in the doctor's presence just moments before walked down the hall toward him. When he saw her he raised his head in acknowledgment, and his face brightened in anticipation of a greeting. At almost the same moment the nurse tilted her head forward and stared at the floor as she walked by briskly. The man's face lost its cheer, and his pace became noticeably slower as he continued on his way with the laundry. Sproul realized that this is what "dropping the head" meant. It was a refusal to acknowledge the other person. It was like saying that the human being was invisible, that he or she did not count.[6]

In the final analysis this is what matters to most people. It is not the position we hold, whether it is high or low, management or labor, or even (in a certain sense) slave or master. What matters is whether we are treated with dignity, whether we are regarded as having real worth. Christianity declares, *"You do have real worth! You are made in God's image! What you do does matter!"* If so, we should do our own work well and value others.

---

[6]Sproul, *The Search for Dignity,* 96–97. The book on Wayne Alderson is titled *Stronger Than Steel* (San Francisco: Harper & Row, 1980).

36

Our Spiritual Warfare

(Ephesians 6:10–12)

Finally, be strong in the Lord and in his mighty power. Put on the full armor of God so that you can take your stand against the devil's schemes. For our struggle is not against flesh and blood, but against the rulers, against the authorities, against the powers of this dark world and against the spiritual forces of evil in the heavenly realms.

Some time ago I came across the statement "A man never forgets his first girlfriend." I do not know whether that is true or not—I suppose it is—but it is equally true, I am sure, that a preacher never forgets his first sermon.

I preached my first sermon when I was thirteen years old, and the text I preached on was the one to which I have now come in this verse-by-verse exposition of Ephesians. I preached that first sermon with visual aids. I played football at the time. So I brought my football equipment into the pulpit and held it up as I developed the parts of the sermon. When I talked about the "breastplate of righteousness" I held up my shoulder pads. When I talked about the "helmet of salvation" I held up my helmet. So it went through the other parts of the Christian soldier's armor. I can visualize how that sermon went, because I had my notes taped to the back of the pieces of my uniform.

It has been almost thirty-five years since I preached that sermon, and in all those years I have preached on these great verses only one other time—in a special series of Sunday evening messages. That strikes me as unfortunate because it suggests that the warfare in which we are engaged as Christians is relatively unimportant, when actually the opposite is the case.

The opposite was obviously the case for Paul. These verses are the culmination of this book, and the point on which they end is that each Christian is engaged in a great spiritual battle and must equip himself for it.

Our Contemporary Problem

Many Christians today would judge the teaching of these verses unimportant. They would encourage us to think positively and peacefully, as if there were no spiritual battles at all. They see Christianity not as an entrance into warfare but as an exit from it. They see it as the solution to our problems. If you are sick, Jesus will make you well. If you are discouraged, Jesus will make you happy. You get the impression from those who talk like this that to believe in Jesus is to enter upon a smooth path and to enjoy smooth sailing.

Another approach to the Christian life does not so much deny the reality of spiritual warfare as insist that, although it exists, it is all over and done with in a certain sense. Watchman Nee's study of Ephesians entitled *Sit Walk Stand* is an example of this.[1] The title of that work is both an outline of Ephesians, as Nee sees it, and an expression of Nee's theology of the Christian life. Christianity begins by *sitting* with Christ in the heavenly places (Eph. 2:6), that is, resting in Christ's achievements. It continues by *walking out* the Christian life (Eph. 4:1, KJV), that is, living Christianity practically. Finally, it involves *standing* on ground Christ has already won for us (Eph. 6:11, 13–14). Nee emphasizes that, because of Christ's victories, our warfare is always a defensive rather than offensive struggle.

There may be some truth in that. But what bothers me is that this thinking has been carried over into expressions of what it means to live the Christian life which suggest that there is nothing (or at least very little) for us to do as Christians. "Let go and let God," some say. That is, the battle is not ours; it is God's. So just let go; let God do the fighting. At the most, you need only stand your ground. It is true, of course, that Paul does use the word "stand." He uses it four times. But when he speaks of our armor he speaks not only of defensive armor such as our helmet, breastplate, and shield, but also of our offensive weapon, our sword. And whether or not he is thinking of fighting offensively or defensively, he *is* thinking of fighting against the most powerful and cunning foes.

In my opinion the proper balance is struck in the first two verses, which contain two commands. First, "Be strong in the Lord and in his mighty power" (v. 10). Second, "Put on the full armor of God so that you can take your stand against the devil's schemes" (v. 11). We are reminded by this combination of commands that we are unequal to the battle. We have no strength; our

strength must come from the Lord. Nevertheless, endued with his strength we are to fight these spiritual forces arrayed against us.

John R. W. Stott shows the inevitability of this struggle, given: (1) the purposes of God expounded in the first five chapters of Ephesians, and (2) the existence of a devil who is opposed to those purposes. Stott writes, "Is God's plan to create a new society? Then they [the hostile spiritual forces] will do their utmost to destroy it. Has God through Jesus Christ broken down the walls dividing human beings of different races and cultures from each other? Then the devil through his emissaries will strive to rebuild them. Does God intend his reconciled and redeemed people to lie together in harmony and purity? Then the powers of hell will scatter among them the seeds of discord and sin."[2]

As Stott shows, the very fact that Paul follows his beautiful and uplifting portrait of peaceful Christian homes and happy Christian relations (in Ephesians 5:22–6:9) with this stark description of warfare indicates that even these things will not be achieved without conflict. Clearly the victories of the Christian life are to be achieved by a relentless and life-long struggle against evil. And even then they are realized only to the extent that we avail ourselves of God's armor.

I love the way William Gurnall, that great seventeenth-century Puritan, approached it. He wrote a book of nearly 1,200 double-column pages (my edition), entitled *The Christian in Complete Armour: A Treatise of the Saint's War Against the Devil*. But that is only the short title! It continues: "wherein a discovery is made of that grand enemy of God and his people—in his policies, power, seat of his empire, wickedness

[1]Watchman Nee, *Sit Walk Stand* (Fort Washington, Pa.: Christian Literature Crusade, 1957).

[2]John R. W. Stott, *God's New Society: The Message of Ephesians* (Downers Grove, Ill.: InterVarsity, 1979), 261–62.

and chief design he hath against the saints—[and] a magazine [is] opened from whence the Christian is furnished with spiritual arms for the battle, helped on with his armour, and taught the use of his weapon, together with the happy issue of the whole war."[3]

In more recent days D. Martyn Lloyd-Jones has made a similar though not equally long attempt at exposition. He has published two books on these verses: *The Christian Warfare*, which contains twenty-six studies on verses 10–13, and *The Christian Soldier*, which contains twenty-six additional studies on the section as a whole.[4]

OUR INVISIBLE FOE

When I approach these closing verses of Ephesians I think of the cartoon that was used on the record jacket of the hit Broadway musical *My Fair Lady*. If you think back to that musical and to the advertisements for it, you will recall the design in which a heavenly being (God, although he looked a great deal like George Bernard Shaw, the author of the play on which *My Fair Lady* was based) was controlling a puppet (who was Henry Higgins, the chief male character in the play) who, in turn, was controlling Eliza Doolittle (the chief female character). The point was that just as Higgins imagined himself to be manipulating Eliza, making her into the "fair lady" he saw her being, so also was God (or George Bernard Shaw) manipulating Higgins.

This is the kind of relationship the apostle Paul has in mind as he begins his description of the nature of the struggle that faces Christian people. He has told us to "be strong in the Lord" and to "put on the full armor of God."

Now he tells why this is necessary. He says, "Our struggle is not against flesh and blood, but against the rulers, against the authorities, against the powers of this dark world and against the spiritual forces of evil in the heavenly realms" (v. 12).

When Paul says that we do not struggle against flesh and blood he is not, in my opinion, denying that we do at times actually struggle on the human level. It is obvious that we do. He is saying that our struggle is not *just* on that level. We do have a physical, visible struggle. But over and above that, over and above what we see, there is an invisible spiritual struggle going on against the devil and his forces. We cannot see the devil or his legions. Yet, as Peter says, "Your enemy the devil prowls around like a roaring lion looking for someone to devour" (1 Peter 5:8). If we are to be successful in this battle, we must be alert to it and equipped to use the armor that is needed.

Right here we have something that sets Christianity off from the philosophies of our world. The world of our day is secular; that is, it operates only within the categories of this age. And it is materialistic, which means that it considers as real only what it can see or touch or measure. For our contemporaries the world is a closed system. That is why talk about the devil is hardly regarded as serious. People still talk about God, of course. He gets some respect out of deference to religious traditions. But the devil? "You can't be serious! A little man in red underwear with a tail and horns? Is that your enemy? He and his little demons?" People laugh at any suggestion that our

[3] William Gurnall, *The Christian in Complete Armour* (1662–65; reprint, Carlisle, Pa.: Banner of Truth Trust, 1979).

[4] D. Martyn Lloyd-Jones, *The Christian Warfare: An Exposition of Ephesians 6:10–13* (Grand Rapids: Baker, 1977), and *The Christian Soldier: An Exposition of Ephesians 6:10 to 20* (Grand Rapids: Baker, 1983). Ray C. Stedman has also published a valuable study entitled *Spiritual Warfare: Winning the Daily Battle with Satan* (Portland, Oreg.: Multnomah, 1975).

warfare is spiritual and, on a more serious note, accuse us of neglecting the real battle which in their opinion should be waged against such tangible things as poverty, oppression, hunger, and various forms of injustice.

We do not want to deny for an instant that those are real problems or that we should do all we can to alleviate or abolish them. But we ask: If the real problems of this world are merely material and visible, how is it that they have not been solved or eliminated long ago? Algernon Charles Swinburne called man "the master of things." All right, then, let him master them! If he cannot—and it is perfectly evident he cannot—let him acknowledge that it is because forces stronger than himself stand behind what is visible. Let him acknowledge that our struggle is not merely against flesh and blood, which we see, but "against the rulers, against the authorities, against the powers of this dark world and against the spiritual forces of evil in the heavenly realms."

I like the way Paul repeats the word "against" in this sentence. It is not the way one is supposed to write, of course. If one of our modern editors had gotten hold of Paul's manuscript, I am sure he would have deleted the repetitions. He would have taken out three occurrences of "against," so the sentence would read: "against the rulers, the authorities, the powers of this dark world and the spiritual forces of evil in the heavenly realms." (And there might even have been some additional shortening!)

But I think Paul knew exactly what he was doing when he repeated that word; and what is more to the point, I think the Holy Spirit had his own clear purpose when he directed the writing. It is a way of saying with emphasis that in the warfare in the Christian life Christians are really "up against it." It is not just a string of things that we should be concerned about. There are

enemies and we must fight against them. We must fight *against* the rulers, *against* the authorities, *against* the powers of this dark world, *against* the spiritual forces of evil in the heavenly realms.

OUR FIELD OF BATTLE

How are we to understand the nouns that occur in this passage: rulers, authorities, powers, and forces? Some have taken them as if they are ranks in Satan's army. At the bottom you have spiritual forces, mere demons. Over these are powers. Powers are governed by authorities, and above these are rulers. Presumably the devil is over all. Or they reverse it: first rulers, then authorities, followed by powers and forces. I do not think Paul is doing that. I think he is using terms which take the powers that are arrayed against us together. The distinction is not between the supposed levels of demonic authority but rather between the various areas of life over which they exert an evil influence.

When Paul talks about rulers, is it not the case that he is thinking about the devil's control of certain regions? A ruler governs a certain territory, a certain portion of land. In human terms, one ruler presides over England, another over France, still another over the United States, and so on. Apparently, the demons also operate that way. In fact, they would have to because, unlike God, they are not omnipresent. That is, they are not everywhere at once as God is. They are finite creatures, though of great power; so they must be in one place or another. When Paul speaks of them as rulers he is probably thinking in this way, regionally. We know, of course, that in some areas of the world the power of Satan is very strong and obvious. In other places, particularly places where the gospel of Jesus Christ has gone, it is comparatively weaker.

What about authorities? Authority is not the same thing as rule. Mother Teresa exercises no physical rule, but she has great authority. Authority has to do with values. So when Paul speaks of authorities he is saying that the values of our culture, as well as specific territory, are demonically controlled. We need to see that the dominant values of our cultures—the "me first" philosophy, pleasure for its own sake, materialism, and other things—are not Christian but are controlled and manipulated by Satan for his own base ends. We are to be at war against them.

Power concerns control. So the powers are those who control what people think and do. I relate this to the secular media, which control so much of our contemporary moral ethos. But not just the media! It also refers to powers that stand behind even these very powerful figures.

The final words make clear that Paul is not just thinking of particularly evil men and women, like Hitler, who somehow control others for their own dark designs. He is thinking rather of "the spiritual forces of evil in the heavenly realms." The emphasis here is upon the evil of this spiritual control. It would be possible to have a holy, beneficial power. In fact, that power exists. It is the power of God in which the Christian is encouraged to be strengthened (v. 10). But the spiritual forces against which we struggle are not holy or beneficial. They are wicked and destructive.

The Christian's warfare is not merely a struggle between truth and falsehood, good and evil, as most people would understand those comparisons. There is a philosophy of history that looks upon struggle between truth and falsehood as being essentially good since, so the thought goes, that is the way progress comes. Truth and error struggle, and truth wins. One philosopher wrote, "Who ever knew truth to be bested in a free and open encounter?" Similarly we are to suppose that good inevitably triumphs. But this is not the case. Truth is often bested. Evil does win. Error and evil will carry the world into a new dark age unless Christians stand firm in the power of God.

OUR MEANS OF SUCCESS

But not in our own strength. Martin Luther had it right when he wrote in one of the best known of all hymns:

Did we in our own strength
    confide,
Our striving would be losing;
Were not the right man on our
    side,
The man of God's own choosing.
Dost ask who that may be?
Christ Jesus, it is he;
Lord Sabaoth his name,
From age to age the same,
And he must win the battle.

We will study precisely what that means in greater detail. But I am sure even at this point that you can see that everything that is given to us to make our victory possible is from Christ. Is it truth (v. 14)? He is the truth; he is the one who said, "I am the way and the truth and the life. No one comes to the Father except through me" (John 14:6). Is it righteousness (v. 14)? He is our righteousness. Paul writes, "Christ . . . has become for us wisdom from God— that is, our righteousness, holiness and redemption" (1 Cor. 1:30). Is it the gospel (v. 15)? The gospel is the gospel of Christ (Mark 1:1). Is it faith (v. 16)? It is faith in him (Gal. 2:20). Salvation (v. 17)? Christ is our salvation; he achieved it by his death on the cross (Acts 4:10–12). Even prayer is by the channel that he has opened up for us (Heb. 10:19–20).

Not one of us can stand against the spiritual forces of evil in our own strength—not even for a moment. But in Christ we can fight on to victory.

37

Our Terrible Enemy

(Ephesians 6:12)

For our struggle is not against flesh and blood, but against the rulers, against the authorities, against the powers of this dark world and against the spiritual forces of evil in the heavenly realms.

M. Scott Peck believes in the devil—not *the* devil necessarily, based on my last reading, but at least in a concentration of spiritual evil that is beyond normal human experience. What convinced him was his participation in two exorcisms which he describes in his best-selling book *People of the Lie*.

Dr. Peck is a psychiatrist. He graduated from Harvard College in 1958, having earned a "high honors" degree. He then went to the Case Western Reserve University School of Medicine for medical training, graduating in 1963, and served in the United States Army as an assistant chief of psychiatry and a neurology consultant to the surgeon general until 1972. From that time he has practiced psychiatry in Connecticut, writing about his experiences, first, in *The Road Less Traveled*, which has sold 1.5 million copies, and now in *People of the Lie*, which is on its way to matching the earlier work's success.

M. Scott Peck, M.D., is no lightweight, as the biographical details show. Yet he believes in an evil spiritual force, Satan, whom he calls "it." In the first of his two books he had not yet reached this conviction, though he had

by the second. It is an interesting (and possibly related fact) that between the first and second of these books Peck not only came to believe in a personal devil—he also became a Christian.[1]

It is an interesting development. Not many years ago belief in Satan would have been a formula for career disaster for anyone but a priest. Yet today, in spite of the fact that ninety-nine percent of all psychiatrists and the majority of all ministers still do not believe in a devil, that is changing. Peck says that since his book came out he has heard of three other highly respected psychiatrists who have also participated in exorcisms, and he agrees with Malachi Martin, an expert on exorcisms, that more than a thousand exorcisms are conducted each year in the United States, without the church's blessing. Many others are ready to discuss demonic possession.

What has produced this change? Peck would argue that it is the sheer reality of evil—viewed in a dramatic way in exorcisms but also to be seen in people who love evil and practice evil for its own sake.

[1] M. Scott Peck, *The Road Less Traveled* (New York: Simon & Schuster, 1978) and *People of the Lie* (New York: Simon & Schuster, 1983).

OUR POWERFUL ENEMY

None of this is the least bit novel to a person well acquainted with the Bible. For whether we turn to the earliest pages of the Old Testament, the prophets, the writers of the four Gospels, the Epistles, or the book of Revelation—at every turn we are reminded of Satan's existence and warned of his activities. This is what Paul is doing in Ephesians. He is describing the Christian's warfare in this world and is showing that it is not merely a struggle against visible enemies. It is a struggle against the devil and those spiritual powers that stand behind the enemies we see. Paul writes, "Put on the full armor of God so that you can take your stand against the devil's schemes. For our struggle is not against flesh and blood, but against the rulers, against the authorities, against the powers of this dark world, and against the spiritual forces of evil in the heavenly realms" (vv. 11–12).

In describing the spiritual forces of evil against whom we must contend Paul says three important things about the devil. First, he is a great and powerful foe. Paul indicates this by the words used to describe his agents—"rulers," "authorities," "powers," and "forces"—and by the fact that he warns us to take arms against them.

When we talk about the devil being great and powerful we must be careful not to overstate the case. Because he is a spiritual rather than a material being, many people are inclined to think of Satan as more or less the equal of God. It is true that he is a counterpart to the greatest of the unfallen angels: Michael or Gabriel. But he is not a spiritual counterpart to God. God is God. Every other being has been created by God and is therefore limited for the simple reason that he or she has been created.

God is omnipotent; that is, he is all-powerful. The devil is not. God can do anything he wishes to do. The devil, like the rest of us, can do only what God permits him to do. This is God's universe, not the devil's. Not even hell is the devil's. God has created hell as the place where he will one day confine Satan and his followers.

God is omnipresent; that is, God is everywhere at once. David said, "Where can I flee from your presence? If I go up to the heavens, you are there; if I make my bed in the depths, you are there. If I rise on the wings of the dawn, if I settle on the far side of the sea, even there your hand will guide me, your right hand will hold me fast" (Ps. 139:7–10). This cannot be said of Satan. Satan can only be in one place at one time. Consequently, he must either tempt one person in one place at one time, or he must extend his influence through one of the other spiritual beings that fell with him. The result is that, although the devil's influence is widespread, it is probably the case that neither you nor anyone you know has ever been tempted by the devil directly. In fact, in all the Bible we know of only six individuals who were tempted by Satan himself: Eve (but not Adam), Job, Jesus Christ, Judas, Peter, and Ananias (but not his wife Sapphira). No doubt there have been many others, but these are the only ones the Bible tells us of specifically.

God is omniscient; that is, he knows everything. This is not true of Satan. Satan does not know everything. True, he knows a great deal, and he is undoubtedly a shrewd guesser. But the ways of God must constantly surprise him, and he certainly has no more certainty about what is going to happen in the future than we have.

Yet Satan is still a powerful enemy. It is not hard to demonstrate this. Reflect on the condition of Adam and Eve before the Fall. They were far more intelligent and much wiser than we can ever hope to be. They were more aware of spiritual issues than we are. They were closer to God. Indeed, there was nothing to separate them from God at all for they had not yet sinned. Yet they fell. And what is even more striking, the devil seems to have had very little trouble bringing their defection about. We are much more foolish than our first parents, as I said. We are spiritually insensitive. We are often far from God. And, as to the other side, the devil is undoubtedly a much better informed and wiser devil now than he was then.

So although Satan is not a spiritual counterpart to God—he is not omnipotent, omnipresent, or omniscient—he is nevertheless a very formidable foe, and a Christian is foolish if he thinks Satan can be resisted by human strength alone.

OUR WICKED ENEMY

The second thing Paul tells us about the devil is that he is wicked and destructive, for he stands behind the powers of "this *dark* world" and the forces "of *evil*" in the heavenly realms.

It is this that got Scott Peck interested in exorcisms. At the beginning, like most psychiatrists, he believed that destructive behavior merely needed to be redirected, which is what most psychotherapy or psychological counseling attempts to do. But his counseling brought him cases in which evil seemed to be existing for its own sake. The crucial case involved a woman he names Charlene. She had been coming to him two-to-four times a week for three years—421 sessions, to be exact—but she never got better, and that was because she did not want to. As Peck came to see it, she only wanted to toy with him.

Peck says, "Charlene's desire to make a conquest of me, to toy with me,

to utterly control our relationship, knew no bounds. It seemed to be a desire for power purely for its own sake. She did not want power in order to improve society, to care for a family, to make herself a more effective person, or in any way accomplish anything creative. Her thirst for power was unsubordinated to anything higher than herself."[2]

It was toward the end of his sessions with Charlene that Peck began to study exorcism.

Paul warns Christians not merely that they may encounter evil people, however, but rather that they are in a struggle against the evil behind such evil, whether they encounter evil people directly or not. If we are to overcome these powers, we must, as John R. W. Stott says, "bear in mind that they have no moral principles, no code of honor, no higher feelings. They recognize no Geneva Convention to restrict or partially civilize the weapons of their warfare. They are utterly unscrupulous, and ruthless in the pursuit of their malicious designs."[3]

OUR CRAFTY ENEMY

The third thing Paul says about Satan is that he is extremely sly and crafty. In the New International Version verse 11 warns us to take our stand against "the devil's schemes." Both the King James and the Revised versions say "wiles." The New English Bible uses the word "devices." What these words mean is that the devil does not always attack us directly or in the same way. On the contrary, he uses a variety of times and methods. Genesis 3 calls him "crafty" (v. 1) and shows how he beguiled Eve. In 2 Corinthians 2:11, Paul says, "We are not unaware of his schemes."

What are these schemes? I think here

---

[2]Peck, *People of the Lie,* 176. The account of Peck's encounters with Charlene is related fully on pages 150–81.

[3]John R. W. Stott, *God's New Society: The Message of Ephesians* (Downers Grove, Ill.: InterVarsity, 1979), 264.

of the work of William Gurnall, the Puritan divine who wrote more on these eleven verses than anybody else in any language. In his 1,200-page study of *The Christian in Complete Armour*, Gurnall exposes Satan's craft in knowing both when and how to make his approaches. Satan attacks:

1. *When the Christian is newly converted.* The early days of our Christian lives are glorious. Before our conversion we were dead in transgressions and sins. Now we are alive. Before, our minds were darkened by the evil spirit of this world. Now we see spiritual things clearly. Before, we did not desire fellowship with God. Now we do. Before, we were discouraged. Now we are filled with optimism and great joy. Ah, but that is when Satan comes— when, like Eve, we are not yet confirmed in any strong path of obedience. He trips us up. Then he says, "I see by your sin that you are not a Christian after all. Your 'conversion' was temporary. You have fallen away. You might as well settle down now and follow me."

2. *When the Christian is afflicted.* When things go well the devil frequently leaves us alone. But when we go through times of affliction, as most of God's children do from time to time, the devil is often quickly there to suggest that God has abandoned us or that we are not really his children. "If God loved you, he wouldn't let you suffer like this," Satan argues. "If God is good, he obviously doesn't care about you. And if he isn't good, well, what's the difference? You might as well curse him for his wickedness and sin as you please."

Job was tempted like this, although the tempting words were channeled through his "friends" and wife. God had permitted Satan to destroy Job's wealth and family and then to afflict him with boils—to show that Job loved God for what God was in himself and not for what he gave Job materially. But when Job lost all these things—possessions, children, and good health—Satan was there to say that it was because of some deep, hidden sin in Job's life. "Job, you just think you're a righteous man," said his friends. "You can't be. This is a moral universe. Bad things don't happen to good people. So if bad things are happening to you, it is because you have done something terrible, whether you know it or not. God is punishing you." His wife was even more outspoken. She said, "Are you still holding on to your integrity? Curse God and die!" (Job 2:9).

3. *When the Christian has achieved some notable success.* This was Peter's experience. Jesus had asked the disciples who they thought he was, and Peter had responded, "You are the Christ, the Son of the living God" (Matt. 16:16). This was a great insight, so great, in fact, that Jesus immediately explained its source, saying, "This was not revealed to you by man, but by my Father in heaven" (v. 17). Jesus then went on to speak about his coming death and resurrection. But Peter, riding high on his good performance, tried to persuade Jesus that his death was unnecessary and occasioned his stinging rebuke: "Get behind me, Satan! You are a stumbling block to me; you do not have in mind the things of God, but the things of men" (v. 23).

4. *When the Christian is idle.* "Idle hands are the devil's hands," says a proverb. "If the devil finds a man inactive, he will soon find some work for him to do," says another. We remember David. The great sin in David's life was his adultery with Bathsheba and the murder of her husband Uriah. It is significant that David's failure began in a time of inactivity. It was the spring of the year when the armies went out to battle, but David (now in his fifties) stayed home from battle, leaving the conduct of the war to

his trusted friend Joab. It was as he was idle in Jerusalem, lounging on the roof of his palace, that David saw Bathsheba and called her to him.

5. *When the Christian is isolated from others who share his faith*. So long as we are with other Christians, our brothers and sisters in Christ, we are with those who can encourage, help, and, if necessary, call us to account. Generally, if we are in such company, Satan recognizes that his time can be better spent elsewhere. But get off by ourselves away from other Christians or, worse yet, get in close, intimate contact with non-Christians—and the devil comes. "I see you are finally away from those hypocrites who have been stopping you from having any fun," he observes. "Well, now you can do what you want to do, and they won't even know about it. Didn't God give you all these [evil] things to enjoy? So enjoy! And even if they are wrong, your doing them is certainly not going to hurt anybody."

6. *When the Christian is dying*. Death is a time of physical weakness, at least if it does not come abruptly, and Satan uses physical weaknesses to afflict us. "At the hour of death, when the saint is down and prostrate in his bodily strength, now this coward falls upon him," writes Gurnall. "As they say of the natural serpent, he never is seen at his length till dying; so this mystical serpent never strains his wit and wiles more, than when his time is thus short. The saint is even stepping into eternity, and now he treads upon his heel, which if he cannot trip up so as to hinder his arrival in heaven, yet at least to bruise it, that he may go with more pain thither."[4]

Satan is subtle in his attacks. But he is not subtle only in the times of his coming. He is also crafty in *how* he attacks. He attacks:

1. *As a roaring lion.* Peter says that the devil comes to us as "a roaring lion, looking for someone to devour" (1 Peter 5:8). I do not think Peter means that Satan always appears as a lion to us, but he sometimes appears before us with a frightful roar—to terrify us into forgetting who we are and whom we are to serve.

2. *As a friend*. At other times the devil appears before us as a friend. This is how Satan came to Eve. He did not come threatening. He came with an offer to help out. He would show them what God was really like. He would help them to become "like God, knowing good and evil" (Gen. 3:5). When Satan comes to you like that, remember that it is Jesus and not the devil who is really your friend. Only Jesus sticks closer than a brother.

3. *As an angel of light*. Oh, how Satan loves to bring "enlightenment." "You don't mean to tell me that you believe those old-fashioned tales you find in the Bible," Satan says. "Nobody believes those myths anymore. Scholarship has disproved all that." I suppose this form of temptation comes from the pulpit more often than from any other place, unless possibly the college or seminary classroom. Martin Luther had it right when he said, "When you look for the devil, don't forget to look in the pulpit." Many have fallen because they have followed the prince of darkness' "light."

HAVING DONE ALL, TO STAND

Satan is indeed a terrible enemy. If it were not for God and the provision he has made for us for this warfare, we would be rightly downcast and discouraged, and we would despair. But we are not to do that. That is why this passage was written. It was written to tell us that, although we face a great

---

[4]William Gurnall, *The Christian in Complete Armor* (1662–65; reprint, Carlisle, Pa.: Banner of Truth Trust, 1979), 74.

and terrible enemy, the victory is not our enemy's but God's. And it is our victory, too, if we arm ourselves as we are told to arm ourselves and persevere to the end.

The conclusion is a simple one—the same conclusion we came to in the previous study. Do not trust yourself. If you trust yourself, as Peter did, you will fall as Peter did. Peter told Jesus, "Even if all fall away, I will not" (Mark 14:29). But that very night, Peter, who considered himself the strongest of all the apostles, denied his Lord three times, on the last occasion even with oaths and cursings (Mark 14:66–72). If we trust to ourselves, we will fall. But if we know our own weakness and therefore turn to God as our necessary defense against Satan, then we will be able to stand against the devil's schemes. The Bible says, "Submit yourselves, then, to God. Resist the devil, and he will flee from you" (James 4:7).

38

Our Only Strength

(Ephesians 6:13)

Therefore put on the full armor of God, so that when the day of evil comes, you may be able to stand your ground, and after you have done everything, to stand.

When I talk about the devil I try, as I did in the last study, to show that he is a finite, and therefore limited, being. He is not an evil counterpart of God. Satan is not omnipotent, as God is. He is not omnipresent, as God is. He is not omniscient, as God is. Consequently, he can only do what God permits. He can only tempt one person in one place at one time, or else operate through those legions of angels, now demons, who fell with him. He does not know the future. At best Satan can make shrewd guesses based on experience.

But none of this means that the devil is not dangerous. He may not be omnipotent, omnipresent, or omniscient. But he is certainly powerful, wicked, and sly. He is so powerful that, according to Jude, even Michael, the archangel, "when he was disputing with the devil about the body of Moses, did not dare to bring a slanderous accusation against him, but said, 'The Lord rebuke you!'" (Jude 9). He is so wicked that he is described in the Bible as "a murderer from the beginning" (John 8:44). He is so sly that we are in constant danger of being tripped up by his wiles. This is why Paul wrote even of an elder in the church that "he must also have a good reputation with outsiders, so that he will not fall into disgrace and into the devil's trap" (1 Tim. 3:7). The devil is not all-powerful, but he is certainly much more powerful than we are. So if we are to resist his evil influences, it must be by the power and provision of God only.

That is why James wrote, "Submit yourselves, then, to *God*. Resist the devil, and he will flee from you" (James 4:7). It is why Paul says, "Put on the full armor of *God*, so that when the day of evil comes, you may be able to stand your ground, and after you have done everything, to stand" (Eph. 6:13).

ELISHA AT DOTHAN

When I think of our need to stand against Satan in the strength of God, I think about the prophet Elisha at Dothan. In those days the northern kingdom of Israel was under attack from the Syrians led by their infamous king Ben Hadad. Israel was the weaker of the two nations, and she would have been overrun by the Syrians had God not been revealing the plans of the Syrian king through Elisha. Whenever Ben Hadad would set a trap for Israel, God would reveal it to Elisha, Elisha would tell the king of Israel, the plans would be changed, and Israel would escape unhurt.

Ben Hadad thought there was a traitor among his officers. So he called them together and demanded to know who he was. They told him the truth: "Elisha, the prophet who is in Israel, tells the king of Israel the very words you speak in your bedroom" (2 Kings 6:12).

When he heard that, Ben Hadad decided that if he was going to make progress in his war with Israel, he would have to capture Elisha first. So he demanded to know where he was. He was told that Elisha was residing at Dothan. Ben Hadad got his troops together, marched to Dothan, and surrounded the city by night. It is an interesting picture: all the armies of Ben Hadad combined to surround and, if possible, capture this one true servant of God.

In the morning the servant of Elisha went out of the city and saw Ben Hadad's soldiers. The story does not tell us anything about him, but I suspect that he was young and even somewhat sleepy as he set out to do his chores—probably to draw water from a city well. I can see him stumbling out of the gate with his eyes half-open, perhaps not even noticing the soldiers until he had first drawn a bucket of water and washed his face. Suddenly he saw them! His eyes opened wide, and, leaving his waterpot, he ran back into the city to tell Elisha they were surrounded. "Oh, my lord, what shall we do?" he asked (v. 15).

Elisha replied in what is surely one of the greatest statements of faith in all the Bible. "Don't be afraid. . . . Those who are with us are more than those who are with them" (v. 16). Then Elisha prayed, and God opened the young man's eyes to see the hills full of horses and chariots of fire around Elisha.

That statement by Elisha is a great statement of the principle we have been studying. On the one hand, it says that the enemy we face is greater even than the enemy we see. The enemy is "them," in this case the combined armies of the Syrians under Ben Hadad. It is also "those who are with them." In view of the revelation given to the servant, this enemy must be the spiritual force of evil that accompanied and stood behind the Syrian forces. But what is on the other side? So far as anything seen is concerned, there were only Elisha and his young servant— two unattended individuals. But, of course, that is not the whole of the equation. On the Syrian side were soldiers plus the spiritual force of evil. On the side of Elisha and his servant were the angels of God here described as "horses and chariots of fire all around Elisha." From a human perspective the Syrians seemed more powerful, but when the spiritual forces were taken into account, God's servants were stronger.

The Lord Our Strength

Paul is not referring to this incident, of course. But the theology of victory, which he is advocating, is the same. Notice how often Paul mentions the Lord in this passage. It is the way he begins: "Finally, be strong *in the Lord* and in his mighty power" (v. 10). When he begins to talk about the armor in which we are to resist the devil's forces, he stresses that it is God's armor: "Put on the full armor *of God* so that you can take your stand against the devil's schemes" (v. 11). So also later: "Therefore put on the full armor *of God*, so that when the day of evil comes, you may be able to stand your ground, and after you have done everything, to stand" (v. 13). It is only by the strength of God that we will be able to stand against these forces.

Although the word "lord" has many uses—it can, for example, be used of a mere human master, as was the case in the servant's cry of alarm to his "lord" Elisha—"Lord" is the word customarily used in the Greek version of the Old

Testament to translate the tetragrammaton, the great name for God (YHWH). This was the name by which God revealed himself to Moses at the burning bush, explaining it by saying, "I AM WHO I AM" (Exod. 3:14). It is a name intended to stretch our minds as we contemplate the nature of God. "Lord" teaches us that the God of the Bible, in whom we are to trust as our only defense against Satan is: self-existent and self-sufficient.

It is most important to see that God is self-existent, because this is what the name "I AM" most naturally points to. Everything we see and know has antecedents. That is, it exists because something existed before it and was its cause. We are here because of our parents. They lived because of their parents, and so on. It is the same with everything else—everything except God. God has no antecedents. Nothing caused God. On the contrary, he caused everything else. Even Satan would not exist if it were not for God. We may be puzzled by this, wondering why God permits Satan and his activity. But even if we do not have the full answers to this question, the fact that God is self-existent begins to put our spiritual warfare in perspective. God, not Satan, is in charge, and in the end everything will be resolved by him and everyone will be answerable to him.

God is also self-sufficient. Self-existence means that God has no origins. Self-sufficiency means that God has no needs. No one can supply anything that God might be supposed to be lacking. No one can teach God anything; he knows all things. No one can stand in for God in any place; he already is everywhere. No one can help God out; he is all-powerful.

When I think of the power of God my mind often goes to the first chapter of Jonah which has a funny little play on words in it relating to God's power. In the fifth verse, after we have been told

that God sent a violent storm after the ship that was carrying Jonah to Tarshish, we read that the sailors were "afraid." That is reasonable enough, of course. Who would not be under those circumstances? They were in danger of losing their lives. But then, just five verses later, in verse 10, after Jonah had been brought up on deck and had identified himself, saying, "I am a Hebrew and I worship the LORD, the God of heaven, who made the sea and the land," we read "this terrified them." The older versions read, "Then were the men exceedingly afraid" (KJV).

Why is it that in verse 5, when they are in danger of losing their lives, the sailors are said to be only "afraid," when in verse 10, after hearing Jonah's testimony, they are said to have been "exceedingly afraid"?

I think it is because these men already knew something about Jonah's God. They were sailors, after all, and sailors get around. They had been in and out of the major ports of the Mediterranean Sea and had heard the port gossip. In the Egyptian ports they would have heard how Jehovah had delivered his people from slavery. He had brought plagues on Egypt: turning the waters of the land to blood, multiplying frogs, gnats, and flies, afflicting cattle, destroying crops, calling out swarms of locusts, eventually blotting out the sun and then killing the firstborn. Nor was that all. When the people prepared to leave Egypt God divided the waters of the Red Sea, making a path for them to pass over. Then he caused the waters to come back and drown the pursuing Egyptians.

Perhaps the sailors heard how Jehovah had cared for his people in the desert—how he had given them manna to eat and water for them and their livestock. He had sent a great cloud to cover them by day, protecting them from the fierce rays of the sun; it turned into a pillar of fire at night to provide both light and warmth. At last God had divided the river Jordan for Israel to cross into Canaan and had destroyed Jericho. He even stopped the sun and moon while the Jewish armies wrought a total destruction on their foes at Gibeon.

This is what the God of the Jews was like. So when Jonah said, "I am a Hebrew and I worship the LORD [Jehovah], the God of heaven, who made the sea and the land," they were terrified and said, "What have you done? . . . What should we do to you to make the sea calm down for us?" (Jonah 1:10–11).

This God is our God too. Only his strength is greater even than that displayed in overpowering Egypt and bringing the Jewish people into the Promised Land. God is the God of *all* power. *Nothing* can stand against him. So although we cannot hope to stand against the forces of Satan in our own strength even for a moment, we can successfully stand against them and defeat them in the power of God. God is our only strength, but he is the only strength we need.

The Armor of God

Still, victory in this spiritual warfare is not automatic, which is why Paul admonishes us to "put on the full armor of God" and "stand [our] ground" against Satan.

Where did Paul get his thoughts about this armor? I suppose that I have never heard a sermon about the Christian's armor that did not point out that Paul probably began to think along these lines while being chained to a Roman guard during his imprisonment. It seems quite plausible. We can imagine him looking at the guard's armor, thinking of the Christian's spiritual warfare, and wondering what the various parts of the guard's armor could illustrate.

It is entirely possible that Paul came by his ideas about the Christian's armor in this way, but I am inclined to think that in this case, as in many others, Paul got his ideas from the Word of God. Paul had filled his mind with the doctrines, words, and images of the Old Testament, and he would have known that in Isaiah 59 there is a picture of God putting on his own armor. Part of it says,

He put on righteousness as his
    breastplate,
  and the helmet of salvation on his
    head (v. 17).

Since those phrases are the exact ones we find in Ephesians 6, I think that Paul got his idea here. That is important, you see. It means that when Paul speaks of the "armor of God," as he does in Ephesians 6, he is not thinking of it only as the armor which God supplies—his in the sense that he gives it—but rather that it is God's own armor, that which he himself wears.

What do we need if we are to fight against Satan? Is it truth? Yes, we need truth, but not just any truth. We need God's own truth: the truth of God, which we find in Scripture. Do we need righteousness? Yes, but not just human righteousness. We need the righteousness of God. The gospel? It is God's gospel, God's good news. Peace? It is God's peace. Faith? It is faith from God, a fruit of the Holy Spirit (Gal. 5:22). Is it salvation? God is salvation. We must be armed with him.

Are you armed with God's armor? The wonderful thing about this, as you will see if you avail yourself of it, is that the armor of God is perfectly suited to us. When we put it on we find that it is just what we need.

When David went out to fight Goliath he was just a young man, and Saul was unwilling to have him fight without armor. So he offered him his own. Saul put his helmet on David's head. He put his breastplate on David's chest. He gave him whatever other pieces of armor he had, but they were all too big. Clothed in Saul's armor David must have looked like a Muppet in William Perry's uniform. So David took Saul's armor off and went out to fight Goliath with his sling.

Only his sling? Yes, in the sense that the sling was the only thing to be seen. But in reality David went out in God's armor. For if ever a man was clothed in God's truth, God's righteousness, God's gospel, God's peace, God's faith, and God's salvation, it was David. And he was invincible. In God's armor David was prepared, not only for physical battle, but for all spiritual battles as well.

Four Great Battles

Some years ago at an early Philadelphia Conference on Reformed Theology, the theme was the biblical terms for salvation, and Dr. John H. Gerstner spoke on "The Language of the Battlefield." In developing this theme Gerstner spoke of four great spiritual battles: (1) the battle of *Satan against God* early in the history of the universe, which Satan lost; (2) the battle of *Satan against man (Adam) without the God-man (Jesus)*, which Satan won; (3) the battle of *Satan against the God-man*, where Satan thought he had won by killing Christ, but had actually lost; and (4) the battle of *Satan against a man (Peter) who was joined to the God-man (Jesus)*, where Satan was also defeated.

The chief contrast in this message was between the second of these battles (Satan against Adam) and the fourth (Satan against Peter). In the first one, Adam seemed to have everything he needed to prevail. He was without sin and had every possible inclination to goodness. Yet he fell, because (we must assume this) he did not avail himself of the strength of Jesus Christ, the God-man, which was certainly not withheld

from him. In the second battle Peter seemed to have nothing. He was sinful, weak, proud, vacillating. He even had the arrogance to tell Jesus, "Even if all fall away, I will not" (Mark 14:29) and "Lord, I am ready to go with you to prison and to death" (Luke 22:33). Peter did fall. He denied his Lord three times, just as Jesus predicted he would. Yet that was not all that happened. Jesus foretold Peter's defection, but he added, "Simon, Simon, Satan has asked to sift you as wheat. But I have prayed for you, Simon, that your faith may not fail. And when you have turned back, strengthen your brothers" (Luke 22:31–32).

In other words, Jesus told Peter, "Peter, you are weak in yourself. Left to your own devices you will certainly fall. You will be no more permanent than chaff when the wind blows upon it. But I am for you. I am on your side; and since you are united to me by saving faith, I have prayed for you, and because of my prayer you will not be destroyed but will instead be strengthened. You will fall, but you will not fall away. You will be turned aside, but you will also be turned back, and when you are you will become a pillar of strength for your brothers."

Gerstner pointed out that there is a hymn we sometimes sing that goes, "Lord, we are able."

"That was written by Peter," Gerstner said. Peter said, "Lord, I am able." But when he was tempted by Satan and fell, Peter discovered that he was not able. So he revised that hymn to read: "Lord, we are not able." He learned that only as he was united to Jesus Christ could he stand his ground and be victorious.

Gerstner adds, "That man, in all his pristine glory, made in the spotless image of God with holiness, righteousness, and knowledge, was able to be brought to ruin by satanic temptation proved that we never of ourselves are *posse non peccare* [able not to sin]. But no matter how weak our faith, how meager our discipleship, how much we shame the name of Christ and have so often to repent and turn home again— no matter how we fail, because we are united to Christ with a love which will never let us go, Satan with all his craft and power cannot stand against us and we can conquer him. . . . Even in our best condition we cannot meet Satan; but in our weakened and debilitated state, sinning far more than we live virtuously, we are able to conquer him because Christ has given us the victory."[1]

---

[1]John H. Gerstner, "The Language of the Battlefield" in *Our Savior God: Studies on Man, Christ, and the Atonement,* ed. James M. Boice (Grand Rapids: Baker, 1980), 161–62. The entire message is on pages 153–62.

39

Our Shining Armor

(Ephesians 6:14–17)

Stand firm then, with the belt of truth buckled around your waist, with the breastplate of righteousness in place, and with your feet fitted with the readiness that comes from the gospel of peace. In addition to all this, take up the shield of faith, with which you can extinguish all the flaming arrows of the evil one. Take the helmet of salvation and the sword of the Spirit, which is the word of God.

I was glancing through some catalogs of secondary schools, and my mind was attracted to the way the sports were classified. I wondered if there would still be "girls' sports" and "boys' sports" in this age of women's liberation. I found that for the most part there still are. There are also "coed sports," "team sports," and "individual sports." There is a category that in my day we used to call "physical education." It is for those who do not play a sport. It is the half-hour every day when fat kids agonize over trying to touch their toes.

This brought to mind a conversation I once had with John Nyland, a former lineman for the Dallas Cowboys and later for the Philadelphia Eagles. He believed there were only two kinds of sports: the "easy" sports everybody else did, and the "contact" sports in which men over two hundred pounds took part.

Thinking of the imagery Paul uses for the Christian's warfare in Ephesians 6, it would be proper to call Christianity a contact sport. The Christian life is no genteel engagement. It is no exercise class. Christianity is warfare, and be-cause of this it is necessary for the Christian soldier to wear armor adequate to resist the spiritual (and sometimes physical) onslaughts of Satan. As I was talking to John Nyland I was thinking that even if I were protected by a steel uniform I would not go into a game against John Nyland. He is so big that I would not go into a game against John Nyland in a tank! In Ephesians 6 Paul is saying that we face an even more formidable foe than that—and not in a mere game either. Satan intends the destruction of our souls. So we must fight him. We will be able to do this successfully only if we avail ourselves of God's armor.

Paul mentioned six pieces of armor in this passage: a belt, a breastplate, shoes, a shield, a helmet, and a sword. They stand for: truth, righteousness, readiness of the gospel of peace, faith, salvation, and the Bible. The first five are defensive in nature. They are the ones we want to look at in this study.

THE BELT OF TRUTH

Strictly speaking, the Roman soldier's belt was more a part of his dress than his armor. It was made of leather and was used to gather his garments together as well as hold his sword. Yet it was part of his war equipment, for it gave him a feeling of inner fortitude and strength when tightened. According to Paul's teaching, the Christian's belt is truth. It is to be his inner strength, what gives him confidence.

Commentators have looked at "truth" in two ways since it can have two basic meanings. First, it can mean "the truth of God." That is, it can refer to Christian doctrine or the specific content of God's revelation in the Bible. Second, since the article "the" is not present, truth can refer to truthfulness or sincerity of heart. I think John R. W. Stott is right, however, when he suggests that "we do not need to choose between these alternatives."[1] As the Bible looks at this area, inner truth or truthfulness begins with a knowledge of God, who is truth, and a knowledge of the truth of God (if it really is known) inevitably leads to a life change consistent with God's character. We must be truthful men and women, of course. But we will become that only as we feast on the revealed truths of God.

It is significant that Paul puts truth first. This suggests that successful spiritual warfare begins with fixing Christianity's great doctrines firmly in our minds. Or to put it another way: it is dangerous to rush into battle without having the great doctrines of the faith fixed firmly in our understanding. Americans especially should hear this, for we have a tendency to think that activity is the important thing and that convictions or truth do not matter or are at least of secondary importance. That is probably not a good approach in any discipline, and it is certainly not a good approach in Christianity. In Christianity truth comes first, then action follows. Without truth, without the doctrines, without the knowledge of who God is, who we are, what we have become in Christ, and what we have been called to do (precisely the kinds of things Paul has been teaching in the earlier chapters of Ephesians)—without this we really do not know what kind of activity in which to engage, and we will be vulnerable to Satan's onslaughts and wiles.

Do you know the great truths of Christianity? Do you study the Bible to apprehend them more deeply?

I think it was Andrew Bonar who first imagined a situation in which a Christian dies and goes to heaven and there meets some of the authors of the biblical books: Ezekiel, for example, and next to him Malachi and Amos and Habakkuk, and maybe Isaiah. They manage to strike up a conversation, and the Christian is glad to meet these men God used to write the Bible. "Ah, Ezekiel, what a pleasure to meet you!" he says.

"I am pleased you are glad to meet me," Ezekiel replies. "Tell me, what did you think about my book?"

The Christian has to answer, "I'm afraid I didn't really read it."

Malachi is there, so he chimes in. "Well, my book is a lot shorter than Ezekiel's. Certainly you read it! What do you think of what I said?"

Again the Christian has to admit that he has not read it. "Malachi? Is that in the Old Testament or the New Testament?"

There was a preacher in Scotland who tried to serve his congregation by teaching some of the illiterate members to read. One was an older Scotsman to whom he had given a number of lessons, helping him through easy portions of the Bible. Circumstances called the pastor away. But a few months later he came back and again went to visit

[1]John R. W. Stott, *God's New Society: The Message of Ephesians* (Downers Grove, Ill.: InterVarsity, 1979), 278.

the home of this man. He was not there, but his wife was. The preacher asked how he was doing with his reading. "Is he getting through the Bible?" he queried.

"Oh, no! He's got out of the Bible and into the newspaper long ago," she answered.

In my opinion many Christians are in precisely that position. They have gotten out of the Bible, if indeed they ever were in it, and they are into the newspapers, magazines, or whatever popular books there may be that strike their fancy. They know more about the box scores of the players in the various baseball leagues than they do about the Gospels, more about football scores than the Sermon on the Mount. Such things should not be. Certainly we are free to learn all we can about everything we can, but lesser things should not keep us from mastering the truths that will make us strong for battle.

The Breastplate of Righteousness

The second piece of the Roman soldier's equipment is his breastplate, which Paul compares to righteousness. Like truth, righteousness can be taken in two ways. It can refer to what in theology is called imputed righteousness, the righteousness of Jesus Christ reckoned to a Christian's account that enables him to stand before God. Or it can refer to specific acts of righteousness—personal holiness, as we might say.

In the third chapter of Zechariah there is a scene in which Joshua the high priest is standing before the angel of the Lord in the temple, and Satan is also standing there to accuse him. Since we are told that Joshua is dressed in filthy clothes, representing his and the people's sin, Satan must have been pointing to these and declaring forcefully that Joshua was not fit to stand before the Lord in this office. It is a clear case of spiritual warfare. But the angel of God intervenes.

"Take off his filthy clothes," says the angel. Then, in place of the filthy clothes he had been wearing, the angel gives him new rich garments and a clean turban for his head. Clearly this symbolizes the righteousness of Christ imputed to him—the clothes were not something Joshua acquired for himself but rather were something given to him—and it is in this righteousness alone that he is enabled to resist Satan's vile accusations.

This is what Count Zinzendorf had in mind when he wrote his great hymn:

Jesus, thy blood and righteousness
My beauty are, my glorious dress;
'Midst flaming worlds, in these
      arrayed,
With joy shall I lift up my head.

Bold shall I stand in thy great day;
For who aught to my charge shall
      lay?
Fully absolved through these I am,
From sin and fear, from guilt and
      shame.

On the other hand, it is significant that immediately after Joshua had been invested with rich robes and a clean turban symbolizing God's righteousness, the angel gave Joshua a charge to be holy. "If you will walk in my ways and keep my requirements, then you will govern my house and have charge of my courts, and I will give you a place among these standing here" (Zech. 3:7).

So imputed righteousness is not to be divorced from actual righteousness. It is because he had been made righteous that Joshua was to live righteously.

If I had to choose between the two possible meanings of righteousness in this passage, I think I would pick the second, for this reason: In this context Paul is urging those who already are Christians to "put on" God's armor. If they are Christians, they have already been clothed with God's righteousness in the first sense. Therefore the only thing they can put on is practical holiness expressed in righteous thoughts and deeds.

I think here of Jesus' words, when he said in reference to Satan, "The prince of this world is coming. He has no hold on me" (John 14:30). I have heard it said that although Satan could find no sin in Christ on which to take hold, he can latch onto plenty in us. That may be true. We are sinful. But what Paul is saying here is that this should not be. We should not give Satan handles to grasp easily. Instead, we must live righteously, as Job did, so Satan and everyone else can see that we are God's true children and his faithful servants.

THE GOSPEL OF PEACE

The most awkward phrase in this list of the Christian's armor is the one about feet: "with your feet fitted with the readiness that comes from the gospel of peace" (v. 15). For one thing, it does not mention the specific piece of armor. We have to assume that Paul means boots or traveling sandals. Again, when he makes the application Paul uses three words ("readiness," "gospel," and "peace"), and it is not immediately clear which one is central. Does Paul want us to be shod with the gospel, with peace, or with the readiness to make the truth known?[2]

In my judgment the emphasis falls upon readiness to make the gospel known. Any Christian already knows the gospel; he would not be a Christian if he did not. So this must go beyond mere knowledge and appropriation. It must involve readiness to share the good news with others. Moreover, Paul links the gospel to the soldier's boots or sandals. Shoes carry us from place to

place, and it is as we go from place to place that we are to be ready to speak about Jesus.

Are you equipped to do that? Do you know how to tell others about the Savior? I think here of that interesting battle involving Gideon, one of the judges of Israel. God told Gideon to collect an army and use it to drive out the occupying Midianites. So Gideon did. He collected an army of 32,000 men. Gideon probably thought that 32,000 soldiers were barely enough for the task ahead of him, but God told him that they were actually too many. So in obedience to the Lord Gideon told any who were afraid to fight to go home. Over 60 percent, 22,000, left. Only 10,000 remained behind. Gideon must have been shaken by that. But still 10,000 soldiers are a large fighting force—if they are good soldiers. He might have thought, "Well, I suppose we can get by with these."

God said, "There are still too many."

"How many more can we spare?" Gideon must have wondered. "Fifty? A hundred?"

God told Gideon to take the army to some water where they could get a drink. He was to watch them. He was to see which ones dropped down on their knees to drink, probably putting down their shield and weapons, and which ones stood ready for battle and merely leaned over to scoop up some water with their hands.

To Gideon's dismay 9,700 men knelt down, dropping their armor. Only 300 stood at attention and scooped the water up. But God took these 300 ready individuals and used them to defeat the Midianites soundly and drive them from the land (see Judges 7).

It does not take a vast number to do God's work, but it does take men and

---

[2]In this case the grammar does not help either. For "of the gospel" can be either an objective or subjective genitive. If objective, the emphasis is on the soldier's readiness to announce the gospel, to make it known. If subjective, the reference is to the firmness or steadiness the gospel gives to those who believe it.

women who are equipped and anxious to share the gospel with others. Are you kneeling (or lying down) on the job? Or are you prepared "always . . . to give an answer to everyone who asks you to give the reason for the hope that you have . . . with gentleness and respect" (1 Peter 3:15)?

THE SHIELD OF FAITH

The Roman soldier had two kinds of shields. There was a small round shield that he would use in hand-to-hand combat when it was important for him to be able to maneuver easily, and there was a large oblong shield that he would use when advancing into battle with other soldiers. This second shield, the one Paul refers to here, was about four or four-and-a-half feet long and about two feet wide, and covered the soldier's body completely. So when the soldiers advanced in rows, as the Romans did, the enemy was faced with a solid wall of shields—row upon row of them. These advancing columns of a Roman army were called phalanxes, and they were the terror of Rome's foes.

Paul is saying that our faith should be like that. It should do three things: (1) it should cover us so that not a portion is exposed, (2) it should link up with the faith of others to prevent a solid wall of defense, and (3) because it does cover our entire person and links up with the faith of our fellow soldiers, it should be able to strike down whatever fiery arrows the enemy may hurl at us.

You have noticed, I am sure, that when Paul speaks of this item of armor he does not say "the shield of *the* faith" as if he were referring to the specific teachings of Christianity—he has already included that in his reference to truth as the Christian's belt—but rather to "the shield of faith," meaning a general confidence in God. Our shield against Satan's arrows is this kind of faith, faith that God can be trusted. It is knowing that when God says that he is

able to keep us from falling and present us before his presence with exceeding joy, he means exactly that and will do it. We do not need to fear when we advance into battle. God will go with us and will bring victory.

THE HELMET OF SALVATION

The final item in the Christian's defensive armor is the helmet that Paul likens to salvation. The helmet of salvation could mean merely that we are saved; that would make sense. But in 1 Thessalonians 5:8 Paul speaks of putting on "the *hope* of salvation as a helmet," and if that is what he is thinking of here, then he is looking to our destiny rather than our present state. He is saying that our anticipation of that end will protect our heads in the heat (and often confusion) of the battle.

It was said of the troops of Lord Cromwell the Protector that they never lost because, being Calvinists, they knew that their destiny was secure and that they were fighting because God had led them to that spot and would prosper them in that work. There is a sense in which that should be true of us. True, we suffer setbacks in our attempts to live the Christian life. Even Paul said that he was sometimes tripped up by Satan's onslaughts: "hard pressed . . . perplexed . . . persecuted . . . struck down" (2 Cor. 4:8–9).

But these momentary setbacks are not the end, nor are they even utter defeats. For Paul said, "We are hard pressed on every side, but not crushed; perplexed, but not in despair; persecuted, but not abandoned; struck down, but not destroyed. . . . Therefore we do not lose heart. Though outwardly we are wasting away, yet inwardly we are being renewed day by day. For our light and momentary troubles are achieving for us an eternal glory that far outweighs them all. So we fix our eyes not on what is seen, but on what is unseen. For what is seen is temporary, but what is unseen is eternal" (2 Cor. 4:8–9, 16–18).

At times the battle presses around the Christian so furiously that he hardly knows where he is or what is happening. That sometimes happens in purely physical warfare too. But what matters is not always that we know where we are or what is happening, but that our great commander-in-chief, the Lord Jesus Christ, knows and has guaranteed the victory.

40

Our Mighty Weapon

(Ephesians 6:17)

Take the helmet of salvation and the sword of the Spirit, which is the word of God.

Sinclair B. Ferguson, assistant professor of systematic theology at Westminster Theological Seminary, has written a book in which he discusses the Christian's warfare against Satan. It is called *Add to Your Faith,* and it is particularly interesting for the way it discusses the Christian's armor. According to Dr. Ferguson, each piece of the armor is directed to one way in which Satan attacks Christians.

Our breastplate arms us against Satan as *accuser.* We have seen from the example of Joshua the high priest, recorded in Zechariah 3, how Satan is present to point an accusing finger at the believer and gloat over his manifold sins. "Look at that sin," he sneers. "No one as wicked as that can serve God." We saw that the righteousness that protects us against these accusations is of two types. First there is the righteousness of Christ imputed to us in justification, symbolized by the rich robes and clean turban given to Joshua. Then there are also those practical deeds of righteousness that are the result of the presence of Christ in our lives; they are referred to in the angel's charge to the high priest after he had been given the new garments.

The next piece of the soldier's equip-ment is his boots or marching sandals. Ferguson thinks of these as protection against Satan as a serpent (Rev. 12:9). A serpent strikes out at the feet or legs of his victims.

Our shield of faith arms us against Satan as tempter. He tells us that we cannot trust God, particularly to deliver us from evil and enable us to live a pure life. Faith in God overcomes these temptations.

The helmet protects us against Satan as deceiver. He would confuse us, if he could. Satan would crush our heads, if it were possible. Actually, it is Satan who is to have his head crushed by Jesus, though Satan was given power to strike his heel, as he did at the cross.

This brings us to the Christian's final piece of armor, the only offensive part: his sword. These others pieces of armor have been defensive. This alone is offensive. It is our means of resisting Satan as liar, according to Ferguson. Jesus said that Satan is "a liar and the father of lies" and "there is no truth in him" (John 8:44). What is sufficient and effective against Satan's untruths? There is only one weapon, and that is the truths of God embodied in the Bible which is God's word.[1]

[1]Sinclair B. Ferguson, *Add to Your Faith: Biblical Teaching on Christian Maturity* (London: Pickering & Inglis, 1980), 104–111.

EVERY WORD OF GOD

In order to understand the nature of Paul's teaching in this area we need to know that the word used for "word" in the phrase "the word of God" is not *logos*, the most common term used in such a phrase, but the word *hrēma*, which is quite different.

Logos is the most exalted word. It was a great word in secular Greek even before it was taken over and used in a special way in the New Testament. Hundreds of years before the time of Christ there was a Greek philosopher named Heraclitus who wrestled with the question of how there could be order in a universe in which everything seemed to be changing. Heraclitus was the philosopher who said, "You can't step into the same river twice." He meant that the water of the river is always moving. So when you step into the river the second time it is no longer the same river. It has changed. To Heraclitus all life was like that. Nothing was stable. All things were changing. But if that is so, he asked, how is it that all things remain the same? Why is the experience of one generation the same as that of people who have gone before? Heraclitus concluded that the *word* of God (he called it the *logos*) stood behind everything we see and governed it. God's *logos* was the ordering principle of the world.

This is the word the apostle John picked up and used with such effect in the opening chapter of his gospel, saying, "In the beginning was the Word, and the Word was with God, and the Word was God. . . . The Word became flesh and made his dwelling among us" (John 1:1, 14). In John's prologue *logos* refers to nothing less than the Lord Jesus Christ. He is God's full and final "word" to mankind. The Scriptures, which are the word of God in a parallel sense, tell us about him.

Hrēma is not like that. While *logos* embraces nearly everything, *hrēma* has a slighter weight. It really means "a saying," in this case, a particular, specific portion of God's written revelation. John 3:16 is a *hrēma*. Romans 3:23 is a *hrēma*, and so on for all the other specific portions of the written "word of God." It is important to see this, as I said, because according to Paul's teaching we are to overcome Satan by the particular words or portions of Scripture.

"IT IS WRITTEN"

What Paul has in mind is modeled by the victory of the Lord Jesus Christ over Satan in the wilderness. The devil approached Jesus after he had been fasting for forty days and was hungry, and said, "If you are the Son of God, tell these stones to become bread" (Matt. 4:3). The idea behind this temptation was not that it was wrong for Jesus to use his supernatural power to make food—his very first miracle was turning water into wine at a wedding in Cana just a few days after this (John 2:1–11), and, later, on at least two occasions, he produced an abundance of bread and fish in Galilee (Matt. 14:13–21; 15:29–39 and parallels). Rather the problem is that it was wrong for him to use his power to test the word of God.

I think R. C. Sproul is right when he suggests that the emphasis in Satan's query was on the word "if": "*If* you are the Son of God, tell these stones to become bread."[2] Immediately before this, in Matthew 3:17, God the Father is recorded as having said at the baptism of Jesus, "This is my Son." This was a direct and unambiguous statement. But now, immediately after this, Satan

<hr />

[2]R. C. Sproul, "Hath God Said?" in *Can We Trust the Bible?* ed. Earl D. Radmacher (Wheaton, Ill.: Tyndale House, 1979), 120–21.

comes to Jesus with the subtle query, "*If* you are the Son of God. . . . " It was a temptation to doubt God's veracity, hidden under what seemed to be a concern for Jesus' physical hunger.

Yet Jesus had no trouble answering Satan. He replied with a quotation from Deuteronomy. "Man does not live on bread alone, but on every word that comes from the mouth of God" (Matt. 4:4; cf. Deut. 8:3). It was as though Jesus was saying, "Satan, it does not really matter much whether I have physical bread to eat. God will preserve my life for as long as he wants, to do with it what he wants. What really matters is whether I believe God or not. If I doubt his word, all is lost."

At this point Satan got into the act, saying, "Well, I see that you are a student of Scripture, having memorized that verse from Deuteronomy. But, of course, I am something of a Bible student myself. When I'm not wandering up and down the earth tempting Job or someone, I have my own periods of Bible study, and not long ago, when I was reading in the Psalms, I came across some interesting verses. Psalm 91:11–12 says, 'He will command his angels concerning you, and they will lift you up in their hands, so that you will not strike your foot against a stone' [Matt. 4:6]. Do you believe that? I believe it. In fact, I believe it so much that I am going to make this suggestion. Let's go up to the highest point of the temple, you and me. You jump off. God will 'bear you up,' and the people who see the miracle will follow you immediately. It will get your ministry off to a rip-roaring start."

Jesus quoted from Deuteronomy a second time. "It is also written, 'Do not put the Lord your God to the test'" (Matt. 4:7; cf. Deut. 6:16). Here Jesus used Scripture to interpret Scripture— an important hermeneutical principle—and said, in effect, "Satan, you want me to put God to the test. But you

have to understand that it is not God who is to be tested. I am the one being tested. My responsibility is not to test but to trust him."

In the third temptation Satan threw off all subtlety and sued for Christ's worship. He showed him the kingdoms of the world and their glory and promised, "All this I will give you . . . if you will bow down and worship me" (Matt. 4:9).

Jesus replied, "Away from me, Satan! For it is written: 'Worship the Lord your God, and serve him only'" (Matt. 4:10; cf. Deut. 6:13). It was another quotation from Deuteronomy. In all Scripture there is no better example of the power of specific sayings of the Word of God to turn Satan aside and preserve the one tempted.

Let me put it very directly. Here is Jesus Christ—the holy Son of the almighty God, the one in whom neither Satan nor man could find any wrong or gain even the tiniest foothold, Jesus, whose eyes were always on the glory of God the Father and who always lived in the closest possible communion with him. If this Jesus, your Lord and Savior, had to know Scripture in order to resist Satan and win a victory over him, how much more do you and I need it to win a like victory! You say, "Well, I have a general idea what the Bible is about. I believe that the Bible is God's Word." That is good. I do not want to discount that in the slightest. But it is not enough. According to Ephesians 6:17, you must know the specific sayings of Scripture—you must have them memorized—if you are to resist and overcome Satan successfully.

I have great admiration for the Navigators at this point because they, of all organizations in this country, are doing most to stress Bible memorization. Everybody stresses Bible study; that is essential. But the Bible memorization is also important, maybe more so. It is because in the heat of temptation, when other external supports are lacking or have been removed by Satan's stratagems, only those specific sayings of God's which are fixed firmly in our minds will remain and will emerge to help us.

Satan will not flee from us simply because we tell him to. He will retreat only before the power of God as he himself speaks his words into the midst of the temptation.

NOTHING MORE POWERFUL

There is nothing in all life more powerful than the specific words of God. You may say, "Surely that is an exaggeration. We know many things that are powerful. What about nuclear weapons?" Well, nuclear weapons are powerful. They can kill you and, if you are not saved, send your soul to hell. But the words of God can impart eternal life and bring you to heaven. "What about gossip, lies, and slander? They do great damage." True, but the truths of God are more powerful than lies, and what is more, they can transform the liar. In times of revival the words of God have transformed whole societies and cultures. Nothing in all of life is more powerful than the words of God.

Think of the accomplishments of God's words.

First, the words of God are *compelling*. That is, they have a way of getting a hold on us and moving us as no other words do. Calvin wrote, "This power which is peculiar to Scripture is clear from the fact that of human writings, however artfully polished, there is none capable of affecting us at all comparably. Read Demosthenes or Cicero; read Plato, Aristotle, and others of that tribe. They will, I admit, allure you, delight you, move you, enrapture you in wonderful measure. But betake yourself from them to this sacred reading. Then, in spite of yourself, so deeply will it affect you, so penetrate your heart, so fix itself in your very marrow, that compared with its deep impression, such vigor as orators and philosophers have will nearly vanish. Consequently, it is easy to see that the Sacred Scriptures, which so far surpass all gifts and graces of the human endeavor, breathe something divine."[3]

Emile Cailliet, a French philosopher who eventually settled in America and became a professor at Princeton Theological Seminary, had a similar testimony. He had received a naturalistic education but had always felt that something was missing in his life. He came to think that what he really needed was "a book that would understand me." He was highly educated, but he knew of no such book. He determined to write one for himself. As he came across particularly moving passages in his studies he would copy them over, index his anthology, and then be able to read his choice passages whenever he was despondent.

The day came when Dr. Cailliet finished his production, and he went out of the small town in France in which he and his wife lived and sat down under a tree to read the book that would understand him. He began with high expectations. But as he read a feeling of disappointment crept over him. The book did not work, and the reason it did not work, as he then realized, was that it was of his own making. It carried no special strength of persuasion. Dejected, he returned the book to his pocket.

At that very moment his wife came up to him with a Bible. He had never seen a Bible in his life, and his wife was almost afraid to give it to him—so insistent had he been about not having such a book in his house. But she had

---

[3]John Calvin, *Institutes of the Christian Religion,* ed. John T. McNeill, trans. Ford Lewis Battles (Philadelphia: Westminster Press, 1960), 1:82.

stumbled upon a small Huguenot chapel earlier that morning and had asked for one, much to her own surprise. Now she was offering it to him.

Cailliet snatched up the book greedily and began to read it. Here is what happened in his own words: "I read and read and read—now aloud with an indescribable warmth surging within. . . . I could not find words to express my awe and wonder. And suddenly the realization dawned upon me: This was the Book that would understand me! I needed it so much, yet, unaware, I had attempted to write my own—in vain. I continued to read deeply into the night, mostly from the gospels. And lo and behold, as I looked through them, the One of whom they spoke, the One who spoke and acted in them became alive to me. . . . To this God I prayed that night, and the God who answered was the same God of whom it was spoken in the Book."[4]

Second, the words of God are *convicting.* Anyone who has faithfully tried to preach or teach the Word of God has had the experience that after the sermon or lesson is over a person will come up and say, "What you were talking about is exactly what I have been doing. Somebody must have told you about me."

Sometimes it is difficult to convince such a person that nobody has said anything about his or her particular sin or situation. It is just that the words of God, carried home by the power of the God who spoke them, have burned into the heart. I think this is what must have happened to the Emmaus disciples when Jesus explained to them out of "Moses and all the Prophets" the things that concerned himself. They said to each other, "Were not our hearts burning within us while he talked with us on the road and opened the Scriptures to us?" (Luke 24:32).

Third, the words of God are *converting.* They change lives as no other power on earth can. Harry Ironside, a great preacher and evangelist from an earlier generation, was in San Francisco once taking part in a Salvation Army sidewalk meeting when he was challenged to debate the subject "Agnosticism versus Christianity" by a well-known socialist of that era. He replied like this:

"I will be glad to agree to this debate on the following conditions: namely, that in order to prove that Mr. _____ has something worth fighting and worth debating about, he will promise to bring with him to the Hall of Science next Sunday [the place and time of the proposed debate] two people whose qualifications I will give in a moment, as proof that agnosticism is of real value in changing human lives and building true character.

"First, he must promise to bring with him one man who was for years what we commonly call a 'down-and-outer' . . . a man who for years was under the power of evil habits from which he could not deliver himself, but who on some occasion entered one of Mr. _____ 's meetings and heard his glorification of agnosticism and his denunciations of the Bible and Christianity, and whose heart and mind as he listened to such an address were so deeply stirred that he went away from that meeting saying, "Henceforth, I too am an agnostic!' and as a result of imbibing that particular philosophy found that a new power had come into his life. The sins he once loved he now hates, and righteousness and goodness are now the ideals of his life. He is now an entirely new man, a credit to himself and an asset to society—all because he is an agnostic.

"Secondly, I would like Mr. _____ to promise to bring with him one

---

[4]Emile Cailliet, *Journey Into Light* (Grand Rapids: Zondervan, 1968), 18.

woman . . . once a poor, wrecked, characterless outcast, the slave of evil passions, and the victim of man's corrupt living [but who also] entered a hall where Mr. _____ was loudly proclaiming his agnosticism and ridiculing the message of the Holy Scriptures. As she listened, hope was born in her heart and she said, 'This is just what I need to deliver me from the slavery of sin!' She followed the teaching and became an intelligent agnostic or infidel. As a result, her whole being revolted against the degradation of the life she had been living. She fled from the den of iniquity where she had been held captive so long; and today, rehabilitated, she has won her way back to an honored position in society and is living a clean, virtuous, happy life, all because she is an agnostic.

"Now," he said, addressing the gentleman who had presented him with his card and the challenge, "If you will promise to bring these two people with you as examples of what agnosticism can do, I will promise to meet you at the Hall of Science at four o'clock next Sunday, and I will bring with me at the very least one hundred men and women who for years lived in just such sinful degradation as I have tried to depict, but who have been gloriously saved through believing the gospel which you ridicule. I will have these men and women with me on the platform as witnesses to the miraculous saving power of Jesus Christ and as present-day proof of the truth of the Bible."

Dr. Ironside then turned to the Salvation Army captain, a girl, and asked, "Captain, have you any who could go with me to such a meeting?"

She exclaimed with enthusiasm, "We can give you forty at least just from this one corps, and we will give you a brass band to lead the procession!"

Apparently the man who had made the challenge had a sense of humor, for he smiled wryly and waved his hand in a deprecating kind of way as if to say, "Nothing doing!" and then he edged out of the crowd while the bystanders clapped for Harry Ironside.[5] There is nothing on earth that convicts people and transforms lives the way the Bible does.

Finally, the words of God are *consoling*. You and I often go through difficult times in life; times that involve sickness or the loss of a job, friends, or a close family member. The world has its way of handling such situations. It says, "Keep a stiff upper lip," "Every cloud has a silver lining," "Things will get better"—profound words like that. But they are not much help. Where does a person who is suffering sickness or loss or persecution or misery find comfort? Let me say it clearly: there is no comfort like that of reading or hearing the very words of God. To hear such words is to hear God himself, and it is God who ministers to the suffering soul through them.

God's Word, My Heart

If we are to resist Satan and find the convicting, converting, and consoling words of God that we need to live and triumph as Christians, we must take the words of God into our minds and hearts. We must pick up the sword of the Spirit and wield it forcefully.

I have seen many swords in my day, having visited scores of war museums, particularly in the British Isles. I have seen beautiful swords, important swords, swords that have been owned and used by kings and warriors of many earlier ages. I have enjoyed looking at them. But they have never done

[5]H. A. Ironside, *Random Reminiscences From Fifty Years of Ministry* (New York: Loizeaux Brothers, 1939), 99–107.

me one bit of good, nor will they. They are not mine. I cannot hold them. They are locked away in those great museums, and there they remain. For a sword to do me any good, I must take it up and use it. So also with the words of God. They are wonderful words, but to be useful to you they must become yours. You must learn them. This is what David was talking about when he said, "I have hidden your word in my heart that I might not sin against you" (Ps. 119:11). Only the words that we know will be useful to us.

41

Our Secret Resource

(Ephesians 6:18–24)

And pray in the Spirit on all occasions with all kinds of prayers and requests. With this in mind, be alert and always keep on praying for all the saints.

Pray also for me, that whenever I open my mouth, words may be given me so that I will fearlessly make known the mystery of the gospel, for which I am an ambassador in chains. Pray that I may declare it fearlessly, as I should.

Tychicus, the dear brother and faithful servant in the Lord, will tell you everything, so that you also may know how I am and what I am doing. I am sending him to you for this very purpose, that you may know how we are, and that he may encourage you.

Peace to the brothers, and love with faith from God the Father and the Lord Jesus Christ. Grace to all who love our Lord Jesus Christ with an undying love.

Several presidencies ago, when Henry Kissinger was secretary of state and often in the news, I saw a cartoon that expressed amazement at his achievements. In those days Kissinger would go to London on Monday, negotiate in the Near East on Tuesday (shuttling back and forth between one eastern capital and another), come home to Washington on Wednesday, and then go off again the next afternoon. He never seemed to get tired. This cartoon showed a very bedraggled Henry Kissinger crawling back into his hotel room after a long day's work, his briefcase trailing behind him. But just as he was coming in through the door, there was another Henry Kissinger springing out of bed, fresh, newly shaved, and smartly dressed, going out to take on a new day's assignments. Outside the hotel room two men were talking, and one was saying to the other, "I just don't know how he does it."

It would be nice if we had that kind of resource for our spiritual battles. Sometimes I wish I were two people—though my secretaries probably wish I were half. We wish we had some secret resource upon which we could draw. But what Paul tells us as he gets to the close of his classic discussion of the Christian's spiritual warfare and armor in Ephesians 6 is that we do have such a resource. Our secret resource is prayer. And what makes it so important is that the weakest Christian can at any period of his life at any moment of the day and in any circumstance cry out to God for help and instantly have the resources of the infinite, sovereign God at his disposal.

Paul is emphasizing this as he gets to the end of his epistle, because he devotes special space to it. The other aspects of our warfare have been mentioned quickly and in passing. Now he says in greater length, "Pray in the Spirit on all occasions with all kinds of prayers and requests. With this in mind, be alert and always keep on praying for all the saints. Pray also for me, that whenever I open my mouth, words may be given me so that I will fearlessly make known the mystery of the gospel, for which I am an ambassador in chains. Pray that I may declare it fearlessly, as I should (vv. 18–20).

THE CHRISTIAN IN COMPLETE ARMOR

Several times in these studies of Ephesians 6:10–18 I have referred to William Gurnall's classic on this chapter, *The Christian in Complete Armour.*[1] Gurnall was a spiritual man, and he understood the emphasis of these verses as well as their precise theological meaning. One thing he understood was the emphasis of these verses on prayer. This great work, as I said before, runs to approximately 1,200 pages in a double-column format (and would be longer in one of today's standard book styles), and Gurnall uses 300 of those 1,200 pages (one-fourth of the whole) to talk about prayer. In Ephesians, three verses are given to prayer, an emphasis in itself. But Gurnall uses 100 pages per verse to explore prayer's significance!

Some years ago, when I was preaching through John, I came to the shortest verse in the Bible, John 11:35: "Jesus wept." I thought it would be a good occasion to demonstrate how much can be found in just one verse of Scripture. So I preached four sermons on that verse. I studied what it taught concerning the nature of God, what it taught about the humanity of Jesus Christ, what it taught about ourselves, and finally, what it taught about how we should relate to others—two sermons per word.

But here was Gurnall devoting one hundred pages to each verse in this section and three hundred pages to the subject overall.

Was Gurnall right in this emphasis? He clearly was. For he wished to show, as Paul himself wished to show, that you and I can be clothed in God's armor—having the belt of truth, the breastplate of righteousness, our feet shod with the readiness that comes from the gospel of peace, the shield of faith, the helmet of salvation, and the sword of the Spirit—and yet fail to triumph because we do not call upon God. A great military disaster of the early Middle Ages was the defeat of the knights of Charlemagne in the approach to a narrow defile in the Pyrenees. It is narrated in the *Song of Roland.*

What makes the story so poignant is that the defeat was unnecessary. Roland, the commander of Charlemagne's rear guard, could have called for help from the main body of the army merely by sounding his great horn Oliphant. But he would not do it. Pride held him back. Because he failed to call upon his secret resource, Roland's troops were massacred. Likewise, many Christians can trace the secret of a defeated life to prayerlessness.

ALL OCCASIONS

How important is prayer? Paul lets us know by repeating the word "all" four times in this passage, as if to say that there is nothing that cannot be prayed for and that there is no situation in which prayer is unavailing. He says that we should pray "on *all* occasions," "with *all* kinds of prayer and requests," "*always*," and finally, "for *all* the saints." It is a helpful and comprehensive outline.

Let us start with the challenge to pray on all occasions. And let me begin by asking: "When do you usually pray?" I suppose there is hardly anybody—

[1] William Gurnall, *The Christian in Complete Armour* (1662–65; reprint, Carlisle, Pa.: Banner of Truth Trust, 1979).

whether a Christian or not—who does not pray in difficulty. Even professing atheists will sometimes break down and pray if things get bad enough. Sometimes they do it unconsciously, as when they exclaim, "O God, what am I going to do?" But what is sad is that the prayer life of genuine Christians is often not much better than that. They will pray in church—sort of. They will often return thanks before plunging into a meal. But the times they really pray, if they do really pray, are when things go bad for them and they find themselves in some difficulty.

They are like the man who was asked what position he assumed when he prayed and who explained how he had once fallen into a well head first and gotten stuck head down in the mud at the bottom. He said, "The prayingest prayer I ever prayed I prayed standing on my head."

Well, it is not wrong to pray in sticky situations, and it may even be true that God puts us in some upside-down situations to get us to pray. But what Paul is saying when he commands us to pray "on all occasions" is that *all* situations in life should draw forth prayer from us. If we are happy, we should express our happiness to God. If we are despondent, we should pray about that. We should pray in work situations. We should pray on vacation. We should pray when we are with friends and when we deal with enemies. There should be no situations in life from which prayers to God are absent.

Because of the context in which Paul here exhorts us to pray, a word should probably be said about prayer and the Christian's armor. Perhaps you remember the line in the hymn "Stand Up, Stand Up for Jesus," that goes

> Put on the gospel armor,
> Each piece put on with prayer;
> Where duty calls, or danger,
> Be never wanting there.

I think George Duffield, the author of that hymn, must have been thinking of these verses in Ephesians as he wrote that, for this is probably what Paul was thinking of as he ended his list of the Christian's pieces of armor with a call to prayerfulness.

Paul calls truth a belt to be buckled around our waist. What is going to keep that belt in place if not prayer? Heresies will work to pull us away from God's truth, and we are always susceptible to the devil's subtle doubts. We must ask God to keep us girded with truth constantly.

Or righteousness? We are prone to sin and will certainly sin and fall farther and farther away from God's righteousness unless God upholds us. Remember how Jesus prayed that he might uphold Peter. Prayer will keep us close to God and keep us from sinning.

If having our feet shod with the "readiness that comes from the gospel of peace" means that we are always to "be prepared to give an answer to everyone who asks [us] to give the reason for the hope that [we] have" (1 Peter 3:15), it is only prayer that will keep us ready. Otherwise we will be immersed in other concerns and miss our opportunities.

So also with the remaining parts of our armor. We will not show faith in God in trials unless we are standing close to God in prayer. We will not be properly protected by our helmet of salvation, nor will we be effective in the use of the Word of God, our sword— unless we are praying. It is in all situations—"on all occasions"—that we are to be prayer warriors.

ALL KINDS OF PRAYERS

The second thing Paul says about prayer is that we are to pray "with all kinds of prayers and requests." What does that mean? Well, there are undoubtedly some who read that phrase and think that its two main nouns are redundant. That is, they think of prayers and requests as being basically the same thing. Are they? This is a case in which one term includes the other but in which this is not true of the reverse. Prayers include requests, but requests do not exhaust prayers. There are many kinds of prayers that we should know about and use effectively.

Do you know that little acrostic that is often used to highlight what the normal steps of a good prayer should be? It is the word ACTS. ACTS stands for Adoration, Confession, Thanksgiving, and Supplications.

Adoration is the place to begin, for our prayers are never worth much unless we begin by praising God. If we do not do that, if we do not let our minds be stretched by the thought of who it is to whom we are praying and what are the resources of this God that are placed at our disposal, we will never really be aware of God's presence and therefore never really pray. Prayer will just be a little ritual we go through. We will say, "Here I am, Lord, and this is what I want." Then we will go away; nothing will have happened to us, and nothing will happen. That is why Reuben A. Torrey says that the most important part of prayer is making sure that we really are coming to *God*, meeting with *him* and requesting of *him* those things we need.[2]

The second word of the acrostic is *confession.* This is an important kind of prayer. For having come into the presence of the holy God and having bowed down to him, it is inevitable that sinful past thoughts and deeds will come to our minds and require confession. We must deal with these things. The final step in the acrostic is supplications, but we will not get far with these if we are still harboring sin in our hearts and clinging to our trespasses. Isaiah 59:1–2 says, "Surely the arm of the LORD is not

too short to save, nor his ear too dull to hear. But your iniquities have separated you from your God; your sins have hidden his face from you, so that he will not hear."

Thanksgiving is a third kind of prayer. We are always ready to ask for things, but like the nine healed lepers, we often forget to thank God for what he has already done for us. When we thank him, one thing we should thank him for especially is the forgiveness and cleansing he has given in response to our confession of sin (cf. 1 John 1:9).

Finally, we may make our requests or *supplications.* Our prayer life will be poor if this is all we do, but it will also be less than it can be if we do not ask God for what we want and lay our needs before him. Jesus himself taught us to make requests, saying, "Give us today our daily bread" (Matt. 6:11). If we come to God as he intends and pray for those things that are according to his will and please him, we can be confident that we will receive those things we ask (cf. 1 John 3:21–22).

PRAYING ALWAYS

The third "all" is embedded in the word "*always.*" It is not just that we are to pray on all occasions (or in all situations) and with all kinds of prayers and requests. We are also to pray always, that is, at all times of the day and sometimes in the night. Paul does not mean that we are to do nothing but pray, of course; we would not get anything else done. Paul himself did not do it. He means that prayer is to be a natural and consistent part of our lives. It is not to be regulated just to special seasons or special days. We are to be people of prayer.

One of the things Gurnall does very well in his three-hundred-page treatment of prayer is to analyze the ways in which the devil tries to get us to stop

[2]R. A. Torrey, *The Power of Prayer and the Prayer of Power* (Grand Rapids: Zondervan, 1955), 74–78.

praying. And one of the things he suggests is that the devil will tell us that while prayer is good for other people— there *are* great prayer warriors—you or I just do not have the "gift" for it. Have you ever thought like that? Have you ever thought that real prayer is probably for other people, not for you?

Some years ago I did a detailed study of the five passages in the New Testament where the gifts of the Spirit are listed, and in doing that study I made a careful listing of the gifts. There were more than twenty items, with some overlap. In my final listing there were nineteen gifts: evangelism, teaching, faith, wisdom, healing, the gift of "helps," and so on. But I noticed this as I worked over these important gifts of the Holy Spirit to the church: *prayer is not among them.* Why is that? Is it because prayer is not important? No. It is because prayer is not a gift. "Gift" is the wrong category in which to consider it. Prayer is a responsibility, an obligation. And this means that you and I are to pray always (in all situations and with all kinds of prayers and requests) regardless of what our other spiritual gift or gifts may be.

So, regardless of what Satan says to you, be a person of prayer. Bathe your life, your family, your friends, your church, and every other concern in prayer, and see how God will honor your prayers and provide blessing.

For All the Saints

The final thing Paul says about the Christian warrior's prayer is that it is "for all the saints." How many saints do you suppose that is? I do not have an answer to that. I do not have a list. I suppose it would be much, much harder to number the saints than it would be to number the hairs on one's head, which Christ himself said was difficult. There are millions of saints in hundreds of this world's countries— and most of us could not even name or

number the countries. How are we to pray for all these people?

We obviously cannot pray for all these Christians by name. But we can pray generally (in cases where we do not know who they are), and we can pray specifically (where we do know who the saints are). To pray even generally will mean more work in preparation for prayer and in prayer than most of us are accustomed to. How about Christians in China? If we are to pray for them, we must know something about the state of Christianity in that country and something about the problems and opportunities they face. How about Christians in North Africa? There is quite a different situation there. We must know what it is if we are to pray intelligently and effectively.

So on for many other groupings of believers: suffering Christians, Christians in positions of power (with their special temptations), isolated Christians, Christians in the East and in the West, Christians of different ethnic and cultural backgrounds. Even in general terms the list is extensive.

But our prayers must also be specific, which Paul shows by bringing in himself as an example. "Pray also for me," he said, "that whenever I open my mouth, words may be given me so that I will fearlessly make known the mystery of the gospel, for which I am an ambassador in chains. Pray that I may declare it fearlessly, as I should" (vv. 19–20).

What a sermon there is right here! When Paul introduces himself as an example of one for whom the Christians at Ephesus could pray, he seems to be saying (because I am sure he was not just self-centered), "Above all, do not forget to pray for ministers of the gospel." Paul was a great man, an apostle of the Lord Jesus Christ. Yet he believed his work would be ineffective unless Christians prayed for him.

He asks that they pray that he might

be given words. This is another point for a sermon. Paul seems to have been more eloquent with words than perhaps any other writer in the Bible. Think of 1 Corinthians 13, the great hymn to love, for example. Paul was a master of words. Yet he knew he needed God's help and blessing that he might choose words that would be effective in reaching others.

Again, he uses the word "fearlessly." Fearlessly? That Paul might be fearless? That seems strange to us, because we think of Paul as eminently fearless— before rioting mobs (as at Ephesus), before kings (like Agrippa and Felix and Nero), in natural disasters (like the storm that overtook the ship bearing the apostle), in prison facing death (as in Rome). But we do not see people's hearts. Just because people seem strong and self-composed on the outside does not mean that they are not trembling within. They still need our prayers. At one point Paul said he was with the Corinthians "in weakness and fear, and with much trembling" (1 Cor. 2:3).

Think of the most fearless person you know, one who presents the gospel of Christ without hesitation in the most difficult circumstances, and then pray that he or she *might remain fearless.* In the same way, pray that the holy might remain holy, the visionary might remain visionary, the great prayer warriors might remain faithful in prayer.

Peace to All

I think Paul's mind was still on prayer as he closed this letter, describing how Tychicus, the bearer of the letter, would fill the Ephesians in on all that Paul was experiencing—that they might pray for him better—and, as he himself prays, that peace, love, and grace might be with his faithful friends and prayer companions at Ephesus.

Do we need peace of mind to live as God wants us to live in this ungodly world? Of course, we do. The way to have it is by asking God for it. Do we need love? Yes. Fuller and fuller measures of the grace of God? Yes, those too. The way to have them is by asking God for them. Jesus said, "Ask and it will be given to you; seek and you will find; knock and the door will be opened to you" (Matt. 7:7). James wrote, "You do not have, because you do not ask God" (James 4:2).

How can we adequately urge the people of God to pray? By the need? Certainly, for there is a great need. By prayer's privilege? Yes, that too. It is a privilege to be able to bring our needs before God.

Maybe the best of all arguments for us today is prayer's results. We are oriented to achievement in our time. Let us remember that prayer will give victory as we go about our tasks and try to live for Jesus. Will the devil attack? Yes, he will—either he or one of his demons, or perhaps through evil influences, teachings, or structures. But what of that? We have a ditty that goes, "The devil trembles when he sees the weakest Christian on his knees." I believe he does, because the praying Christian is calling upon the inexhaustible and irresistible power of God.

Subject Index

Scripture Index